ACCOUNTING
At Your Fingertips
SECOND EDITION

George R. Murray, CPA, and Kathleen Murray, CPA

ALPHA
A member of Penguin Group (USA) Inc.

ALPHA BOOKS

Published by Penguin Group (USA) Inc. • Penguin Group (USA) Inc., 375 Hudson Street, New York, New York 10014, USA • Penguin Group (Canada), 90 Eglinton Avenue East, Suite 700, Toronto, Ontario M4P 2Y3, Canada (a division of Pearson Penguin Canada Inc.) • Penguin Books Ltd., 80 Strand, London WC2R ORL, England • Penguin Ireland, 25 St. Stephen's Green, Dublin 2, Ireland (a division of Penguin Books Ltd.) • Penguin Group (Australia), 250 Camberwell Road, Camberwell, Victoria 3124, Australia (a division of Pearson Australia Group Pty. Ltd.) • Penguin Books India Pvt. Ltd., 11 Community Centre, Panchsheel Park, New Delhi—110 017, India • Penguin Group (NZ), 67 Apollo Drive, Rosedale, North Shore, Auckland 1311, New Zealand (a division of Pearson New Zealand Ltd.) • Penguin Books (South Africa) (Pty.) Ltd., 24 Sturdee Avenue, Rosebank, Johannesburg 2196, South Africa

Penguin Books Ltd., Registered Offices: 80 Strand, London WC2R ORL, England

International Standard Book Number: 978-1-61564-203-8
Library of Congress Catalog Card Number: 2012930862

14 13 12   8 7 6 5 4 3 2 1

Interpretation of the printing code: The rightmost number of the first series of numbers is the year of the book's printing; the rightmost number of the second series of numbers is the number of the book's printing. For example, a printing code of 12-1 shows that the first printing occurred in 2012.

Printed in the United States of America

Note: This publication contains the opinions and ideas of its authors. It is intended to provide helpful and informative material on the subject matter covered. It is sold with the understanding that the authors and publisher are not engaged in rendering professional services in the book. If the reader requires personal assistance or advice, a competent professional should be consulted.

The authors and publisher specifically disclaim any responsibility for any liability, loss, or risk, personal or otherwise, which is incurred as a consequence, directly or indirectly, of the use and application of any of the contents of this book.

Trademarks: All terms mentioned in this book that are known to be or are suspected of being trademarks or service marks have been appropriately capitalized. Alpha Books and Penguin Group (USA) Inc. cannot attest to the accuracy of this information. Use of a term in this book should not be regarded as affecting the validity of any trademark or service mark.

Most Alpha books are available at special quantity discounts for bulk purchases for sales promotions, premiums, fund-raising, or educational use. Special books, or book excerpts, can also be created to fit specific needs. For details, write: Special Markets, Alpha Books, 375 Hudson Street, New York, NY 10014.

Publisher: **Marie Butler-Knight**	Copy Editor: **Cate Schwenk**
Associate Publisher: **Mike Sanders**	Cover/Book Designer: **Kurt Owens**
Executive Managing Editor: **Billy Fields**	Indexer: **Brad Herriman**
Senior Acquisitions Editor: **Brook Farling**	Layout: **Ayanna Lacey**
Development Editor: **Mark Reddin**	Senior Proofreader: **Laura Caddell**
Senior Production Editor: **Kayla Dugger**	

Contents

Introduction

We all need good information—particularly on a topic as specialized as accounting. And fortunately, there's a lot out there, a veritable avalanche once you start looking: beginners' guides, reference books, hefty manuals, how-to websites … the list goes on and on.

Yet now more than ever, who's got the time to be buried under all that information? You need answers to your questions, and you want them now—not after you've waded through 10 pages on the finer points of financial statements or spent an hour sifting through Google search results only to discover you're more confused than when you started.

That was the thinking when we originally wrote *Accounting at Your Fingertips* in 2007. We wanted to cut through the clutter to the essentials—so you wouldn't have to. Our goal was to create a simple but practical reference to basic accounting, and reader response suggests we did.

It's interesting what can happen in 5 years. While the rules for keeping books and producing financial reports are fairly standardized, changes in the tax code and a veritable boom in the number of small businesses using computerized accounting made us think it might be time for an update. So *Accounting at Your Fingertips, Second Edition,* has been revised to reflect the most current accounting rules and procedures. In addition, we've expanded our discussion of how accounting software and online programs work and might help make your job easier. At the same time this book, like the original, remains easy to navigate, with built-in shortcuts to get you to the information you want quickly and easily.

Who This Book Is For

This book is designed to be a quick reference on accounting for anyone with limited time but an unlimited appetite for solid and useful information.

Entrepreneurs: Maybe you're starting a new business and want some quick pointers on setting up a simple accounting system.

Bookkeepers: Perhaps you're handling accounting duties for a company and need a review of the basics.

Accountants: You're well past the beginner stage, but could use a primer on a transaction you've never handled before.

Whether you fit into one of these categories, or you just want to learn more about accounting, this book is for you. We promise not to waste your time with windy explanations, because we know you have work to do. Instead, we put the answers right where you want them: at your fingertips.

How This Book Is Organized

The book is designed to take you from setting up an accounting system to handling day-to-day transactions, financial statements, and troubleshooting. We've organized it to mirror the accounting cycle, but you can dive in anywhere—by account, type of transaction, or process—to get the answer you need. The first page of every chapter contains a table of contents so you can quickly see what's covered in the chapter.

✓ _____

These are quick definitions of accounting terms discussed in the chapter to enhance your understanding of the material covered.

In addition, the following reference features should help you zero in on what you want quickly:

SEE ALSO references quickly direct you to other sections in the book that relate to what you're trying to do.

Where to Get More Information

In the back of the book, you'll find two appendixes: a glossary and a list of useful organizations and websites for further information.

Acknowledgments

The authors would like to thank Mike Wojtysiak, CPA, for his time and generosity in reviewing the original manuscript. Any errors are ours alone.

Trademarks

All terms mentioned in this book that are known to be or are suspected of being trademarks or service marks have been appropriately capitalized. Alpha Books and Penguin Group (USA) Inc. cannot attest to the accuracy of this information. Use of a term in this book should not be regarded as affecting the validity of any trademark or service mark.

1

Accounting System Setup

1.1 Accounting Basics

The Functions of Accounting

Accounts

The Accounting Equation

Financial Statements

The Rules of Accounting

Internal Controls

In this subchapter, we explain the function of accounting and who benefits from the information it provides. We also introduce the building blocks of an accounting system—assets, liabilities, and owner's equity—and show how transactions affecting these accounts are summarized into key financial statements.

The Functions of Accounting

Accounting has been called the language of business, and rightly so. Every day, companies complete numerous transactions: selling products or services, paying employees, buying supplies, collecting outstanding bills, and so on. Accountants take all this information—the numbers, the documents, the headaches, really—and translate it into a format that provides a pretty good picture of how the business is doing.

The financial reports generated through accounting provide decision-making data for a host of users, including …

- Potential investors weighing whether to put money into an operation.
- Bankers determining a company's suitability for a loan.
- Suppliers assessing a company's creditworthiness.
- Customers deciding whether to place an order.
- Government looking at taxes paid.

Perhaps the most important user, however, is you, the business owner or employee. Accounting provides answers to some of the most basic questions you have about your company.

- Is the business profitable? Are you making money?
- Do you have enough cash to meet your expenses?

- Should you discontinue or add a product?

- Are you carrying too much debt?

- Can you afford to invest in a new facility?

- How much would you have to sell to make a profit?

- As a "going concern," is the business able to pay you a reasonable salary, provide a return on your investment, and sustain reasonable growth in the future?

You can see why it's in your interest to set up an accounting system that accurately reflects how your business is doing. After all, the better information you have, the better decisions you'll be able to make and the better your company is likely to do financially.

Accounts

To make sense of all the random financial data a business processes daily, accountants classify like items or transactions into accounts. There are five types of accounts:

- Assets

- Liabilities

- Equity

- Revenues

- Expenses

Assets, liabilities, and equity are permanent accounts that carry a running balance. Revenues and expenses are activity accounts that are closed out into equity at the end of the period. In this section, we focus on permanent accounts. We cover revenue and expenses in the next subchapter.

SEE ALSO 11.5, "Opening New Books"

The Accounting Equation

Your company's **assets** are the things it owns—the equipment, the cash in the bank, the products it's selling. **Liabilities,** on the other hand, are monies owed—to the employees who assemble your product or the bank that helped finance your manufacturing plant. **Owner's equity** is what's left over of your investment after debt is taken into account.

Accounting gets a bad rap for being difficult to understand, but its basic premise is really quite simple:

What you own (minus What you owe) = Your investment in the company

Or in accounting terms:

Assets (minus Liabilities) = Equity

To put it in more concrete terms: if Sam Smith deposits $5,000 in a business bank account to open Sam's Car Repair:

Sam's assets ($5,000) = Sam's equity ($5,000)

This formula is known as the *accounting equation* and is at the root of the **double entry system.** One of the basic tenets of accounting is that every transaction has two sides, and that a change in one account affects another. Investing in a business increases its cash on the one hand and the owner's investment on the other.

✓ _____

Assets are items owned by a business.

Liabilities are monies owed by a business.

Owner's equity, sometimes referred to as capital, is an investment plus or minus accumulated profit and losses.

The **double entry system** is a method of recording business transactions so each transaction has both a debit (left) and credit (right) side. The two sides must be equal.

The accounting equation is often shown this way:

Assets = Liabilities + Equity

To continue with our previous example, if Sam Smith purchased $5,000 worth of equipment on account for his repair shop:

Sam's assets = Sam's liabilities + Sam's equity

$10,000 ($5,000 cash + $5,000 equipment) = $5,000 + $5,000

The balance sheet is derived from the accounting equation. No matter how many accounts are added or how many transactions take place, the asset side must always "balance" the liabilities and equity.

Financial Statements

The primary method of communicating business results is through financial statements. Indeed, a chance encounter with a complex-looking page of numbers might have been what initially drove you to pick up this book. Here we offer a quick review of the basic reports—the balance sheet and the income statement—and what each can tell you.

SEE ALSO 13.1, "Analysis Methods"

SEE ALSO 13.2, "Assessing Profitability"

SEE ALSO 13.3, "Determining Ability to Pay Debt"

SEE ALSO 13.4, "Measuring Liquidity"

The Balance Sheet

The balance sheet is a report that shows the financial position of a company at a given point in time. One quick glance reveals quite a bit about what the company has (assets) and what it owes (liabilities) with the difference representing net worth or owner's equity. A deeper analysis of a balance sheet's numbers can tell a seasoned investor or manager much more.

SEE ALSO Chapter 13, "Analyzing Financial Results"

The following example shows a balance sheet for Every Day Adventure Company. The firm markets survival training courses and equipment to corporations. Every Day's accountant has prepared this balance sheet as part of the company's year-end financial statements. Note that assets, liabilities, and owner's equity are put in separate sections, with current (or short-term) assets and liabilities listed first.

SEE ALSO 1.4, "Establishing the Chart of Accounts"

EVERY DAY ADVENTURE COMPANY
BALANCE SHEET
DECEMBER 31
Current Assets

Cash	$5,000
Accounts Receivable	$20,000
Inventory	$2,000
Prepaid Expenses	$1,200
Total Current Assets	**$28,200**

Fixed Assets

Office Equipment	$27,000
Less: Accumulated Depreciation	$2,500
Total Noncurrent Assets	**$24,500**
TOTAL ASSETS	**$52,700**

Liabilities

Accounts Payable	$13,500
Long-Term Notes Payable	$10,000
Total Liabilities	**$23,500**
Owner's Equity	$37,400
Owner's Drawing Accounting	($8,200)
Total Owner's Equity	**$29,200**
TOTAL LIABILITIES AND OWNER'S EQUITY	**$52,700**

The Income Statement

The **income statement,** also called a profit and loss statement, or P&L statement, reports **revenues** and **expenses** of a business for a certain period of time, usually a month or year. If revenues exceed expenses, it shows a profit; if expenses exceed revenues, it is said to post a loss. Expenses on the income statement of a company that sells a product will include **cost of goods sold.**

An **income statement,** also called profit and loss statement, shows revenues and expenses for a specific period of time.

Revenues, often referred to as sales, are the proceeds from sales or services.

Expenses are the costs of doing business.

Cost of goods sold, often called cost of sales, is the cost of merchandise or product sold to the customer.

Take a look at the following income statement for Every Day Adventure Company. Note that net income is derived by subtracting the cost of goods sold from sales less operating expenses, interest, and taxes.

SEE ALSO 5.1, "Accounting for Inventory"

SEE ALSO 5.5, "Cost of Goods Sold"

SEE ALSO 9.1, "Time Value Basics"

SEE ALSO 12.4, "Income Taxes"

SEE ALSO 14.4, "The Operating Expenses Budget"

EVERY DAY ADVENTURE COMPANY
INCOME STATEMENT
FOR THE YEAR ENDED DECEMBER 31

Sales, Net	$101,000
Cost of Goods Sold	$59,000
Gross Profit	$42,000
Operating Expenses	$29,000
Operating Income	$13,000
Interest Expense	$2,000
Income Before Taxes	$11,000
Income Tax Expense	$2,300
Net Income	$8,700

The Statement of Cash Flow

The third key financial statement is the **statement of cash flow,** or the cash flow statement. This tells you about a company's cash position; about cash received and payments made in the course of doing business for loans and investments; and about its ability to meet future financial obligations.

SEE ALSO 11.4, "Generating Financial Statements"

✓

A **statement of cash flow,** also called the cash flow statement, details a company's cash position by showing its major sources and uses of cash.

The cash flow statement is prepared after the balance sheet and income statement, because some figures on these reports are necessary to determine cash flow. Following is the year-end cash flow statement for Every Day Adventure Company.

EVERY DAY ADVENTURE COMPANY
STATEMENT OF CASH FLOWS
FOR THE YEAR ENDED DECEMBER 31
Operating Activities

Collections from Customers	$96,000
Payments to Suppliers	($64,000)
Payments for Operating Expenses	($29,000)
Payments for Income Taxes	($2,300)
Payments for Interest	($2,000)
Cash Used by Operating Activities	($1,300)

Investing Activities

Purchase of Equipment	($5,000)
Cash Used by Investing Activities	($5,000)

Financing Activities	
Proceeds from Loan	$5,000
Payment on Loan	($2,000)
Cash Provided by Financing Activities	$3,000
Net Decrease in Cash	($3,300)
Beginning Cash	$8,300
Ending Cash	$5,000

Numbers in ( ) are credit balances.

The Rules of Accounting

When setting up accounts and preparing financial statements, accountants must follow certain rules. These **Generally Accepted Accounting Principles (GAAP)** are updated from time to time, but some basic assumptions about how accounting is done never change:

- *Be consistent.* Keep the same method of accounting for something from year to year.

- *Be conservative.* Overestimate potential liabilities, and underestimate revenues.

✓

Generally Accepted Accounting Principles (GAAP; pronounced *gap*) are the rules accountants must follow when preparing financial statements. They're handed down by the Financial Accounting Standards Board (FASB), the rule-making body for the profession.

Internal Controls

GAAP requires that financial statements be stated fairly. One means to help achieve this is by having adequate **internal controls.**

✓

Internal controls refer to the system of procedures and policies that help safeguard a company's assets and reduce the risk of irregularities or errors in its financial records.

Internal controls are important no matter how big or small the organization. Internal controls basically fall into these categories:

Physical, mechanical, or technological internal controls keep assets protected from theft or misappropriation. This category contains things like storing money in a safe, using timecards, or requiring computer passwords to access certain systems.

Establishing responsibility. Assigning certain duties to certain individuals creates accountability over processing transactions. An example would be making sure only the petty cash custodian makes disbursements from the fund.

Segregating duties means no one individual has too much access to or control over any one asset. For example, the individuals responsible for keeping track of inventory shouldn't also handle purchases and shipments, the rationale being it would be easier for this person to cover up any errors or irregularities.

Independent verification establishes that each employee's computations and work are checked by another employee. For example, a manager verifies cash collected with the cash register tape.

Good documentation procedures ensure that all transactions can be accounted for. These include controls like prenumbered invoices and forwarding documents to the accounting department.

We cover specific internal control procedures for various assets in later chapters.

SEE ALSO 3.1, "Classifying Cash"

SEE ALSO 4.3, "Accounts Receivable"

SEE ALSO 5.1, "Accounting for Inventory"

SEE ALSO 7.1, "Property, Plant, and Equipment"

1.2   Determining a Form of Entity

Sole Proprietorships

Partnerships

Limited Liability Companies

C Corporations

S Corporations

Before you set up any accounting system, you need to decide what kind of business you are or are going to be. That classification will determine the way your chart of accounts, books, and files should be organized. You can choose among a number of legally recognized structures, or forms of entity, to operate your business depending on your risk tolerance and desired tax situation. The most common forms include these:

- Sole proprietorship
- Partnership
- Limited liability company
- C corporation
- S corporation

To determine the right one for you, you need to weigh your desire for simplicity and ease of operation against the importance of being protected from liability.

Sole Proprietorships

Going into business as a sole proprietor is the simplest way to operate a business. It eliminates the need to pay yourself a fixed salary, but you can still withdraw cash as needed as a capital withdrawal, which is tax-free. As owner, you'll report profit or loss from the business on your own federal income tax return (on Schedule C) without regard to cash withdrawals during the year.

The drawbacks? The assets of the business, as well as everything else you own, are not protected in the event of a successful judgment against the business. It's as if you and the business are one in the court's eyes. Even your personal property is fair game if your company runs into trouble.

Partnerships

A partnership requires two or more owners. It operates much like a proprietorship, except that decisions such as opening a bank account, for example, must be approved by all the partners. As a partner, you're also entitled to draw on the capital account as needed. You also report profit or loss on your federal income tax return Schedule E (cash withdrawals not included).

A con: as is the case with a sole proprietor, personal assets as well as business assets are unprotected in the event of any lawsuits or judgments against the business.

Limited Liability Companies

Limited liability companies (LLCs) are entities created by state law that may operate as a partnership, but without the personal liability issues. So that means successful judgments against the business are limited to the assets of the business. You're not included.

LLCs have drawing accounts—distributions may be made to owners, and there's no requirement that they be based on your share of the business. Profits or losses pass through to shareholders and are treated the same way as with partnerships.

C Corporations

A C corporation is a separate taxable entity that limits liability to the business's assets. (C refers to the tax code section that pertains to this particular entity.) Owners are required to be on the payroll just like any other employee, so there are no drawing accounts. C corporations pay taxes on their own net income. Owners pay taxes on their salaries.

S Corporations

An S Corporation is also a pass-through entity that limits the liability to the assets of the business. (S refers to part of the applicable tax code.) The net income or losses are passed through to the shareholders' individual income tax returns. Owners are salaried employees, as with C corporations. S corporations are limited to 100 shareholders and follow strict election rules.

Because of the many legal and tax ramifications involved with forming an entity, it's worth consulting an expert on this one. If you have any questions, an attorney or CPA can thoroughly explain the particular business attributes of each form of entity.

1.3   Creating a Filing System

Accounting Documents

Setting Up Your Filing System

When you know what your business is going to be and you've found your location, you're ready to organize your office. That means ordering appropriate accounting documents and setting up your files. For the purposes of this book, our initial explanations will assume you're using a manual bookkeeping system. Although current accounting software is inexpensive, easy to use, and saves time, it never hurts to understand the basics, and your knowledge of a manual system will come in handy in selecting the right software and using it properly. Because more and more business people are choosing to automate, however, we have included descriptions in this edition of how a computerized system would handle certain transactions and processes. We also address computer software and online accounting programs in more detail later in the book.

SEE ALSO Chapter 15, "Computerized Accounting"

Accounting Documents

Here are the basic documents you should have in your accounting kit:

- *Checks*. We recommend sequentially numbered, imprinted, three-part check vouchers, which include an original and two copies.

- *Deposit slips*. Get two-part so there's a copy for your records.

- *Sales invoices*. Use sequentially numbered four-part invoices, which include an original and three copies.

- *Purchase orders*. Also prenumbered and with copies.

You can order accounting documents through a supply store, or in the case of checks and deposit slips, from your bank. You won't need to order shipping or receiving documents. The bill of lading that comes with a shipment, or the invoice you fill out with your shipper, serves as your documentation.

In computerized systems, many of these documents will be automatically generated when a transaction occurs. Sequentially numbered sales invoices, for example, will be produced when a sale is recorded. Similarly, checks can be generated when a payment is due.

Setting Up Your Filing System

Let's deal with paper files first. You can set up computer files as well for convenience, but you'll still want to keep the hardcopy documentation. The IRS requires documentation going back at least 3 years for most business transactions. If you do your accounting via computer, a record of all of your transactions will be kept in the system and will be readily accessible in the event you get audited or want to review something. Obviously, you'll need to be sure to back up your system regularly.

Customer Files

For starters, you'll need a file folder for each customer, in which you'll store paid invoices for that customer, as well as any pertinent customer data. This could include credit reports, terms, purchasing history, shipping specifications, etc.

You'll also want to create an unpaid invoices file which will contain all customers' invoices that have not been paid. Here is where you'll put bills that have not yet come due as you receive them. Check these files periodically to determine whether customers are up-to-date on their payments and to ensure nothing falls through the cracks. At any given time, the total of all the unpaid invoices in the file will add up to your company's accounts receivable.

Vendor Files

Set up a file folder for each vendor, in which you store paid invoices for that vendor, as well as details, terms, etc. In addition to individual files for each vendor, you'll also want to set up your unpaid file by due date. This means creating separate file folders for each day of the month, containing invoices due to be paid that day. That way, you'll have all the bills due on a particular date at your fingertips. To be sure you capture any discounts, file bills by the earlier date.

1.4   Establishing the Chart of Accounts

Balance Sheet Accounts

Revenue and Expense Accounts

A Sample Chart of Accounts

The **chart of accounts** is your road map. Here's where you take stock of what you have and the kind of business you expect to do and decide for which accounts you'll need to classify your transactions. In this subchapter, you learn more about revenue and expense accounts, as well as how to develop your own chart of accounts.

✓

A **chart of accounts** is the list of all the different accounts you have for your business.

Balance Sheet Accounts

Balance sheet accounts include all asset, liability, and equity accounts. This means everything from the cash you have in the bank and inventory on hand to amounts you owe creditors and employees. In addition, this section includes accounts to record any investments you made in the company or monies withdrawn for personal use.

Determining Assets

Assets are the things you own. Typically, assets are divided into two categories:

- Current assets
- Noncurrent assets

Current assets are those you expect to either use, sell, or convert to cash within a year at the most. Accounts receivable that you're owed from customers is an example of a current asset. A prepayment for something such as rent or insurance is also a current asset. Noncurrent assets are those you expect to have for more than a year. Land, building, and any property you need to do your business would qualify, as would intangible assets, like a brand name.

Determining Liabilities

Like assets, liabilities can also be qualified as current and long-term. Current liabilities are those debts you expect to pay within the year, such as accounts payable, which is money you owe to creditors for purchases on account. Employee salaries are another common current liability.

SEE ALSO 6.1, "Accounts Payable"

SEE ALSO 8.5, "Recording Payroll"

Long-term notes payable and mortgage debt are examples of long-term liability. You will be making payments on these loans for a number of years.

Calculating Equity

Equity can include everything from a sole proprietor's investment and withdrawals from the business to different classes of stock sold on a public exchange. For sole proprietorships and partnerships, equity is typically divided into three accounts:

- *Capital*. This account reflects the total investment in the business and usually has a credit balance.

- *Drawing*. Amounts the owner or owners withdraw from the business are recorded in this account, which typically has a debit balance.

- *Profit and loss* (also called retained earnings). This is the account where net income for the year is recorded. It is closed into the capital account at the end of the year.

For corporations, the equity includes different classes of stock and profit and loss (or retained earnings accounts). But corporations do not have drawing accounts.

Revenue and Expense Accounts

Revenue and expense accounts are temporary accounts set up to track business activity on a yearly basis. At the end of the year, they are closed into retained earnings (also called profit and loss account) on the balance sheet, so they have a zero balance at the start of the next period. Like asset and liabilities, revenue and expense accounts are denoted by a separate series of numbers in the chart of accounts. Sales accounts are 300 series. Expenses are 400s.

Sales Accounts

Sales and income accounts represent proceeds from sales of goods or services. They can also be called *revenue accounts*. Accounts holding interest income, such as from a short-term loan to an employee or a payment extension to a customer, also fall into this category.

Expense Accounts

These accounts record your costs of doing business. They include fixed charges you must regularly pay out, like employee salaries and utilities, and other more variable charges like fees for advertising or supplies. The purchases account would go here as well. Also included in this category are noncash expenses such as **depreciation.**

SEE ALSO 7.2, "Depreciation"

✓

Depreciation is used to account for the decline in value of an asset through wear and tear, deterioration, and obsolescence by allocating its cost over its useful life.

A Sample Chart of Accounts

The following sample chart of accounts would be suitable for most small businesses. Some companies have fewer accounts than this; others have more. It depends on the business, the size, and the type of industry. A service company, for example, might have very little inventory (manuals to sell to customers, perhaps) or none at all. You could add other account categories as needed.

Numbering can vary. In this case, we've broken down the accounts as follows:

Assets	100s
Liabilities	200 to 289
Equity	290 to 299
Sales	300s
Expenses	400s and 500s

Computerized systems, however, typically use four- to seven-digit account numbers, so if you used QuickBooks, for example, cash in bank might be A/C #1010. We've included a sample Chart of Accounts for an automated system in Chapter 15, as it may be beneficial to see the difference. In the end, how you choose to number your accounts matters little as long as you're consistent and know your own system. No matter how it's set up, any organization benefits from having a chart of accounts customized to their business. In our example, we've also included a brief definition and chapter references where you can find more detail on particular accounts.

SEE ALSO 15.5, "Customizing and Using Your Software"

EVERY DAY ADVENTURE COMPANY
CHART OF ACCOUNTS

Number	Category	See Also
101	Cash on Hand (cash and receipts at company)	Chapter 3
102	Cash in Bank (funds deposited in bank account)	Chapter 3
105	Petty Cash (fund for small business expenses)	Chapter 3
130	Notes Receivable (promissory notes)	Chapter 4
140	Accounts Receivable (amounts customers owe you)	Chapter 4
150	Inventory (items for sale or to go into mfg. goods)	Chapter 5
160	Prepaid Expenses (amount paid in advance for future expenses)	Chapter 1
170	Land (land or acreage owned by company)	Chapter 7
175	Building (buildings owned by company)	Chapter 7
176	Accumulated Depreciation—Building*	Chapter 7
180	Machinery and Equipment (machinery and equipment used in creating product or service)	Chapter 7
181	Accumulated Depreciation—Machinery and Equipment*	Chapter 7
185	Office Equipment (computers, desks, copiers, etc.)	Chapter 7
186	Accumulated Depreciation—Office Equipment	Chapter 7
190	Automotive Equipment (company cars, etc.)	Chapter 7
191	Accumulated Depreciation—Automotive Equipment	Chapter 7
195	Other Assets (investments, leases, etc.)	Chapter 7

Liabilities

Number	Category	See Also
201	Notes Payable—Short-Term (promise to repay company)	Chapter 6
210	Accounts Payable (amounts owed to creditors/suppliers)	Chapter 6
230	FICA Withheld (Social Security/Medicare taxes owed)	Chapter 8
231	Federal Income Tax Withheld (federal income tax owed)	Chapter 8
232	State and County Income Tax Withheld (state and county tax owed)	Chapter 8
235	Accrued Payroll Taxes (payroll taxes owed)	Chapter 12
240	Other Accrued Liabilities (other liabilities owed)	Chapter 11
270	Long-Term Notes Payable (amounts owed creditor >1 year)	Chapter 9

Number	Category	See Also
	Capital Section	

(For Sole Proprietorship)

Number	Category	See Also
290	Proprietor's Capital (owner's investment in company)	Chapter 1
295	Proprietor's Drawing (owner's withdrawals from company)	Chapter 1
299	Profit and Loss (the amount your company made or lost in the period)	Chapter 1

(For Partnership)

Number	Category	See Also
290	Partners' Capital (partners' investment in company)	Chapter 1
295	Partners' Drawing (partners' withdrawal from company)	Chapter 1
299	Profit and Loss	Chapter 11

(For Corporation)

Number	Category	See Also
290	Common Stock (ownership shares in company)	Chapter 1
295	Retained Earnings (profit and loss)	Chapter 11
299	Profit and Loss (amount made or lost by operations)	Chapter 11
301	Sales (revenues or total brought in by operations)	Chapter 4
305	Interest Income (interest earned on investments)	Chapter 4
310	Cash Discounts Allowed (discounts on sales)	Chapter 4
401	Purchases (materials purchased for mfg. or resale)	Chapter 6
402	Cash Discounts Earned (discounts earned on purchases)	Chapter 6
410	Staff Salaries (cost of paying staff for period)	Chapter 8
415	Payroll Tax Expense (cost payroll taxes paid by employer)	Chapter 8
420	Automotive Expenses (costs such as gas/mileage related to used auto business)	Chapter 6
425	Insurance (costs of insuring the business)	Chapter 6
430	Utilities (cost of electricity, water, heating, and cooling)	Chapter 6
432	Telephone (phone charges for the period)	Chapter 6
435	Repairs and Maintenance (cost of repairing and maintaining assets)	Chapter 6
440	Advertising (cost of advertising product)	Chapter 6
448	Commission Expense (amounts earned by company salespeople)	Chapter 6
450	Travel and Entertainment (expenses for business travel and entertaining)	Chapter 6
452	Promotion (cost of promoting and publicizing services)	Chapter 6
455	Shipping Expenses (cost of shipping product/purchases)	Chapter 6
460	Bad Debts (cost of customer accounts in default)	Chapter 4
501	Office Supplies and Expense (cost of supplies used in period)	Chapter 6
505	Depreciation (expense for asset decline)	Chapter 7
510	Contributions (charitable contributions made by firm)	Chapter 8

Continues

Continued

Number	Category	See Also
520	Pension/Profit-Sharing Expense (amounts paid for employee benefits)	Chapter 8
525	Postage (cost of postage)	Chapter 6
530	Professional Fees (cost of association memberships, continuing professional education, etc.)	Chapter 6
595	Interest Expense (interest costs incurred on debt)	Chapter 6
599	Miscellaneous (business expenses that don't fall into other categories)	Chapter 6

*Write-off of asset over useful life.

1.5 Opening the General Ledger

General Ledger Setup
A Sample General Ledger Page

When you've developed your chart of accounts, you're ready to set up your **general ledger.** This is where you keep a record of all activity and changes in your accounts. It's also the book you'll use as the basis for generating your financial statements. In this subchapter, we show you how to set up your general ledger and post the opening amounts for individual accounts.

✓

A **general ledger** is the complete set of a company's accounts. This record shows increases and decreases in each account and the current balance.

General Ledger Setup

The general ledger is set up in the same order as the chart of accounts. Each account is given its own number and page, where you can record transactions and summaries of transactions from the various journals. In this way, the general ledger enables you to keep a running total of each account's balance.

SEE ALSO 2.4, "Recording in Journals"

The ledger's pages list the account name on a line across the top and show the account's increases and decreases on separate sides of a chart. For this reason, they're called T accounts—the horizontal and vertical line form a T. A simple version looks like this:

ACCT. 102   CASH IN BANK

12/31 Balance $5,000	

Any amounts posted on the left side of the T-line are considered **debits** to the account. Amounts on the right side are **credits.** Each line item represents a separate journal entry and should be dated and referenced to the source journal. In some cases, when setting up the ledger or carrying forward an opening balance, only a date is necessary. Debit and credits are discussed in more detail when we discuss recording transactions.

SEE ALSO 2.3, "Analyzing Transactions"

✓ _____

Debit is the left side of an account. For an asset, it represents an increase; for a liability, a decrease.

Credit is the right side of an account. For an asset, it represents decreases; for a liability, increases.

The following example shows how you would open a general ledger. If we were starting with an actual company, the opening amounts would be drawn from supporting documentation and journals. Here we're using the 12/31 balances for Every Day Adventure Company as opening balances for the next period beginning 1/1. Some accounts on Every Day's books currently carry zero balances, but that will change as monthly transactions are recorded, so we still need to create the ledger page. Most companies use a modified version of the T-account. Here is a common format, which includes labeled columns for the date, reference, debits, credits, and balance. The posting reference refers to the journal where the posting originated.

SEE ALSO 2.4, "Recording in Journals"

EVERY DAY ADVENTURE COMPANY
GENERAL LEDGER
Assets

ACCT. 101   CASH ON HAND

Date	Reference	Debit	Credit	Balance
1/1	Opening Balance			$0

ACCT. 102   CASH IN BANK

Date	Reference	Debit	Credit	Balance
1/1	Opening Balance	$5,000		$5,000

ACCT. 105   PETTY CASH

Date	Reference	Debit	Credit	Balance
1/1	Opening Balance	-0-		$0

ACCT. 140   ACCOUNTS RECEIVABLE

Date	Reference	Debit	Credit	Balance
1/1	Opening Balance			$20,000

ACCT. 150   INVENTORY

Date	Reference	Debit	Credit	Balance
1/1	Opening Balance			$2,000

ACCT. 160   PREPAID EXPENSES

Date	Reference	Debit	Credit	Balance
1/1	Opening Balance			$1,200

ACCT. 185   OFFICE EQUIPMENT

Date	Reference	Debit	Credit	Balance
1/1	Opening Balance			$27,000

ACCT. 186   ACCUMULATED DEPRECIATION: OFFICE EQUIPMENT

Date	Reference	Debit	Credit	Balance
1/1	Opening Balance			($2,500)

Liabilities

ACCT. 210   ACCOUNTS PAYABLE

Date	Reference	Debit	Credit	Balance
1/1	Opening Balance			($13,500)

ACCT. 270   LONG-TERM NOTES PAYABLE

Date	Reference	Debit	Credit	Balance
1/1	Opening Balance			($10,000)

Owner's Equity

ACCT. 290   PROPRIETOR'S CAPITAL

Date	Reference	Debit	Credit	Balance
1/1	Opening Balance			($37,400)

ACCT. 295   PROPRIETOR'S DRAWING

Date	Reference	Debit	Credit	Balance
1/1	Opening Balance			$8,200

The complete general ledger for Every Day Adventure Company would continue with accounts for revenue and expenses, but because these have zero balances at the beginning of the period, we have not included them here.

SEE ALSO 2.5, "Posting to the General Ledger"

SEE ALSO 10.2, "Closing Cash Journals"

SEE ALSO 10.3, "Closing Employee Accounts"

A Sample General Ledger Page

As transactions occur, accountants enter them first to a journal and then post the monthly totals to the general ledger. By the end of the period, a general ledger page for a cash account might appear as follows:

ACCT. 102   CASH IN BANK

Date	Reference	Debit	Credit	Balance
5/31	Balance			$13,300
6/30	CR (Cash Receipts Journal)	$2,300		
6/30	CD (Cash Disbursements Journal)		$5,000	
6/30	General Journal		$1,600	$9,000

Note that each posting is given a reference to the journal where it originated. The balance need not be computed after each entry. The end of the period is fine.

In this instance we have computed the balance after each entry to illustrate the effect of each addition or subtraction from the account. A computerized system would include updated balances as well. However, if you are familiar with the mathematics of debits and credits, running a balance at the end of the period is fine.

SEE ALSO 2.4, "Recording in Journals"

Recording Business Transactions

2.1 The Accounting Cycle

In this subchapter, we explain the **accounting cycle,** or how **transactions** are recorded, summarized, and translated into useful financial information. Understanding the accounting cycle is essential to knowing how financial transactions are converted into hard data about a company.

✓

The **accounting cycle** is the series of events from the execution of a transaction to its ultimate reflection in the financial statements.

A **transaction** for accounting purposes is a business event that alters a company's financial position.

The **operating cycle** is the average length of time between buying inventory and receiving cash proceeds from its sale.

Unlike the **operating cycle,** which may vary by company or industry, the accounting cycle is the same for all entities. It can be broken down into the following steps:

1. Executing a transaction
2. Analyzing the transaction
3. Recording the transaction in the appropriate journal
4. Posting the transaction to the general ledger
5. Preparing a trial balance
6. Making adjustments
7. Preparing financial statements

SEE ALSO Chapter 11, "Year-End Reporting"

2.2 Timing

Accounting Periods

Cash vs. Accrual

When setting up for business, a company needs to make at least two important timing-related decisions: choosing an accounting period or fiscal year, and deciding whether to record transactions as they occur (**accrual basis**) or when cash is received or paid out (**cash basis**). This subchapter covers the factors to consider in making these choices.

✓

In **cash basis** accounting, transactions are recorded and reported only when cash is received or paid.

Accrual basis accounting requires recording transactions when they occur. Sales, for example, are recorded when the merchandise exchanges hands, even if paid for using credit.

Accounting Periods

An accounting period is the length of time for which transactions are recorded, summarized, and reported—typically a year. For tax purposes, this is also the period upon which taxes are computed. Many large public firms publish monthly and quarterly reports and statements as well, but their primary accounting period as far as the IRS is concerned is the fiscal year. Companies often choose to have their accounting period coincide with the calendar year for simplicity and convenience, but this is not required. Retailers, for example, typically use January 31 as the end of their fiscal year because this encompasses their peak season (Christmas), as well as the costs related to it.

Sole proprietors are the owners of their businesses, and their profit and loss must be reported on their personal tax return on Schedule C at the end of the calendar year. For this reason, their accounting fiscal year needs to end on December 31. Otherwise, there are no hard-and-fast requirements for deciding when to begin and end an accounting period, but it should reflect the business cycle. If you want to change accounting periods, you need to get permission from the IRS.

Cash vs. Accrual

A company also must determine at the outset whether to use a cash basis or accrual basis for recording transactions and filing taxes. From a financial statement standpoint, the accrual basis is more informative, because it clearly matches revenue and expenses. When you receive and are billed for an item you purchase, it makes sense that you should be required to record a liability for the amount you owe. The IRS requires most established businesses with revenues over a certain amount to use the accrual method, and that is the focus of this book.

However, for small and start-up businesses, it's worth knowing that there are advantages to the cash basis, including ...

- *Ease of tax payment.* Because an entity must pay tax only on income received in cash, the company should have the funds on hand.

- *Reduced taxes.* A cash basis taxpayer is better able to control taxable income by delaying cash deposits or speeding up the payment of expenses.

- *Efficiency.* Bookkeeping throughout the year on the cash basis is simpler and less time-consuming.

Many small businesses maintain their records on a cash basis throughout the year to take advantage of cash basis tax filing while preparing the financial statements on the accrual basis for more meaningful reporting. You can do this, but you need to make a few adjusting entries at year-end to convert cash basis records to the accrual basis.

Note: If you use an accounting software program, you'll be asked to select your preferred method—cash or accrual—for recording transactions. However, you still have the option of producing individual reports in the other method. Some business owners find this useful when starting out to see the differences in their financial reporting.

SEE ALSO 15.2, "Evaluating Computerized Systems"

2.3 Analyzing Transactions

Understanding Debits and Credits

Documentation

Before any activity can be properly recorded, transactions must be analyzed to determine what accounts they affect. In this subchapter, you learn about debits and credits and the importance of recording transactions in the proper period.

Understanding Debits and Credits

In accounting, every transaction affects at least two accounts—increasing one and decreasing the other. This is the basis for the double entry bookkeeping and the first step in analyzing any transaction.

SEE ALSO 1.1, "Accounting Basics"

SEE ALSO 1.4, "Establishing the Chart of Accounts"

For example, if you paid $1,500 to buy two new laptops for your company on January 5, your cash account would decrease by $1,500. At the same time, you've acquired two computers, so your office equipment account would increase by $1,500.

Remember, the general ledger shows two sides for each account so additions and subtractions are recorded separately. The left side of an account is the debit side; the right side is the credit side.

SEE ALSO 1.5, "Opening the General Ledger"

Recording Assets

Assets typically have debit balances. Increases in assets are shown on the left, or debit, side. Decreases in assets are shown on the right, or credit, side. Liabilities are the opposite, with increases coming on the credit side and decreases being debits. This may seem counterintuitive to how it is in everyday life, where your bank account is credited with deposits and debited with withdrawals, but it actually isn't. From your bank's point of view, when you deposit money, this increases their liability to you (credit) and when you withdraw money it reduces their liability (debit).

So after our laptop purchase, the transaction would be reflected in the accounts as follows:

ACCT. 102   CASH IN BANK

Date	Reference	Debit	Credit	Balance
1/2	Balance			$4,240
1/6	CD Cash Disbursements Journal		$1,500	$2,740

ACCT. 185   OFFICE EQUIPMENT

Date	Reference	Debit	Credit	Balance
1/2	Balance			$2,000
1/6	CD Cash Disbursements Journal	$1,500		$3,500

The cash in bank account now has a balance of $2,740 ($4,240 – $1,500). Meanwhile, the $1,500 debit to the office equipment account has increased the account to $3,500 ($2,000 + $1,500).

Recording Liabilities

Liability accounts typically have credit balances. Record an increase in a liability on the right side, or as a credit to the account. A decrease in a liability is debited to the account.

Continuing our laptop example: if instead of paying cash, you bought the computers on account with one of your suppliers, you would record an increase in accounts payable (a liability) as opposed to a decrease in cash.

SEE ALSO 6.1, "Accounts Payable"

This would be reflected in your general ledger accounts as follows:

ACCT. 185   OFFICE EQUIPMENT

Date	Reference	Debit	Credit	Balance
1/2	Balance			$2,000
1/6	CD Cash Disbursements Journal	$1,500		$3,500

ACCT. 210   ACCOUNTS PAYABLE

Date	Reference	Debit	Credit	Balance
1/2	Balance			($1,600)
1/6	CD Cash Disbursements Journal		$1,500	($3,100)

The balance in office equipment increased $1,500 to $3,500, while accounts payable also increased $1,500 to $3,100.

Recording Owner's Equity

Owner's equity, like liabilities, is a claim on assets. Consequently, increases in owner's equity are recorded on the right or credit side, while a decrease is considered a debit. For example, if the owner invested more of his own cash into the business, this would ultimately affect the equity and cash accounts as follows:

ACCT. 102   CASH IN BANK

Date	Reference	Debit	Credit	Balance
1/2	Balance			$4,240
1/6	CD Cash Disbursements Journal		$1,500	$2,740
1/15	CR Cash Receipts Journal	$2,000		$4,740

ACCT. 290   PROPRIETOR'S CAPITAL

Date	Reference	Debit	Credit	Balance
1/2	Balance			($5,000)
1/15	CR Cash Receipts Journal		$2,000	($7,000)

The cash account would now have $4,740, while the equity account, called proprietor's capital here because this is a sole proprietorship, would have a balance of $7,000. Note that balances don't ordinarily need to be calculated after each entry, but we are doing it here for purposes of illustration. In a computerized system, the accounts would automatically be updated as the entries are recorded and saved.

SEE ALSO 15.1, "Benefits of Computerized Accounting"

Recording Revenue

Revenue (income) accounts usually have credit balances. Increases in revenues are credited to the right side, while decreases are debited on the left. If our company had credit sales of $3,275 for the week, this would be recorded in the accounts as follows.

ACCT. 140 ACCOUNTS RECEIVABLE

Date	Reference	Debit	Credit	Balance
1/2	Balance			$2,600
1/18	CR Cash Receipts Journal	$3,275		$5,875

ACCT. 301 SALES

Date	Reference	Debit	Credit	Balance
1/2	Balance			$0
1/10	CR Cash Receipts Journal		$4,500	($4,500)
1/18	CR Cash Receipts Journal		$3,275	($7,775)

The balance in accounts receivable is now $5,875, while our month-to-date sales are $7,775.

Recording Expenses

Expenses generally have debit balances. An increase in an expense goes on the left or debit side. A decrease in an expense is credited to the right side of the account. So if we are billed for advertising expenses of $1,400 on January 20, this would be reflected as follows:

ACCT. 440 ADVERTISING EXPENSE

Date	Reference	Debit	Credit	Balance
1/2	Balance			$0
1/20	CR Cash Disbursements Journal	$1,400		$1,400

ACCT. 210 ACCOUNTS PAYABLE

Date	Reference	Debit	Credit	Balance
1/2	Balance			($1,600)
1/15	CR Cash Receipts Journal		$1,500	
1/20	GJ General Journal		$1,400	($4,500)

So advertising expense is charged $1,400 for the month, and accounts payable increases to $4,500. Note that advertising expense did not have an opening balance. This is because revenue and expense accounts are closed into the equity at the end of the period.

SEE ALSO 11.3, "Preparing a Trial Balance"

Is It a Debit or Credit?

The second part of analyzing a transaction is determining whether the accounts involved are debited or credited. Sometimes accounts won't have the usual balance, but this is a temporary state. The following table provides a quick reference:

Account	Usual Balance	Debit	Credit
Asset	Debit	+	−
Liability	Credit	−	+
Equity	Credit	−	+
Revenue	Credit	−	+
Expense	Debit	+	−

Documentation

Every accounting transaction is going to be initiated by some sort of documentation. This is usually your first clue as to how to classify it. A sales receipt, for example, obviously represents a sale. It also tells you whether the sale was made for cash or on credit. At the end of the day, a cash register tape lists total sales and also breaks down sales between cash and credit. This makes it easy to decide what accounts will be affected.

If the tape for 4/15 shows sales of $2,654, and $1,200 of that was cash and the rest was store credit, you know that the following accounts will have changes:

Sales:	+ $2,654
Cash:	+ 1,200
Accounts Receivable:	+ $1,454

In accounting, there's a specific way of writing down this transaction that mirrors the effects on the left and right (debit and credit) sides of the account:

	Debit	Credit
4/15　Cash	$1,200	
Accounts Receivable	$1,454	
Sales		$2,654
To record sales for 4/15.		

This is called a **journal entry** because the **journal** is the book where it is recorded. The journal is the first place a transaction is recorded. It is the only place in accounting where both sides of the transaction are shown together, so it is an important link in the process. Remember, postings to the general ledger only show the debit or credit in the particular account. In our preceding example, accounts receivable would only reflect a debit for $1,454. The other parts of the transaction would be recorded in the cash and sales accounts.

✓

The **journal,** or the book of first or original entry, is the first place a transaction is recorded or "journalized." It's also the only place where the entire transaction is recorded together with an explanation. This is called a **journal entry.**

A number of different journals exist, and sometimes postings are summaries of days' or months' worth of transactions. We cover journals in the next subchapter.

2.4 Recording in Journals

The General Journal

The Sales Journal

The Cash Receipts Journal

The Purchases Journal

The Cash Disbursements Journal

In accounting, the journal is the book of first entry, where all transactions are recorded and explained. But there's more than one journal:

- The general journal, which records transactions that don't fit into any of the other four journals

- The sales journal, which records credit sales

- The cash receipts journal, which records any cash received (sometimes combined with the sales journal)

- The purchases journal, which records purchases on account

- The cash disbursements journal, which records cash payments of any kind (sometimes combined with the purchases journal)

In this subchapter, we describe each of these different types of journals and teach you how to know where to record what.

The General Journal

A small business that has few transactions might use the general journal as the only journal, but this is extremely rare in our experience. Let's take a look at a sample general journal page. Note that one column refers to the general ledger account number. This enables you to trace each entry to its ultimate reflection in the general ledger.

SEE ALSO 1.5, "Opening the General Ledger"

BRIGHT IDEA MANUFACTURING COMPANY
GENERAL JOURNAL

Date	Account Explanation	Acct.#	Debit	Credit
8/1	Prepaid Insurance	160	$1,200	
	Accounts Payable	210		$1,200
To record renewal of annual insurance policy for the year.				
8/6	Notes Receivable	130	$2,500	
	Accounts Receivable—Lee	140		$2,500
To record conversion of accounts receivable for Lee Co. to a notes receivable.				
8/31	Insurance Expense	425	$100	
	Prepaid Insurance	160		$100
To record insurance expense for August.				
8/31	Depreciation Expense	186	$500	
	Accumulated Depreciation	505		$500
To record depreciation expense on office equipment for August.				

Notice that many of the transactions recorded here are noncash transactions. Any activity affecting cash would be recorded in the cash receipts or cash disbursements journal.

The Sales Journal

In most large businesses, the sales journal is used to record credit sales only. However, in some small businesses, the sales journal and cash receipts journal are combined so all sales of any type are recorded in one place. For the purposes of this example, assume that Bright Idea Manufacturing Company is a large-enough concern to warrant a separate sales journal.

BRIGHT IDEA MANUFACTURING COMPANY
SALES JOURNAL

Date	Customer	Invoice #	Reference	Amount
8/2	Lee Company	4233	X	$2,500
8/4	J. Jones	4239	X	$1,300
8/5	P. Gupta	4242	X	$3,850
8/14	R. Sanchez	4259	X	$4,120
8/16	S. Mellings	4263	X	$1,980
8/20	F. Bachman	4267	X	$5,300
8/21	Field Co.	4268	X	$2,600

Date	Customer	Invoice #	Reference	Amount
8/23	A&A Corp.	4271	X	$6,800
8/30	S. Toth	4276	X	$1,500
Total August Sales				**$29,950**

Each entry in the journal reflects a transaction with one customer and, as such, should be debited to that customer's account in the accounts receivable subsidiary ledger. The X in the Reference column denotes this has been done. In addition, you would want to put the open invoice in the customer's paper file.

SEE ALSO 4.3, "Accounts Receivable"

SEE ALSO 1.3, "Creating a Filing System"

The postings to sales in the general ledger would not be made individually, unless the company had very few, high-dollar sales. Instead, all sales for the month would be totaled, and the totals would be posted to the general ledger at the end of the month. The effect of this summary posting is represented in the following entry.

	Debit	Credit
3/31 Accounts Receivable	$29,950	
Sales		$29,950
To record credit sales for August.		

The Cash Receipts Journal

The cash receipts journal is where you record any receipt of cash, whether from a sale, payment on account, or any other reason.

BRIGHT IDEA MANUFACTURING COMPANY
CASH RECEIPTS JOURNAL

Date	Description/Account	PR	General Account (Credit)	Sales (Credit)	Accounts Receivable (Credit)	Cash Discounts* Allowed (Credit)	Cash Debit
8/5	Accounts receivable—Wong Co.				($9,700)		$9,700
8/17	Sales			($29,550)			$29,550
8/21	Accounts receivable—Nelson				($2,000)		$2,000
8/22	Accounts receivable—Hadley Corp.				($4,500)		$4,500
8/28	Sale of land	170	($100,000)				$100,000
Total 8/31			($100,000)	($29,550)	($16,200)		$145,750
			{170}	{301}	{140}		{102}

*Also called sales discounts.

Numbers in ( ) are credit balances. Numbers in { } are account numbers.

You can easily customize the cash receipts journal for your business by taking out credit accounts and substituting your own. Small businesses with a limited accounting staff often use a combined cash/sales journal that includes both cash and credit sales and all cash receipt transactions. This saves time, and if one accountant handles both, there's no need for separate journals.

Regardless of which format you choose, the mechanics are the same. At the end of the month, you post totals from the cash receipts journal to the general ledger. The following journal entry summarizes the net effect.

	Debit	Credit
8/31 Cash	$145,750	
Land		$100,000
Sales		$29,550
Accounts Receivable		$16,200
To record cash receipts activity from August.		

WILSON AND COMPANY
CASH AND SALES JOURNAL

Date	Customer	Cash Deposit	Accounts Debit	Receivable Credit	Sales Tax	Sales	Sales Discounts	Sales Returns and Allowances	Shipping Expenses	Misc.	Acct. #	Other Debit	Other Credit
5/1	A. Terra		$1,500			($1,500)							
5/2	C. Lewis	$2,649		($2,649)									
5/5	Tom's Recycling		$500							Office Equip.	185		($500)
5/10	L. Riley	$1,500		($1,500)									
5/20	I. Palmer	$430				($450)	$20						
5/25	Party Palace		$1,285		($56)	($1,229)							
Total		$4,579	$3,285	($4,149)	($56)	($3,179)	$20						($500)
		{102}		{140}	{599}	{301}	{310}						{185}

Numbers in ( ) are credit balances. Numbers in { } are account numbers.

The Purchases Journal

The purchases journal is similar to the sales journal, in that all credit purchases of merchandise are recorded here. Anything purchased for cash, on the other hand, goes in the cash disbursements journal.

2.4

BRIGHT IDEA MANUFACTURING COMPANY
PURCHASES JOURNAL

Date	Vendor	Invoice Date	Reference	Amount
8/4	Tolley Corp.	8/4	X	$4,700
8/8	Smith and Brill	8/7	X	$9,370
8/11	J. Maxwell	8/10	X	$5,100
8/12	Geoff Steel	8/12	X	$7,700
8/25	Plastics, Inc.	8/24	X	$5,200
8/30	Signs and Things	8/30	X	$2,460
Total				$34,530
				{401}

Numbers in { } are account numbers.

At the end of the month, the total amount of purchases on credit would be recorded to account 401, purchases, as referenced at the bottom of the Amount column. The individual vendor accounts would be updated at the time of each sale by crediting the appropriate account in the individual accounts payable subsidiary ledger. The unpaid invoice would be put in the file for the appropriate date due. The net effect to the accounts is represented by the following journal entry.

	Debit	Credit
8/31 Purchases	$34,530	
Accounts Payable		$34,530
To record purchases on account for August.		

The Cash Disbursements Journal

Cash payments of any type are recorded in the cash disbursements journal.

BRIGHT IDEA MANUFACTURING COMPANY
CASH DISBURSEMENTS JOURNAL

Check #	Account Description	PR	Purchases	Account Debit	Payable Debit	Discounts Earned* (Credit)	Cash (Credit)
325	Purchases	401	$3,600				($3,600)
326	Office Equipment	185		$25,000			($25,000)
327–331	Staff Salaries	410		$9,100			($9,100)
332	Purchases	410			$5,800		($5,800)
333–337	Staff Salaries	410		$9,100			($9,100)
8/31	Total		$3,600 {401}	$43,200	$5,800 {210}		($52,600) {102}

*Also called purchase discounts.

Numbers in { } are account numbers.

As with the cash receipts journal, you can easily customize the cash disbursements journal for your business. The number of columns you include is up to you and depends on your chart of accounts and the activities of your particular business.

Small businesses with a limited accounting staff often use a combined cash disbursements/purchases journal that includes both cash and credit payments and all cash disbursement transactions, including payroll and the related taxes. This saves time, and if one accountant handles both, there's no need for separate journals unless the volume of transactions recorded becomes cumbersome.

Regardless of which format you choose, the mechanics are the same. At the end of the month, the activity in the journal would be totaled by individual accounts and posted to the general ledger. The net effect could be summarized as follows:

	Debit	Credit
8/31 Purchases	$9,400	
Staff Salaries	$18,200	
Office Equipment	$25,000	
Cash		$52,600
To record cash disbursements for August.		

SEE ALSO 6.4, "Cash Disbursements"

BRIGHT IDEA MANUFACTURING COMPANY
PURCHASES AND CASH DISBURSEMENTS JOURNAL

Date	Check #	Account Description	PR	Cash Amount	FICA w/held	Federal w/held	State w/held	Payroll	Purchases	Debit	(Credit)	Maintenance	Earned (Credit)	Misc.	Account #	(Credit)
															Accounts Payable → Purchases / Debit / (Credit); **Cash* Discounts** → Maintenance / Earned (Credit); **Other Debit** → Account # / (Credit)	
8/2	325	Purchases	401	($3,600)				$401	$3,600							
8/4		Purchases							$4,700		($4,700)					
8/6	326	Office Equipment	185	($25,000)										Office Equip.	185	$25,000
8/7	327–331	Staff Salaries	410	($9,100)	($550)	($1,820)	($780)	$12,250								
8/8		Purchases							$9,370		($9,370)					
8/11		Purchases							$5,700		($5,700)					
8/12		Purchases							$7,700		($7,700)					
8/19	332	Purchases		($5,800)						$5,800						
8/22	333–337	Staff Salaries	410	($9,100)	($550)	($1,820)	($780)	$12,250								
8/25		Purchases							$5,200		($5,200)					
8/30		Purchases							$2,460		($2,460)					
8/31		Total		($52,600)	($1,100)	($3,640)	($1,560)	$24,500	$38,730	$5,800	($35,130)					$25,000
				{102}				{410}	{401}	{210}						{185}

*Also called purchase discounts.

Numbers in ( ) are credit balances. Numbers in { } are account numbers.

2.5 Posting to the General Ledger

After transactions are entered in the journal, the next stop is the general ledger. In this subchapter, we show you how to summarize and make postings to the general ledger.

Note in the following examples we list the journal with its abbreviation to avoid confusion when we start out. In practice, the abbreviation is sufficient. Here's what we're using:

General Journal	GJ
Sales Journal	SJ
Cash Receipts Journal	CR
Purchase Journal	PJ
Cash Disbursements Journal	CD

BRIGHT IDEA MANUFACTURING COMPANY
GENERAL LEDGER

ACCT. 102   CASH

Date	Reference	Debit	Credit	Balance
7/31	Balance			$3,200
8/31	CR	$145,750		$148,950
8/31	CD		$52,600	$96,350

ACCT. 130   NOTES RECEIVABLE

Date	Reference	Debit	Credit	Balance
7/31	Balance			$0
8/6	GJ	$2,500		$2,500

ACCT. 140   ACCOUNTS RECEIVABLE

Date	Reference	Debit	Credit	Balance
7/31	Balance			$4,000
8/6	SJ	$29,950		$33,950
8/6	GJ		$2,500	$31,450
8/31	CR		$16,200	$15,250

ACCT. 150   INVENTORY

Date	Reference	Debit	Credit	Balance
7/31	Balance			$8,260
8/31	PJ	$34,530		$39,730
8/31	GJ Cost of Goods Sold*		$33,000	
8/31	CD		$9,400	$16,130

Note: Purchases must be adjusted with adjusting entry for cost of goods sold.

SEE ALSO 10.5, "Adjusting Entries"

ACCT. 160   PREPAID EXPENSES

Date	Reference	Debit	Credit	Balance
7/31	Balance			$0
8/1	CD Cash Disbursements Journal	$1,200		
8/20	GJ		$100	$1,100

ACCT. 170   LAND

Date	Reference	Debit	Credit	Balance
7/31	Balance			$100,000
8/31	CR Cash Receipts Journal		$100,000	$0

ACCT. 185   OFFICE EQUIPMENT

Date	Reference	Debit	Credit	Balance
7/31	Balance			$14,000
8/31	CD Cash Disbursements Journal	$25,000		$39,000

ACCT. 186   ACCUMULATED DEPRECIATION—OFFICE EQUIPMENT

Date	Reference	Debit	Credit	Balance
7/31	Balance			($1,500)
8/31	GJ General Journal		$500	($2,000)

Liabilities

ACCT. 210 ACCOUNTS PAYABLE

Date	Reference	Debit	Credit	Balance
7/31	Balance			($6,600)
8/31	GJ General Journal		$1,200	
8/31	CD Cash Disbursements Journal		$34,530	($42,330)

ACCT. 270 LONG-TERM NOTES PAYABLE

Date	Reference	Debit	Credit	Balance
7/31	Balance			($10,000)
8/31	Balance			($10,000)

Equity

ACCT. 290 PROPRIETOR'S CAPITAL

Date	Reference	Debit	Credit	Balance
7/31	Balance			($112,300)
8/31	Net Income		$3,700	($116,000)

ACCT. 301 SALES

Date	Reference	Debit	Credit	Balance
8/1	Balance			$0
8/31	SJ Sales Journal		$29,950	($29,950)
8/31	GJ General Journal	$4,500*		($25,450)
8/31	CR		$29,550	($55,500)

*Last-minute entry made to adjust sales for damaged merchandise returned (other side of entry to cost of sales).

ACCT. 401 PURCHASES

Date	Reference	Debit	Credit	Balance
7/31	Balance			$0
8/31	PJ Purchases Journal	$34,530		
8/31	CD	$9,400		$43,930

ACCT. 410   STAFF SALARIES

Date	Reference	Debit	Credit	Balance
7/31	Balance			$0
8/31	CD Cash Disbursements Journal	$18,200		$18,200

ACCT. 425   INSURANCE EXPENSE

Date	Reference	Debit	Credit	Balance
7/31	Balance			$0
8/31	GJ General Journal	$100		$100

ACCT. 505   DEPRECIATION EXPENSE

Date	Reference	Debit	Credit	Balance
7/31	Balance			$0
8/31	GJ General Journal	$500		$500

As you can see from this example, posting to the general ledger from your journals is a fairly straightforward process. Some smaller companies might choose to post individual entries as they occur during the month; however, most organizations post summary totals for items like sales or cash disbursements at the end of the month. However you decide to proceed, what's important is having a consistent system so you can go back to your journals to check or verify transactions.

2.6 Generating Financial Statements

At the end of the period (a month, a year, etc.), the general ledger is used as the basis for generating financial statements. Here we offer a quick preview of how general ledger balance totals become part of the balance sheet and income statement.

Notice that we've taken some liberties. In the actual closing process, we would make sure the numbers in the ledgers balance first. We would then make any adjustments, which would include taking the beginning inventory + purchases – the cost of goods sold to arrive at ending inventory. The net result would then be added or subtracted to inventory, with the offset going to cost of goods sold. We'd also close an income of $3,200 into the profit and loss account 299 (not shown here) and add it to proprietor's equity to arrive at total owner's equity.

SEE ALSO 1.4, "Establishing the Chart of Accounts"

SEE ALSO 10.4, "Developing a Trial Balance"

SEE ALSO 10.5, "Adjusting Entries"

SEE ALSO 10.6, "The Adjusted Trial Balance"

BRIGHT IDEA MANUFACTURING COMPANY BALANCE SHEET AUGUST 31	
Cash	$96,350
Notes Receivable	$2,500
Accounts Receivable	$15,250
Inventory	$16,130
Prepaid Insurance	$1,100
Total Current Assets	$131,330
Office Equipment	$39,000
Less: Accumulated Depreciation	$2,000
Total Fixed Assets	$37,000
TOTAL ASSETS	$168,330
Accounts Payable	$42,330
Long-Term Notes	$10,000
Total Liabilities	$52,330
Owner's Equity	$116,000
TOTAL LIABILITIES AND OWNER'S EQUITY	$168,330

Following is an income statement for Bright Idea Manufacturing Company. If you've posted properly to your general ledger and accurately tallied totals for each account, you should be able to simply put these balances into your preliminary financial statements (known as a trial balance). We don't show that step here, because no additional adjustments were required, but we do further explain trial balances in a later subchapter.

SEE ALSO 10.4, "Developing a Trial Balance"

BRIGHT IDEA MANUFACTURING COMPANY
INCOME STATEMENT FOR THE MONTH ENDING 8/31

Sales		$55,500
Cost of Goods Sold		$33,000
Gross Profit		$22,500
Less: Operating Expenses		
Staff Salaries	*$18,200*	
Insurance	*$100*	
Depreciation	*$500*	
Total Operating Expenses		$18,800
Operating Income		$3,700
Interest Expense		$0
Income Before Taxes		$3,700
Taxes		$0
Net Income		**$3,700**

In this chapter, we've taken you through the accounting cycle. After an accounting transaction has been executed, it must be analyzed and recorded in the appropriate journal. Journal entries are then summarized and posted to the general ledger. At the end of the month, general ledger balances are reconciled to any subledgers and tallied on a trial balance before the figures are transferred to the income statement and balance sheet. Following this process should provide you with financial statements that accurately reflect your company's business transactions and financial results for the period.

Note: If you use a computerized system, the biggest difference will be that sales, payments, and other transactions need only be recorded a single time. Once you input the data, any posting to or reconciling with subledgers, summary to trial balance, and update to financial statements will be done automatically. This is obviously a huge time-saving benefit provided all transactions have been entered properly.

SEE ALSO Chapter 15, "Computerized Accounting"

3

Accounting for Cash

3.1 Classifying Cash

What's Included in Cash

What's Not Included in Cash

Different Accounts for Cash

In this subchapter, we discuss what you can legitimately consider cash for accounting purposes. We also help you decide how to classify items that seem like cash but belong in a different account.

What's Included in Cash

For most businesses, **cash** consists of currency and coin on hand or in the bank. It may also include **petty cash**—a small fund kept at the company to pay miscellaneous expenses. In addition, foreign currency, bank drafts, checks, cashier's checks, electronic fund transfers, and money orders all count toward your cash balance.

Cash equivalents, such as certificates of deposit (CDs) or Treasury bills with maturities of 3 months or less, are also considered cash because of the ease with which they can be converted to cash. It's fairly common practice now for many banks to automatically invest your excess cash balances in these types of instruments so you can earn interest. If you need to withdraw the funds, the bank automatically converts them back to cash.

✓

Cash is any funds on hand or in the bank, as well as cash equivalents and petty cash.

Petty cash is a small fund, typically $100 or less, kept on hand to meet miscellaneous expenses without going through the payment approval process.

Cash equivalents are short-term investments such as CDs and Treasury bills that can be easily converted into cash and have an original maturity of no more than 3 months.

As a general rule, if the bank will accept it for deposit, you can consider it cash.

What's Not Included in Cash

Just because you can quickly liquidate an asset, doesn't mean it counts as cash on the balance sheet. Your buddy's IOU might seem as good as cash to you, but until you have the money in hand, his promissory note must be classified as a **receivable.**

> ✓
>
> A **receivable** is an amount a party (usually a customer) has agreed to pay within a period of time. An *accounts receivable* is a verbal agreement. A *notes receivable* is a written promise to pay.

The following table lists some items often mistaken for cash, along with their appropriate account classification.

CASH CONFUSED?

Item	Account Classification
Post-dated check	Accounts Receivable
Postage stamps	Office or Prepaid Expense
Uncollected promissory note	Notes Receivable
Travel advances:	
Deducted from employee salary	Accounts Receivable
Not deducted	Prepaid Expense
Credit lines	Notes Payable

Different Accounts for Cash

Often businesses have more than one account for cash. This makes it easier to keep track of cash in different places (bank or company) or with different uses. For example, your chart of accounts might look like the following.

SEE ALSO 1.4, "Establishing the Chart of Accounts"

ROYAL LANDSCAPE COMPANY
CHART OF ACCOUNTS

Acct. #	Account
101	Cash in the Bank
102	Cash on Hand
105	Petty Cash

The balances and activity for each of these accounts are kept separately in the general ledger. Similar cash accounts can also be set up in a computerized system, although, as noted previously, they would likely have four- to seven-digit account numbers. At the end of the period, the amounts are combined on the balance sheet under a "Cash" heading.

SEE ALSO 15.4, "Converting to an Automated System"

ROYAL LANDSCAPE COMPANY
BALANCE SHEET (PARTIAL)
DECEMBER 31

Assets	
Current Assets:	
Cash*	$2,500
Accounts Receivable	$6,650
Less: Allowance for Doubtful Accounts	$220
Net Receivables	**$6,430**
Inventory	$3,100
Prepaid Assets	$1,200
Total Current Assets	**$13,230**

* Cash on Hand ($800) + Cash in Bank ($1,500) + Petty Cash ($200)

Cash can refer to many things, which is important to remember when you're totaling it for a balance sheet. In addition to cash in the bank, a company might have cash or cash receipts on hand, and possibly even a petty cash fund for meeting small business expenses. Short-term investments such as CDs or Treasury bills also are classified as cash.

3.2   The Business Bank Account

Separating Business from Personal

Opening an Account

Managing Cash Levels

In this subchapter, you learn some quick do's and don'ts for setting up a business bank account, and the importance of monitoring how much money you keep in it.

Separating Business from Personal

Many an entrepreneur has started off paying company expenses through his or her personal checking account, but we don't recommend it. A separate business account, often called the **operating account,** provides the best picture of the actual cash activity in your enterprise. It's also a big plus for record-keeping purposes because you won't have to separate business and personal expenses at tax time. And it's highly recommended in the event of an audit by the IRS.

✓
___

An **operating account** is a company's main bank account for meeting operating expenses and depositing money earned.

Opening an Account

At the minimum, your business should have a checking account to pay bills and receive payments. Some companies set up a separate savings account as well, but with the wide availability of interest-earning checking accounts, this may be unnecessary, particularly for a small business. Before you even start shopping around for an account, however, you'll need to take care of some procedural items, such as getting a federal ID number and obtaining authorization for an account.

Obtaining a Taxpayer ID Number

Before opening a business bank account, you'll need a federal taxpayer ID number, also referred to as an employer identification number. To get one you should obtain form SS-4 from the IRS website, irs.gov. You may fill it out and register online, or mail or fax in the printed form. Sole proprietors who have no employees may use their Social Security number as a taxpayer ID number.

Getting Authorization

If you're a sole proprietor, when you have your taxpayer number, you're ready to go. If you're part of a partnership or corporation, you first need further authorization.

In a partnership, both principals—you *and* your partner—must sign off on the account. For a corporation, you'll need to have a **corporate board resolution** authorizing the bank account with specific signatures.

✓

A **corporate board resolution** is a documented vote by board members authorizing the company to take a certain action.

Recording a New Account

Recording the opening of your bank account is fairly straightforward. The net effect of this transaction is reflected in the following journal entry. In actual practice, the $5,000 increase in your cash balance would be one of many entries made to the check register and then summarized to cash receipts journal before posting to the general ledger cash account at the end of the month, but we wanted to illustrate the change separately. The cash account increases by $5,000 and is offset by an entry to record your investment (equity) in the business.

		Debit	Credit
2/1	Cash	$5,000	
	Owner's Equity		$5,000
	To record initial deposit to open bank account.		

This entry is entered in the check register, because that's where all transactions involving cash are recorded.

SMITH, INC.
CHECK REGISTER

Date	Payer/Payee	Debit	Credit	Balance
4/1	M. Smith, owner	$5,000		$5,000
4/6	Speedy Clean, Inc.		$500	$4,500
4/9	Pacific Electric Co.		$375	$4,125
4/29	Franchise Fee		$500	$3,625

The transaction would be entered in the cash receipts journal as well:

SMITH, INC.
CASH RECEIPTS JOURNAL

Date	Sales	Cash	Accounts Receivable	Discounts	Account #	Other Account	Amount
4/1		$5,000			290	Equity	($5,000)

At the end of the month, all transactions within the journal would be summarized (additional deposits added in, or payments subtracted) and posted to the appropriate accounts in the general ledger. Let's assume Smith, Inc., had no further transactions involving the bank account or equity for the month:

ACCT. 102   CASH IN BANK

Date	Reference	Debit	Credit	Balance
3/31	Balance			$0
4/1	CR (Bank Deposit)	$5,000		$5,000

ACCT. 290   OWNER'S EQUITY

Date	Reference	Debit	Credit	Balance
4/1	Opening Balance			$0
4/1	CJ (Bank Deposit)		$5,000	$5,000

The new balances in these accounts at the end of the month will be carried forward on the trial balance to become the basis for the cash and owner's equity line items on the balance sheet. However, the cash balance per the general ledger will still need to be reconciled to the cash balance in the bank, to be sure all transactions for the period have been recorded correctly.

SEE ALSO 3.4, "Preparing a Bank Reconciliation"

Managing Cash Levels

In addition to keeping proper records of cash transactions, it's important to monitor cash to ensure you have enough funds available to meet current operating needs, pay bills, and cover emergencies.

Most banks now offer checking accounts that automatically shift excess funds to an interest-bearing account, so having too much cash in the bank, not earning much interest, isn't the problem it used to be. Still, if you're consistently carrying a balance well over your operating needs, you'll want to evaluate whether the money might be better invested in a longer-term investment with a potentially higher payback.

While there's no rule of thumb about how much cash to keep on hand, preparing a cash budget for the year can help you stay on track. If you estimate your planned receipts and disbursements for each month, you can better gauge how much to keep in your account.

SEE ALSO 14.6, "The Cash Budget"

3.3 Implementing Internal Controls Over Cash

Types of Theft and Fraud

Physical Safeguards

Procedural Safeguards

Sample Procedures

Cash is highly transferable, meaning it has a high degree of **liquidity,** which also means it's easy to steal. The U.S. Chamber of Commerce estimates that **embezzlement** alone costs businesses $4 billion a year, showing that perhaps even the most trusted employees aren't immune to the temptations that come with handling cash.

✓

Liquidity describes a company's ability to meet debt payments and operating expenses.

Embezzlement is the process of stealing cash from a company while trying to cover it up by omitting transactions or otherwise falsifying accounting records.

This subchapter deals with setting up a system of policies and procedures to help safeguard the cash in your operations and minimize the opportunity for theft and errors.

Types of Theft and Fraud

It's not that we mean to focus on the negative, but being aware of what could go wrong might help you prevent it from happening at your organization. The businesses most susceptible to cash misappropriation are those that handle large volume of cash daily—bars, casinos, and similar operations. They're particularly vulnerable to a crime known as **skimming,** when employees pocket some of the receipts and record a lower amount in the books. So management needs to take extra precautions to help ensure cash is processed and recorded properly.

Other companies may receive more of their customer payments by check, but this won't necessarily stop a resourceful bookkeeper with too much responsibility. Cash shortages can be concealed by **kiting** checks, or **lapping** customer payments.

✓

Skimming is when an employee or business pockets part of cash receipts before recording a smaller amount in the books.

Kiting is an attempt to hide a cash shortage in one account by depositing a check from another and exploiting the float time between then and when it clears the bank.

Lapping can happen when an employee handles both receipt of cash and paying bills. Here the bookkeeper would deposit a customer check in his personal account and then use the next payment to reduce the previous customer's bill, and so on.

Physical Safeguards

One of the most obvious ways to protect cash is by putting it in the bank, or making sure that cash on hand is secured and access is restricted to as few people as possible. Other protective measures include cameras, direct deposit of payments, and bonding of employees so theft is covered by insurance. Because some of these measures can be obtrusive, the key is to strike a balance between safeguards and the efficient operation of your business.

Daily Deposits

Cash receipts (which include cash and checks) should be deposited in the bank daily. Any cash on hand should be strictly controlled—preferably kept in a locked cash register for retail operations or stored in a safe with access limited to appropriate personnel.

This might seem obvious, but in start-up businesses in particular, procedures for handling cash often remain dangerously casual. Entrepreneurs focused on the business can be tempted to turn over cash duties to one employee or clerk, often with little or no oversight. This is a prescription for trouble.

Other Deterrents

Businesses that handle large amounts of cash often have cameras on the premises to discourage theft. Cash registers automatically record sales and keep a running tally, which can be reconciled with cash in the drawer. If improper check handling is a concern, customer payments can be sent directly to a lockbox at the bank. Some retail operations use "secret shoppers" to double-check that sales are being recorded correctly.

If your employees handle large amounts of cash, you should also have them **bonded,** which is a form of insurance against theft. To get bonded, potential hires must go through a background check. In addition to screening employees for previous problems, listing bonding as a requirement of the job might discourage people with marginal backgrounds from applying in the first place.

✓

> **Bonding** is purchasing insurance in the event of employee theft or dishonesty.

Using preprinted checks is another visible way of discouraging misappropriation, as all check numbers must be accounted for.

Procedural Safeguards

Locking cash up isn't the only way to prevent theft. How and to whom you assign duties can also help discourage irregularities and make it easier to catch mistakes or errors as they happen. The key is to not vest too much responsibility for handling cash in any one person. Spreading duties around and setting up a system where employees have their work checked by other employees can be one of your most effective safeguards over cash or any asset.

Assigning Responsibilities

All companies should have written policies and procedures for how cash is handled and by whom. This helps track money received and paid as well as providing a way to retrace a transaction in the event of a discrepancy. These procedures can be elaborate or very basic, depending on the size of your business, as we demonstrate in the upcoming examples.

Separation of Duties

How you distribute the tasks involved in handling cash might prove your best safeguard against sticky fingers. By assigning different employees the responsibility for the receipt, recording, and payment functions, you'll make it more difficult for cash shortages or mistakes to be made without someone noticing.

Independent Verification

Where possible, duties should be assigned so each employee's work is checked by another employee. This is the best way to catch irregularities or errors in the early stages. A shortage of cash in the till, for example, could be quickly rectified by having a manager compare cash totals with the register tape before depositing the day's receipts.

Check the Books

Keep running totals in the check register. If you keep balance after each addition or subtraction, you're more likely to catch errors. Also, perform a bank reconciliation monthly to check for any errors or discrepancies. That procedure is addressed in the following section.

Cash-Handling Checklist

Here's a quick checklist of internal control procedures over cash:

- ❏ Deposit all receipts daily.
- ❏ Bond all employees handling large amounts of cash.
- ❏ Independently verify all daily cash totals.
- ❏ Use prenumbered checks to pay bills.
- ❏ Keep employees handling cash receipts or payments from being involved in keeping accounting records for cash.
- ❏ Restrict employees recording cash transactions in books from also having access to cash.
- ❏ Reconcile bank accounts monthly.
- ❏ Limit access to the signature stamp for checks.
- ❏ Require regular vacations for employees who record cash transactions.
- ❏ Be sure the owner receives and reviews bank statements directly.

Internal controls alone won't inoculate you against theft or misappropriation; no policies can realistically prevent **collusion.** Like any safeguards, they're only as good as the people implementing them, so it's important for a business owner to remain involved with day-to-day operations and keep an eye out for irregularities.

✓

Collusion is when two or more employees conspire to embezzle money or otherwise defraud the company.

Sample Procedures

In the following sections, we've included a set of sample procedures for handling cash receipts and disbursements. Obviously, you have more leeway with a larger company, because you have more employees to divide responsibility among. But this doesn't mean you can't set up some checks and balances in a small business, as our example shows. So don't use few employees as an excuse for vesting too much responsibility in one person.

Large Companies

In an ideal world, an established company with a full accounting staff and plenty of employees among whom to divide responsibilities might use a procedure such as this for handling cash:

For cash receipts:

A receptionist opens the mail and removes the checks. She endorses the checks with a dated deposit stamp, adds the checks to the daily check summary, and forwards the checks to the cashier.

A cashier compares the daily summary sheet to the total checks and prepares a deposit slip.

A treasurer makes a bank deposit and forwards a copy of the checks and deposit slip to the accounts receivable department.

An accounts receivable clerk records the total cash received from the daily check summary to the cash receipts journal. The clerk subtracts the individual check payments from the customer account balances in the subsidiary ledgers.

For cash disbursements:

An accounts payable clerk reviews bills coming due in the **accounts payable** file, prepares a **voucher** and attaches it to the invoice, and sends them to the cashier for approval.

SEE ALSO 6.1, "Accounts Payable"

✓

Accounts payable is an amount that's owed a creditor within a certain time period.

A **voucher** is an authorization form, usually prenumbered, that's required before a check can be approved for payment.

The cashier compares the bill to the voucher, approves it for payment, and sends it all to the treasurer.

The treasurer cuts the check and returns it to the cashier to be signed with the signature stamp. Remember, regardless of the size of the business, there are dangers inherent in using a stamp. Therefore, if checks are not signed, safeguards and security checks that limit access need to be put in place when using a signature stamp.

The cashier stamps the check with the signature stamp and forwards it to the receptionist to mail.

The receptionist mails the check to the vendor.

Small Companies

Small companies don't have the luxury of such a large, organized staff. So start-ups and small businesses with few employees must allocate duties and provide for adequate checks and balances as best they can. For example, Parties by Paula, Inc., is a catering company that has been in business for almost 3 years. Including its founder, Paula Stone, the company has four permanent employees—an additional chef, a party planner/hostess, and a bookkeeper. Customers usually make a cash deposit in advance of the event and pay by check or credit card at the time of the party, or mail in a check.

Obviously, there aren't many people to divide responsibilities among, so Ms. Stone sets up the system as follows:

For cash receipts:

The owner receives all payments and compiles a summary.

The party planner checks her math and makes the bank deposit.

The bookkeeper receives the deposit slip and details and enters the receipts in the journal and the customer accounts.

The owner endorses the checks.

For cash disbursements:

The bookkeeper prepares the invoices for payment.

The owner approves the vouchers.

The bookkeeper cuts the checks and supporting documentation.

The owner signs the checks.

Notice that by juggling responsibilities among three individuals, Parties by Paula is still able to maintain control over cash receipts and disbursements.

SEE ALSO 6.4, "Cash Disbursements"

3.4 Preparing a Bank Reconciliation

Book-to-Bank Differences

Bank Reconciliation Steps

Troubleshooting

Adjusting Entries

3.4

A big part of effective internal controls over cash is performing a bank reconciliation each month to ensure that the amount shown in the books agrees with what's in the bank. In this subchapter, we explain why bank and book differences occur and how to reconcile them should you find them.

Book-to-Bank Differences

Because of timing differences and bank charges, the amount recorded as cash on your books at the end of the month usually won't match the amount listed on your bank statement. To get the true value of cash for the end of each month— the amount you can accurately list on your balance sheet—it's necessary to make adjustments by adding and subtracting these differences.

Certain items have to be adjusted to bring the amount shown on the bank statement in line with the actual balance, including the following:

Deposits in transit are deposits made before the end of the month but are not reflected in the bank statement. These amounts must be added back into bank balance.

Outstanding checks are those checks that have been written but have not yet cleared the bank by the date of the statement.

Bank errors are amounts that might have been recorded incorrectly, for example, if the bank transposed the numbers on the check. This would require a call to the bank to notify them of the error.

Overdrafts are the proverbial "bounced" checks, or checks written for amounts exceeding the balance in the bank account.

Automatic deposits are those amounts automatically debited directly to your bank account on a regular basis. This is often how payroll is handled.

Electronic funds transfers (EFTs) are payments you've set up to be automatically deducted from your account.

Automatic loans are amounts advanced to you by the bank to cover potential overdrafts. Also called *automatic overdraft protection.*

Monthly service charges are those amounts the bank charges to process your account.

NSF (insufficient funds) checks are checks you've received that are drawn on an account with insufficient funds to cover it.

Bank Reconciliation Steps

You can prepare a bank reconciliation using the following steps:

1. It used to be standard procedure to compare your cancelled checks with the checks listed on the bank account statement. That way you could be sure the bank has correctly recorded the check amounts. Today, banks typically no longer return cancelled checks to their customers. However, you can still obtain an image statement from the bank, which is essentially a copy of all your cancelled checks, though there is often a fee for this. If you find an error, you should notify the bank and adjust the bank balance for that amount.

2. Compare the check register with the checks on the bank account statement. Deduct those checks still outstanding from the bank balance.

3. Match the deposit slips against the deposits per the books. Add any deposits in transit back to the bank balance.

4. Check the bank statement for electronic fund transfers, and deduct any that have not been recorded from the book balance.

SEE ALSO 3.1, "Classifying Cash"

5. Deduct any bank service charges or loan fees from the book balance.

6. Subtract any checks returned for insufficient funds from the book balance.

7. Be sure the adjusted book and bank balances now agree. If they don't, recheck your work as suggested in our troubleshooting section.

Following is the February end-of-month bank reconciliation for ABC Services Corp., a corporate cleaning service. Note how the reconciliation is done in two parts. The first section takes the balance from ABC's bank statement and reconciles it to the cash balance in its accounts (the book balance). After adjusting it for items that may have been recorded on the books but not reached the bank yet because of timing differences—in this case a last-minute deposit and some checks that have been written but not yet cashed—ABC arrives at the actual cash balance.

In the second half of the reconciliation, ABC takes the amount of cash on its books and adjusts for items that the bank knows about—charges and an unrecorded automatic deposit for a tax refund—but that ABC did not have to figure into its calculations.

ABC SERVICES CORP.
BANK RECONCILIATION
FEBRUARY 28

Balance per Bank	$12,424
Add: Deposits in Transit (2/28)	$2,600
Subtotal	$15,024
Deductions:	
Outstanding Checks:	
1431	*$5,619*
1503	*$400*
1522	*$125*
Subtotal	**$6,144**
Revised (True) Balance per Bank	$8,880
Balance per Book:	$10,920
Add: Automatic Deposit Not Recorded (Tax Refund)	$1,685
Subtotal	$12,605
Deductions:	
Bank Service Charge	*$30*
Automatic Loan Fee	*$25*
NSF Check	*$3,670*
Subtotal	**$3,725**
Revised (True) Balance per Book	**$8,880**

Troubleshooting

If the bank reconciliation is done correctly, the adjusted book and bank balances should now be equal, as they are in the preceding example. If they aren't, you will need to go back and recheck your work. Here are some double-checking tips:

Do the math, and look at the difference. If it's divisible by 9, you might have transposed the numbers. Check all the deductions and additions to be sure you have recorded them properly. For example, let's say the revised bank balance in preceding reconciliation came to $8,808, while you still had a revised book balance of $8,880. The difference is $72, which is divisible by 9 (72 ÷ 9 = 8). So you suspect one of the numbers may not have been recorded correctly. On closer examination it turns out that check # 1431 for $5,619 was erroneously recorded as $5,691, a $72 difference. When you correct this, the book and bank balances both equal $8,880.

For the bank balance, double-check that you have included all outstanding checks or deposits. Outstanding checks should be subtracted and deposits added back. For the book balance, scan the bank statement again to be sure you've deducted any charges from the book balance and captured deposits from outside sources.

Note that most accounting software and online programs include troubleshooting tips and other features to help you identify and correct bank reconciliation errors.

SEE ALSO 15.1, "Benefits of Computerized Accounting"

Adjusting Entries

After you've completed and verified the bank reconciliation, you'll need to make an adjustment to the books to reflect the correct balance. In the case of ABC Services, the journal entry to record the adjustment would be as follows:

	Debit	Credit
2/28 Accounts Receivable	$3,670	
Bank Charges and Fees	$55	
Automatic Deposit—Tax Refund		$1,685
Cash		$2,040
To adjust cash balance from reconciliation.		

This journal entry would be made at the end of the period—in this case, in time for the February monthly financial statements.

3.5 Petty Cash

As we mentioned earlier in this chapter, businesses often find it convenient to keep a small amount of cash on hand to pay miscellaneous expenses without having to go through the hassle and paperwork of the regular payment process. This fund, known as petty cash, often covers minor expenditures like delivery fees, coffee and donuts, taxi fares, and emergency supplies. It's set up using an **imprest system.**

✓

An **imprest system** or **imprest account** is a method of controlling expenditures by setting up a fund at a fixed amount and requiring supporting documentation for reimbursement to replenish the fund to the fixed amount.

To set up the petty cash account, you would make the following entry:

		Debit	Credit
1/2	Petty Cash	$200	
	Cash		$200
To set up the petty cash fund.			

In administering the petty cash fund, many of the same rules that apply for cash apply to petty cash. Petty cash should be stored in a locked box with controlled access to the key. Any disbursements should be recorded on a record sheet, and a receipt for the expense should be kept for verification.

Following is an example of a record sheet to keep track of petty cash disbursements. Each addition or disbursement to the fund should be written down on a separate line in a dated entry.

PETTY CASH

Date	Explanation	Debit	Credit	Balance
1/1	Beginning Balance			$0
1/2	Deposit from Cash	$200		$200
1/26	Office Supplies *(copy paper and stamps)*		$55	$145

The person who administers the petty cash fund is known as the fund custodian. At the end of the month, if the fund is in need of replenishing, he or she can debit the appropriate expenses and credit cash in bank to restore to the original amount.

	Debit	Credit
1/31 Office Supplies Expense	$55	
Auto Expense	$40	
Delivery Charge	$25	
Cash in Bank		$120
To replenish petty cash fund.		

Petty cash is set up as an imprest account, so all the payments are made from the fund and only recorded in the accounts when the fund is replenished. As an internal control, someone other than the petty cash custodian should reconcile the fund's receipts at the end of the period to be sure all monies disbursed are properly accounted for. Any shortfalls or overages should be investigated and recorded to a cash over and short account.

	Debit	Credit
1/31 Office Supplies Expense	$55	
Auto Expense	$40	
Freight-In	$25	
Cash Over and Short	$10	
Cash in Bank		$130
To show the net effect of replenishing the petty cash fund and record shortage.		

Cash, for accounting purposes, includes any money or funds a company has on hand or in the bank, as well as certain short-term investments. It's also the easiest asset to misappropriate if you don't take the proper precautions, including making daily deposits, safeguarding cash on hand, and performing a monthly bank reconciliation to catch any problems quickly.

Sales and Accounts Receivable

4.1 Recording Sales

Timing of Sales

Recording Cash Sales

Recording Credit Sales

How and when can you record a sale? This subchapter answers that question and explains how to handle exceptions.

Timing of Sales

Under accounting's accrual basis, sales revenue is recognized and can be legitimately recorded on the books in the period in which it is earned. For service businesses, this typically means when the services have been performed. For a manufacturing or merchandising business, sales occur when goods have been handed over or shipped to the customer in return for cash or the promise of cash in the future (a receivable). This is known as the **revenue recognition principle.**

✓ _____

> The **revenue recognition principle** holds that sales revenue should be recorded when earned, i.e., services performed or goods exchanged.

SEE ALSO 3.1, "Classifying Cash"

For example, say HappyTimes DayCare ordered a washer and dryer from EZ Appliances, Inc., to clean children's clothing that becomes dirty during the school day. EZ receives the order, but cannot record the sale at that point. Only when EZ has delivered the goods to the school would the sale be considered completed for accounting purposes.

The revenue recognition principle applies to most companies, for most sales, with a few exceptions:

Installment sales. These sales of furniture and other large items allow customers to pay for the product in separate payments or installments. Because complete collection is not considered as certain as regular credit sales (the buyer's debt is not backed by a credit card company or bank), you should only book sales revenue and cost of goods sold as the payments are made.

Certain long-term construction contracts. Because these building projects can take several months or even years to complete, contractors and construction firms are allowed to recognize revenues using a percentage of completion method, recording sales as portions of the contract are completed, as shown in the following formula:

Percentage estimated completed × Contract = Revenue recorded in price period

End of production. In businesses involving commodities, where prices can fluctuate, management is allowed to recognize revenue when production is completed even if customers haven't taken possession of the product.

Recording Cash Sales

With cash sales, your main issue is having adequate internal controls to ensure that cash is safeguarded and all transactions are recorded properly. You've probably already taken steps in this direction with several common business practices:

- Using a cash register that locks after each sale
- Using preprinted and numbered invoices
- Daily reconciliation of cash receipts and checks with register tape or invoice copies by someone other than the cashier in order to spot discrepancies early

SEE ALSO 3.3, "Implementing Internal Controls Over Cash"

Recording cash sales is fairly straightforward. Assume Fun Furniture, Inc., sold four table and chair sets, six cribs, and two high chairs to the newly opened HappyTimes DayCare. The proprietor of HappyTimes paid by check upon delivery on May 1. Fun Furniture, like most businesses, records cash sales in the cash receipts journal:

	Debit	Credit
5/1 Cash	$3,250	
Sales		$3,250
To record furniture sales to HappyTimes.		

If your company does a high volume of cash sales, you might not list each sale individually. Retailers, for example, generally make one posting of total sales for the day based on the cash register tape or daily sales report, as shown in the following example.

FUN FURNITURE
CASH RECEIPTS JOURNAL

Date	Description	PR	General A/C	Sales	Accounts Receivable	Cash
5/1	Sales			($3,250)		$3,250

Recording Credit Sales

Businesses generally deal with two types of credit sales: purchases on account (**trade credit**) or those with credit cards (**consumer credit**).

✓

> **Trade credit** is when a customer buys something on account for which he or she agrees to pay a certain amount within a certain time.
>
> **Consumer credit** is when the customer pays with credit card and a third party handles collections and remits the money to the company, less a fee.

Typical terms for business trade accounts are 2/10, net 30. This means you receive a discount of 2 percent if you pay within 10 days, and the balance must be paid in 30 days. It's your company's responsibility to collect trade credit amounts, so it's important to have a means to evaluate the creditworthiness of potential new customers.

SEE ALSO 4.4, "Selling Accounts Receivable"

With consumer credit cards, the bank or financial institution backing the card remits the amount owed, less a fee, to you. Collection of the debt and the risk if the customer doesn't pay become their responsibility.

A credit sale is recorded as an accounts receivable until the money is paid. The exceptions are sales with MasterCard or Visa, which can be recorded to cash because the remittance is made so quickly. For purposes of this example, assume Brennan's Seafood purchased a new customized kitchen on account with Master Chef Appliance, Inc.

		Debit	Credit
3/6	Accounts Receivable—Brennan's Seafood	$96,000	
	Sales		$96,000

To record purchase of Chef's Kitchen model #57834 by Brennan's Seafood, terms 2/10, n/30.

When cash is received, the accounts receivable is reduced and the payment increases cash:

	Debit	Credit
4/5 Cash	$96,000	
Accounts Receivable—Brennan's		$96,000
To record customer payment of accounts receivable.		

Master Chef sells one or two of its industrial-style kitchens a week. For accounting purposes, management records the individual sales as they occur. On March 6, when the company sold kitchen equipment to the Kiddie Gourmet chain for $18,000, the following was recorded in the sales journal:

4.1

MASTER CHEF APPLIANCE, INC.
SALES JOURNAL

Date	Account Debited	Terms	Invoice #	PR	Amount
1/9	Romero's Café		85		$20,000
2/13	Salads in a Sack		86		$32,000
2/22	Brennan's		87		$96,000
3/6	Kiddie Gourmet		88		$18,000

Had Master Chef been selling smaller items, or in the case of retailers who do a high volume of business daily, it would be more typical to wait until the end of the day and post total sales to the cash receipts journal.

SEE ALSO 4.2, "Adjusting and Summarizing Sales"

SEE ALSO 2.4, "Recording in Journals"

4.2 Adjusting and Summarizing Sales

Understanding Discounts

Sales Returns and Allowances

Monitoring High Levels of Returns

In this subchapter, we discuss discounts and sales returns, and you learn how to adjust sales and summarize these transactions for financial reporting.

Understanding Discounts

Customers who pay on account are often offered a discount if they pay by a certain time. The terms are typically listed as 2/10, n/30, which means they get a 2 percent discount if they pay within 10 days and owe the balance 20 days later (30 days after the purchase). Most customers like to take advantage of discounts if at all possible, as this is most cost-efficient. There are two types of discounts:

- Cash discounts
- Sales discounts

Cash vs. Sales Discounts

Sales discounts, sometimes called bulk discounts or trade discounts, are a reduction in price. They do not necessarily have to be tied to payment terms, but may instead be tied to quantity purchased. Sales discounts are automatically taken off the price, so the sales and accounts receivable the seller records already reflect the discount and do not require adjustment.

Cash discounts are reduction in debt if you pay your bill early. Typically, when we refer to discounts in this book, we are referring to cash discounts. The account we use is 310, cash discounts allowed.

Recording Discounts

Discounts are recorded at the time of payment as a reduction in the accounts receivable. For example, Off Road Company buys $5,000 worth of tires from Otto Auto Supplies with terms 2/10, n/30. Otto's original entry to record the sale would be:

	Debit	Credit
5/2 Accounts Receivable	$5,000	
Sales		$5,000
To record sale to Off Road Co., 2/10, n/30.		

Off Road Co. remits payment at day 9, earning the discount. So Otto has to reflect the reduced sales price in its accounts. Because the sale has already been recorded, he doesn't reverse it, but records it to an account called **cash discounts allowed:**

	Debit	Credit
5/12 Cash	$4,900	
Cash Discounts Allowed	$100	
Accounts Receivable		$5,000
To record payment from Off Road Co., net of discount.		

Some companies show these discounts on their financials as a deduction from sales to arrive at net sales. More often, particularly with small businesses, cash discounts allowed on sales are reflected in the income statement as an expense because they really represent a finance decision (a choice to accept less for cash received more quickly) rather than a sales price adjustment.

✓

> A **cash discounts allowed** account is used to record a percentage reduction in price earned by a customer who pays his or her bill within a certain time.

Sales Returns and Allowances

Sometimes customers want to return items because they're defective, damaged, or unacceptable in some other way. As a general practice, most businesses accept returns or remit an allowance for damages if they are notified within a specific time period, say 10 days.

It's important to have procedures in place for properly handling and accounting for these transactions. Most businesses use a **contra account, sales returns and allowances,** to track these expenses. Merchandise returns or allowances given on damaged items are also recorded in an account for sales returns and allowances.

✓

A **contra account** is an offset account deducting a reserve or other amount from another account so both amounts can be shown on the financial statements. Examples include sales returns and allowances and allowance for doubtful accounts.

A **sales returns and allowances** account offsets against sales and is debited with customer returns of merchandise or refunds.

As an example, let's say HappyTimes DayCare seeks to return four cribs worth $2,000 after discovering a safety problem with the side gates. Fun Furniture would adjust its books with the following entry:

	Debit	Credit
6/2 Sales Returns and Allowances	$2,000	
Accounts Receivable		$2,000

To refund HappyTimes DayCare for crib return, credit memo #139.

Note that the original sale is not reversed for the merchandise return. The purpose of a separate, or contra, account is to help keep track of the total amount of returns and allowances a company grants. On Fun Furniture's next monthly income statement, the total amount in sales returns and allowances, together with any discounts given, will be deducted from sales to arrive at net sales for the period, as follows:

FUN FURNITURE, INC.
INCOME STATEMENT
JUNE 30

Sales	$185,400
Less: Sales Returns and Allowances	$4,620
Net Sales	$180,780

Monitoring High Levels of Returns

Businesses need to pay particular attention to the level of sales returns and allowances they're experiencing. Larger-than-usual balances in this account can hint at other issues that need to be examined, such as problems in the production process, for example, or delayed delivery times. It's important to get a reason from the customer.

Too many sales returns can also be a sign of malfeasance, and it's worth calling customers to verify balances if you have any concerns. One way employees can defraud a company is by generating phony **credit memorandums** and then pocketing the cash.

✓

> A **credit memorandum** is the document given by the seller to a buyer of merchandise to let him know that his account is being credited for a certain amount (typically, the price of the item returned).

4.2

In this case, too, internal controls are important. In particular:

- Use of prenumbered checks and credit memorandums
- Supervisory checks on employees who process credits
- Review of daily sales transactions

SEE ALSO 1.1, "Accounting Basics"

A company can record a sales invoice when services have been rendered or goods have been given or shipped to the customer and when the customer has paid, or promised to pay. Customers who pay within a certain time may qualify for a cash discount, which is recorded in a separate account (cash discounts allowed). Sales returns and allowances also go into a separate account. Both sales returns and cash discounts allowed reduce net income.

4.3 Accounts Receivable

Deciding on Your Credit Policy

Tracking Customer Accounts

The Accounts Receivable Aging Schedule

Accelerating Collections

Estimating Uncollectibles

In this subchapter, we tell you everything you always wanted to know about accounts receivable, commonly abbreviated by accountants as A/R. You learn how to set up credit policy and track customer accounts, speed collections, and deal with those funds you can't collect.

Deciding on Your Credit Policy

If you're going to allow sales on account, which is essential for most businesses, you're going to have to decide how much credit you're going to extend and to whom. This can be more challenging than it looks. If your credit terms are too lenient, your sales may be high, but you also may pay the price in higher customer defaults. So it's important to strike the right balance.

Some factors you'll want to address in setting your credit policy include:

Credit limits. How much credit are you willing to extend to customers and what parameters will be used to determine who qualifies for what?

Credit terms. When will payment be due and what discounts, if any, are given for early payment? Will you charge late payment penalties? For guidance you might check with trade associations to see what terms other companies in your industry are offering.

Deposit policy. Will you require a deposit prior to delivering the product or service? Will it be refundable? This often comes into play in personal service or consulting contracts, where a deposit or down payment is standard procedure to cover the seller for costs incurred and to encourage the buyer to honor the contract.

Customer evaluation criteria. What will you want to know about customers before extending credit? Factors to consider include the company's finances, how long it has been around, volume of business expected, etc. In most cases, this involves a credit check. A large company has a separate department for this. Smaller businesses often find it beneficial to subscribe to a credit service such as Dun and Bradstreet to do these checks for them, as it's a lot less expensive than bad debt.

It's also important that your policy is well-documented and that both you and the customer have agreed to the terms.

Tracking Customer Accounts

When you've determined your credit policy, you'll need to set up a system to monitor individual customer accounts. Each time you add a new customer, you should set up a file with credit information, outstanding orders, and a record of unpaid invoices. You could do this on the computer, but you should also have the documents filed in hardcopy by customer name.

If you work with a computerized system, you can create records for individual customers with contact info, addresses, terms, outstanding invoices, and other pertinent data. These records, which become part of a master list, enable you to automatically generate invoices and make it easier to track customer accounts.

SEE ALSO 1.3, "Creating a Filing System"

SEE ALSO 15.1, "Benefits of Computerized Accounting"

You also need to set up a page for the customer in the accounts receivable subsidiary ledger. This account is directly debited when you record a credit sale in the sales journal. When the customer makes a payment, this amount is credited to his or her account in the accounts receivable subledger. A computerized system will automatically post to a customer's account when an entry is made to the sales journal. In a manual system you must make two postings, first to the sales journal and then a separate posting to the customer's account.

ACCOUNTS RECEIVABLE SUBLEDGER
LYNCH, 1551

	Date	Debit	Credit	Balance
Sales Invoice	4/2		$1,500	($1,500)
Payment	6/2	$1,000		($500)

At the end of the accounting period, the combined totals in the subsidiary ledgers should reconcile with the total in the accounts receivable control account in the general ledger. These records also make it easy for you to quickly see how much a customer has purchased and where he or she is on payments.

SEE ALSO 10.2, "Closing Cash Journals"

The Accounts Receivable Aging Schedule

The **accounts receivable aging schedule** offers a clear idea of who owes what to your company and for how long. It is the single best way to gauge how you're doing in terms of collecting monies outstanding and identifying customers who might be lagging or having problems with payments. It's also often useful as a basis for determining how much of a reserve to create for uncollectible accounts.

✓

> The **accounts receivable aging schedule** is a way of categorizing receivables to see how much is outstanding and for what period of time. It shows who is paying and who isn't, and what amounts are in danger of becoming uncollectible.

For example, Visual Arts Limited is a graphics company that provides advertising and graphics services to a variety of businesses. On December 31, Visual had a balance of $31,330 in accounts receivable. Visual's accountant prepared the following aging schedule to look at their outstanding receivables.

VISUAL ARTS LIMITED
AGING SCHEDULE
DECEMBER 31

| Customer | Balance 12/31 | Current | Days Past Due | | | |
			31 to 60	61 to 90	91 to 120	Over 120
C. Nelson	$3,400	$1,600	$1,800			
MLM Services	$4,900	$1,100	$2,300	$1,500		
Dial-A-Map	$1,200					$1,200
Jean Smith	$1,920	$1,920				
Tap Co.	$4,590	$3,590	$1,000			
Jones & Jones	$6,750	$3,200	$1,550	$1,200	$800	
Worth More, Inc.	$8,570	$5,200	$1,300	$2,070		
Totals	$31,330	$16,610	$7,950	$4,770	$800	$1,200

Note: A computerized system will generate the aging schedule for you, which can save time over producing it manually, particularly if you have a high volume of customers.

SEE ALSO 15.1, "Benefits of Computerized Accounting"

Accelerating Collections

The aging schedule is also a good way to see whether you need to devise a means of accelerating collections. It helps you identify problem accounts and amounts and shows you where to target your collection efforts.

Looking at the preceding schedule for Visual Arts Limited, for example, it's clear that at least two of the accounts, Dial-A-Map and Jones & Jones, are very late and worth investigating. Of the two, Dial-A-Map might be the bigger concern because its whole balance is overdue and it's not done further business with Visual. Jones & Jones continued to bring new projects to Visual, so presumably it's looking for a long-term relationship and is less likely to just stop paying or is looking at you as his or her banker.

When looking at aging, people sometimes tend to not worry until an item gets in the far right column (over 120 days). By then, it's uncollectible. You have to start contacting customers when their bills are over 30 days past due. Make notes of their promises to pay, and follow up to be sure they do what they say they're going to.

Estimating Uncollectibles

Despite your best efforts at screening customers and meeting their needs, you'll probably have customers who can't or don't pay. For this reason, you should make some provision for **uncollectible accounts.**

✓

Uncollectible accounts are those amounts customers are unlikely to pay.

Businesses use one of two methods to provide for uncollectible accounts:

- Setting up an allowance for projected unpaid amounts
- Directly writing off accounts you don't expect to collect

The Allowance Method

Under the allowance method, you make an estimate of how much you expect to remain uncollected and record that amount to an account called **allowances for doubtful accounts.** This account is an offset (or contra) account to accounts receivable. Much like sales returns and allowances that offset sales, it's shown separately on the balance sheet to provide information about the amount of accounts receivable deemed questionable. The other side is written off as an expense to **bad debts expense.**

SEE ALSO 10.2, "Closing Cash Journals"

The allowance is not a **direct write-off** of any particular account, but a conservative estimate of historical collection losses.

✓
___

The **allowance for doubtful accounts** is a reserve for accounts receivable that is expected to be uncollectible.

Bad debts expense is a charge for accounts receivable expected to be uncollectible.

A **direct write-off** is an outstanding account taken off the books because the customer is not expected to pay.

How much to put into the allowance is based on your previous collection experience, volume of sales and credit sales, and economic conditions. This reserve is usually computed as a percentage of sales or as a percentage of accounts receivable. Accountants often make the argument that using accounts receivable as a basis is the better choice because it matches accounts and the estimate most closely, while sales could also include cash sales.

For example, DJ Corp. has sales of $11,000 this year and wants to estimate uncollectibles based on its accounts receivable balance. The following table shows its percentage of uncollectible sales in each of the previous 4 years.

	Year 1	Year 2	Year 3	Year 4
Bad Debts	$500	$540	$480	$600
Total Accounts Receivable	$10,000	$9,000	$12,000	$12,000
% Accounts Receivable	5%	6%	4%	5%

As this table shows, bad debts have averaged 5 percent at DJ Corp., so if the next year it has accounts receivable of $11,000, it will have an allowance of $550.

Another way to estimate uncollectibles uses the accounts receivable aging schedule and looks at accounts by how long they've been outstanding. This method is often more precise, as accounts typically become more difficult to collect as they age. In the case of Visual Arts, we would slightly expand our analysis:

VISUAL ARTS LIMITED
AGING SCHEDULE
DECEMBER 31

Customer	Balance 12/31	Current	31 to 60	Days Past Due 61 to 90	91 to 120	Over 120
C. Nelson	$3,400	$1,600	$1,800			
MLM Services	$4,900	$1,100	$2,300	$1,500		
Dial-A-Map	$1,200					$1,200
Jean Smith	$1,920	$1,920				
Tap Co.	$4,590	$3,590	$1,000			
Jones & Jones	$6,750	$3,200	$1,550	$1,200	$800	
Worth More, Inc.	$8,570	$5,200	$1,300	$2,070		
Totals	$31,330	$16,610	$7,950	$4,770	$800	$1,200

4.3

Here we look at balances by age and apply historical rates to them. For example, we know that in the past, 4 percent of Visual's current accounts have gone uncollected, while 30 percent of accounts over 120 days have had to be written off. Using the data in the preceding table, let's look at the past and compute these historical rates:

Age	Amount	% Estimated* Uncollectible	Balance in Allowance
Current	$16,610	4%	$664
31 to 60	$7,950	10%	$795
61 to 90	$4,770	20%	$954
91 to 120	$800	25%	$200
Over 120	$1,200	30%	$360
Year-End Balance Allowance for Doubtful Accounts			$2,973

Based on past experience.

Assuming you already have a balance of $758 in allowance for doubtful accounts, you would make the following entry to credit the account with the difference between that and your projected reserve of $2,973:

		Debit	Credit
12/31	Bad Debts Provision	$2,215	
	Allowance for Doubtful Accounts		$2,215
	To record bad debts provision.		

You would likely make this entry at the end of the period; many companies do this once a year. The allowance is roughly 9 percent of the total receivables at 12/31. If you chose to use the percentage of receivables method, it would not be out of line to use 9 percent in the following year. Be conservative and consistent, without wildly over or underestimating your bad debts expense.

SEE ALSO 10.5, "Adjusting Entries"

The Direct Write-Off Method

The other method of recognizing bad debts is by directly writing off accounts you deem uncollectible:

		Debit	Credit
12/31	Bad Debts Expense	$1,200	
	Accounts Receivable—Dial-A-Map		$1,200
To write off bad debt.			

This method is the one more commonly used by small businesses. It encourages keeping on top of accounts so as soon as one looks problematic, you can start trying to collect it. You shouldn't rush to write off an account until you have exhausted collection efforts, of course. But once you have deemed an account uncollectible, the direct write-off method has the advantage of being specific and conservative. If you err, it's on the side of understating profits. If the account later proves collectible, the account can be reinstated.

Reinstating Written-Off Accounts Receivable

What if you run into a situation where you have written off an account, but the customer ends up paying the bill? If Dial-A-Map were to have a turnaround and pay its bill 3 months from now, where do you record the payment, as its account no longer exists? First, you'd need to reestablish the accounts receivable for Dial-A-Map:

		Debit	Credit
12/1	Accounts Receivable—Dial-A-Map	$1,200	
	Allowance for Doubtful Accounts		$1,200
To reinstate accounts receivable for Dial-A-Map.			

Then, you need an additional entry to record the receipt of payment:

	Debit	Credit
12/1 Cash	$1,200	
Accounts Receivable—Dial-A-Map		$1,200

To record payment of Dial-A-Map accounts receivable.

As an alternative, skip the step of reinstating A/R, debit cash $1,200, and credit allowance for doubtful accounts for the same.

4.3

If the Dial-A-Map accounts receivable was originally written off using the direct write-off method, you would need another way to reinstate it because there was no allowance created and you can't reverse an expense from a previous period. In this case, you would credit the amount to a revenue account, as follows:

	Debit	Credit
12/1 Cash	$1,200	
Recoveries of Bad Debt (or Bad Debt Expense)		$1,200

To record payment of accounts receivable written off as uncollectible.

Most businesses sell to customers on account, allowing them to pay by a certain time in the future. Still, a certain percentage of those accounts receivable become uncollectible. Companies provide for these bad debts in two ways, either by setting up an allowance for uncollectible accounts or by directly writing off old accounts. The best way to reduce bad debts is by using credit checks for customers and monitoring past due accounts.

4.4 Selling Accounts Receivable

To Sell or Not to Sell?

Understanding Factoring

Accepting Major Credit Cards

This subchapter deals with ways to accelerate the collection of accounts receivable by selling them to another entity so you can receive the cash more quickly. It might sound unusual, but if your company takes major credit cards, it's something you already do.

To Sell or Not to Sell?

Companies that choose to sell receivables typically do so because collection costs and billing costs are high. In many cases, it's just as easy, and less expensive, to have MasterCard and Visa handle these functions than for companies to do it themselves, even if it means you pay a fee. For this reason, most companies that have been in business for any length of time, particularly retailers, take major credit cards.

Understanding Factoring

Selling accounts receivable is also known as *factoring*, because the financial institution that bought accounts receivable used to be called a *factor*. The purchasing financial institution charges a commission to collect the account, often up to 3 percent. The good part about selling accounts receivable is that you receive your money right away, as opposed to having to wait until the customer gets around to paying you. The bad news is you pay a fee for the privilege.

For example, if Acme Printing decides to factor its $45,000 in total receivables with the Centaur Financing Co., Centaur immediately pays Acme $40,500 for its receivables and then collects from them on its own. The $4,500 difference between the $40,500 and $45,000 is the 10 percent commission Acme pays for the service. But the money Centaur collects for them may be better used elsewhere, and Acme might find that the process pays for itself.

Accepting Major Credit Cards

Another way of selling accounts receivable is by accepting major credit cards like Visa and MasterCard. In this case, the banks that handle the collections remit payment to your company as soon as they receive the credit card receipts. MasterCard and Visa sales are even recorded as cash sales by most retailers because the bank immediately credits the seller's account for the amount, less the service charge, as soon as the slips are received.

4.4

4.5 Notes Receivable

Recording Notes Receivable

Computing Notes Receivable Interest

Collecting Notes Receivable

Notes receivable are written agreements to pay a certain amount by a certain date. In this subchapter, we show how to value and compute interest on these receivables and what to do if they can't be collected.

Recording Notes Receivable

Notes receivable are often used with customers who want to extend the payment for a purchase beyond the usual terms. A note can be required of new or high-risk customers. For example, say The Boat Company loans Jacob Snelling $3,000 on June 9. In return, Snelling signs a promissory note for $3,000 at 10 percent due in 90 days. The Boat Company then records the following entry:

	Debit	Credit
6/9 Notes Receivable	$3,000	
Cash		$3,000

To record notes receivable with Jacob Snelling for 90 days at 10 percent (annual) interest.

When Snelling repays the note 3 months later, The Boat Company updates its records as follows:

	Debit	Credit
9/7 Cash	$3,075	
Notes Receivable		$3,000
Interest Earned		$75

To record repayment of Snelling notes receivable plus 10 percent interest.

Computing Notes Receivable Interest

Different types of interest are calculated on notes receivable—ordinary interest charges and the discount rate on notes sold to the bank for early collection. Ordinary interest is stated at an annual rate on most notes receivable, so the amount must be prorated for the number of days or months the note is outstanding. So if your company accepted a note receivable with a face value of $6,000 for 90 days at 12 percent interest to replace an accounts receivable from customer Jack Smith, it would be recorded as follows:

		Debit	Credit
5/1	Notes Receivable—Smith	$6,000	
	Accounts Receivable		$6,000
	To record notes receivable from Mr. Smith.		

When Mr. Smith repays the note on 7/31, the interest he owes would be computed as follows:

Principal × Interest = Annual interest
$6,000 × .12 = $720

Annual interest ÷ 12 months = Monthly interest
$720 ÷ 12 = $60

Monthly interest × 3 months = Interest owed
$60 × 3 = $180

Interest can also be calculated based on days in the year, for which 360 is often used. In this case:

90 ÷ 360 = .25 × $720 = $180

As you can see, the amounts would be the same. You would record payment with the following journal entry:

		Debit	Credit
7/31	Cash	$6,180	
	Notes Receivable		$6,000
	Interest Income		$180
	To record collection of notes receivable—Smith, plus 12 percent interest.		

SEE ALSO 9.1, "Time Value Basics"

SEE ALSO 9.4, "Long-Term Receivables"

Collecting Notes Receivable

Notes receivable, like accounts receivable, are recorded at their net realizable value—their face value minus any allowance for bad debts. You can use the same procedures for estimating uncollectible notes as you do for regular accounts receivable—either a percentage of sales or a percentage of notes outstanding.

Discounting Notes Receivable

Sometimes a company sells a note to a bank for earlier collection. This process is called **discounting notes receivable** and is similar to selling or factoring accounts receivable. In the case of discounting a note, the fee charged for the service is known as the **discount rate.** For example, suppose Computers R Us needed money and wanted to discount a note for $10,000. The bank charges a discount rate of 13 percent. The **discount value** of the note is computed as follows:

SEE ALSO 4.4, "Selling Accounts Receivable"

Face Value of Note:	$10,000
Interest on Note (90 Days at 10%):	$250
Maturity Value:	$10,250
Discount Period:	36 days
Discount on Maturity Value (36 Days at 13%):	$133
Proceeds	$10,117

SEE ALSO 9.1, "Time Value Basics"

✓

Discounting notes receivable is when a company sells a note receivable to a bank for collection, paying a fee (**discount rate**), which is a percentage of the note's maturity value (note plus interest). The proceeds that the company will receive are known as the **discounted value** of the note.

You can use the following entry to record collection:

	Debit	Credit
6/24 Cash	$10,117	
Interest Income		$117
Notes Receivable		$10,000

To record bank collection of note receivable.

If the proceeds had been less than face value, you would have recorded interest expense.

Writing Off Notes Receivable

A notes receivable deemed uncollectible is called an uncollectible or a dishonored notes receivable. A dishonored note can be handled in one of two ways. It can be directly written off to the allowance for doubtful accounts: notes receivable.

	Debit	Credit
7/31 Bad Debts Expense	$2,000	
Allowance for Doubtful Accounts: Notes Receivable		$2,000

To write off dishonored note receivable.

Or it can be converted to an accounts receivable:

	Debit	Credit
7/31 Accounts Receivable	$2,060	
Notes Receivable		$2,060

To record dishonored note receivable plus interest.

The accounts receivable would then be written off according to your usual procedures for customer accounts. If a note that has been discounted proves uncollectible, it reverts to the original holder with interest.

Inventory and Cost of Goods Sold

5.1 Accounting for Inventory

Major Inventory Issues

Classifying Inventory

Employing Inventory Systems

This subchapter offers a quick primer on the major issues related to inventory. We take you through how it's classified and accounted for and help you choose an inventory system that works for your company.

Major Inventory Issues

Unless you're in the service business, **inventory** is likely to be one of your company's most significant assets. Inventory systems can be intimidating in their complexity, yet managing inventory isn't that difficult if you stay focused on the major issues—valuation and costing.

✓ _____

Inventory represents items held for resale or product that will go into the manufacturing of goods to be sold.

Two separate accounting systems are reserved for inventory, and you have several different methods you can use to value it, the most common of which we deal with in this subchapter. But the basic equation involved in tracking this asset is a simple one:

Quantity × Cost = Inventory value

To figure out the value of your inventory at the end of a period, you need to know how much you have in stock, by product. To determine this, you can count it in what is known as a **physical inventory,** or you can estimate it. Then you need to determine the cost per unit. This includes the price you paid to buy or make the product, plus additional costs that relate to getting it ready for sale, like advertising and freight costs.

These terms might be unfamiliar right now (although we hope to help you around that), but the basic idea of what you're trying to do all comes back to this equation:

Quantity × Cost = Inventory value

✓
──────────────────────────────────────

> **Physical inventory** is the process of taking an actual physical
> count of the items you have in inventory.

Classifying Inventory

The way you classify your inventory depends a great deal on what kind of business you own or work for. If you're a retailer like Target or The Home Depot or a grocer like Ralph's, you're likely to have hundreds of very different products at varying costs, all with one thing in common—they can all be recorded as merchandise inventory. Manufacturers record inventory at different stages, depending on how far along it is in the production process.

Merchandising Inventory

5.1

Merchandisers might list inventory in a single account, but it must be owned (not consigned) and substantially ready for sale; this means the inventory does not require further processing. For example, you wouldn't include fabric that was cut out to make dresses but not sewn together as merchandising inventory for a retail store. These items would be considered work in process until they were completed. On the other hand, a bike that requires the customer to assemble it and can be sold that way qualifies as merchandise inventory.

Following is a balance sheet for the Right Stuff Co., a retailer that sells sporting goods and equipment for the serious outdoorsman. As you can see, Merchandise Inventory is a single line item in current assets.

RIGHT STUFF CO.
BALANCE SHEET
DECEMBER 31
Current Assets

Cash	$2,500
Accounts Receivable, Net	$5,600
Merchandise Inventory	$6,350
Prepaid Assets	$1,200
Total Current Assets	**$15,650**
Property, Plant and Equipment	$3,200
Less: Accumulated Depreciation	$600
	$2,600
	Continues

Continued

Long-Term Receivables	$1,000
Intangible Assets	$1,000
Total Noncurrent Assets	**$4,600**
TOTAL ASSETS	$20,250

Current Liabilities

Accounts Payable	$2,700
Accrued Salaries and Wages	$3,500
Total Current Liabilities	**$6,200**
Long-Term Notes Payable	$1,100
Total Noncurrent Liabilities	**$1,100**
Total Liabilities	*$7,300*
Owner's Equity	$12,950
TOTAL LIABILITIES AND OWNER'S EQUITY	$20,250

Merchandise inventory is made up of goods bought for resale that are just that—ready to sell. Any business that sells a product that it doesn't have to make, build, manufacture, mine, or process generally has this type of inventory on its balance sheet.

Manufacturing Inventory

Manufacturers divide inventory into three different types:

- Raw materials
- Work in process
- Finished goods

Raw materials are the components, ingredients, and parts that go into making the company's product. The steel needed to make cars, for example, would be considered a raw material. Work in process (W-I-P) is the second stage of manufacturing inventory and consists of products partially made or assembled. For example, a truck wheel assembly or unpainted pottery would be work in process. W-I-P would include the cost of raw materials used plus any labor or **overhead** costs expended to date. Finished goods are just that—manufactured goods that are complete and ready for sale. Finished goods include raw material, labor, and overhead costs.

✓

> **Overhead** refers to expenses related to the production process, such as rent, utilities, and insurance. These costs are usually allocated based on a percentage of direct labor hours.

Occasionally, a company might set up a separate account for manufacturing or factory supplies inventory, which would include items like nails, oil, and cleaning supplies that might not be a main component of the product but are used in production. However, it's more common for these items to be expensed and become a component of overhead.

Employing Inventory Systems

5.1

Two accounting systems are used to track inventory—the perpetual inventory system and the periodic inventory system.

The Perpetual Inventory System

The perpetual inventory system is perhaps the most accurate inventory system in terms of tracking costs in and out of inventory. Inventory records are maintained continuously, so any item purchased is immediately recorded into inventory at actual cost and any item sold is immediately deducted from inventory, again at cost (usually, the purchase price plus shipping charges). Computerized accounting operates on the perpetual inventory system and always maintains an up-to-date inventory count.

For example, Factory Flatscreen Ltd. purchased three televisions—a 51-inch screen for $800, a deluxe 65-inch for $1,900, and another deluxe 80-inch for $2,750. The entry to record these purchases into inventory would be as follows:

	Debit	Credit
7/15 Merchandise Inventory	$5,450	
Accounts Payable		$5,450

To record the inventory purchase of three widescreen TVs from Factory Flatscreen Ltd.

In the perpetual inventory system, you won't have a separate "Purchases" account for inventory. All stock purchases are debited directly to inventory when they're made. **Freight-in,** purchase returns and allowances, and purchase discounts (cash discounts earned) are also recorded directly to the inventory account.

✓

Freight-in refers to shipping charges paid by the purchaser that become part of the cost of the product.

SEE ALSO 6.2, "Accounting for Purchases"

Companies that manufacture and/or sell high-dollar items that can easily be tracked by price frequently use a perpetual inventory system. For example, on September 6, Factory Flatscreen Ltd. sold the deluxe 80-inch television for $5,999. The company would make the following journal entries to record the sale and cost of sales and subsequent reduction in inventory:

	Debit	Credit
9/6 Sales	$5,999	
Accounts Receivable		$5,999
To record sale of deluxe widescreen television.		
9/6 Cost of Goods Sold	$2,750	
Merchandise Inventory		$2,750
To record cost of goods sold and reduce inventory for television sold.		

Scanners at stores have made perpetual inventory systems cheaper and accessible to many businesses. Freight-in is debited directly to inventory. Purchase returns and all discounts are deducted directly from inventory.

SEE ALSO 6.2, "Accounting for Purchases"

The Periodic Inventory System

Under a periodic inventory system, the actual quantity of inventory on hand is determined only at the end of the period. Unlike the perpetual system, purchases of inventory are usually recorded to an actual "purchases" account, with the total in that account being transferred to inventory at the end of the month. However, smaller businesses using a perpetual system may prefer to charge purchases directly to inventory for simplicity's sake. This is acceptable, as long as you remain consistent. We cover both approaches in this section.

SEE ALSO 6.2, "Accounting for Purchases"

Using purchases account: Cost of goods sold is not determined product by product. Instead, it's derived at the end of the period as follows:

Beginning inventory + Purchases = Goods available for sale

Goods available for sale – Ending inventory = Cost of goods sold

As an example, let's assume the manager of Al's All Sports Shop has determined the store has an inventory of $8,500 on hand at the end of the month. During the period, the store purchased $4,500 of merchandise, mostly seasonal baseball gear. Inventory at the beginning of the month was $6,200. In April, the store had sales of $9,100. Using the preceding formula, we can compute the cost of goods sold for Al's:

Beginning inventory + Purchases = Goods available for sale
$6,200 + $4,500 = $10,700

Goods available for sale – Ending inventory = Cost of goods sold
$10,700 – $8,500 = $2,200

At the end of the month, Al's All Sports Shop would make the following entries:

	Debit	Credit
4/15 Purchases	$4,500	
Accounts Payable		$4,500
To record purchases for April.		
4/30 Accounts Receivable	$9,100	
Sales		$9,100
To record April sales.		

At the end of the period, Al also would need to close the purchases account into inventory, because purchases is only a temporary account. The company could then recognize cost of goods sold for the income statement. This transaction is reflected in the following entry.

5.1

	Debit	Credit
4/30 Inventory (Ending, Physical Count)	$8,500	
Cost of Goods Sold	$2,200	
Purchases		$4,500
Inventory (Beginning)		$6,200

To record cost of goods sold and adjust inventory for the month.

Without purchases account: If Al chooses not to use a purchases account, he would record the purchase directly to inventory.

	Debit	Credit
4/15 Inventory	$4,500	
Accounts Payable		$4,500

To record purchase of merchandise inventory.

The only entry Al's All Sports would have to make at the end of the period would be to adjust the inventory to the inventory balance per the physical count. The difference would be the cost of goods sold for the month.

	Debit	Credit
4/30 Cost of Goods Sold	$2,200	
Inventory		$2,200

To adjust physical inventory and record cost of goods sold.

Of the two accounting systems used for inventory, the perpetual system, is perhaps the most accurate because it records and deletes the actual cost of items as they move in and out of inventory. But even with sophisticated computer systems for tracking prices of multiple goods, the perpetual system is not always practical. That's why many companies use a periodic system, where regular verifications of actual physical count of inventory are used to determine inventory value and the cost of goods sold.

5.2 Determining Inventory Quantity

Taking Physical Inventory
Estimating Quantities

One of the basic issues of inventory valuation is determining the quantity of goods to be included. In this subchapter, you learn how to take a physical inventory and ways to monitor inventory levels when counting all your stock isn't feasible.

Taking Physical Inventory

5.2

If you've chosen to use a periodic system to account for inventories, you need to physically count your inventory at the end of the period. Even with a perpetual system, you should take an annual inventory to be sure the stock listed on your books and what you have on hand is roughly equal. Small differences can be attributed to **shrinkage,** but large gaps may point to a more serious problem, like theft.

✓

Shrinkage is a decline in inventory quantities due to breakage, damage, or loss.

Timing

Because it's impractical for most businesses to count inventory monthly, the end of the year (or close to it) is the best time to take inventory. Most businesses either close for the day or choose a very slow period for doing the inventory to avoid having goods going in and out while they're counting.

Inventory Procedures

How and when inventories are taken can vary by company, but certain standard procedures are followed each time. These are designed to enable you to get an accurate and verifiable count in the most efficient manner.

The following list of procedures can be applied in most cases:

- Choose employees who do not normally handle inventory to do the counting. Some companies hire outside contractors to ensure independence for this specific job.

- Put prenumbered tags on items as you count them. Large items should have their own tags. For smaller items, bolts, or diodes that must be weighed or measured, one tag is sufficient if all are together.

- Physically inspect any packages, boxes, containers, and locked storage sheds to be sure they contain what they say they do.

- Counts should be verified by a second employee and tags signed.

- A supervisor should make sure every item is tagged and that nothing is tagged more than once.

- All numbered tags should be accounted for.

- When the physical counting is concluded, quantities for each item should be listed on the inventory summary sheet. A separate employee should verify the accuracy of this sheet.

Following is a sample inventory summary sheet for Al's All Sport Company, a sporting goods store. Notice how the tags are recorded in order and all are accounted for and the employee counting the items has initialed the Verified column.

AL'S ALL SPORT COMPANY
INVENTORY SUMMARY SHEET 1/15

Tag #	Item	Serial #	Count	Verified
001	Aluminum Bats	SP2303	120	TLP
002	Wooden Bats	AD3994	180	TLP
003	Wooden Bats—youth	AD3992	92	TLP
004	Wilson Gloves	WI-606	45	DC
005	Easton Gloves	EA416	20	DC
006	Rawlings Gloves	RA1113	25	DC
007	Balls—Easton	EA225	400	DC
008	Balls—Wilson	WI4434	550	DC
009	VOID	—	—	—
010	Baseball caps	RA939	102	TLP

Inventory tag 009, which was damaged during count, would be marked VOID and attached to the inventory sheet.

What to Include

An important aspect of taking inventory is making sure it's complete and up to date. Because of timing differences in shipping and receiving, you might have to take out certain items and add others in. You'll want to verify ownership of goods, too. Remember, only goods that are actually owned by the company on the inventory date should be included in its inventory.

Here's a quick list of what's included and what's not:

Included:

Goods in transit shipped **FOB shipping point**

Goods at different facilities in showrooms, or at convention booths, for example

Goods out on consignment

Goods contracted for that have not yet been separated and applied to the contract

Not included:

Consigned goods

Goods in transit shipped **FOB destination**

Goods ordered for future delivery

5.2

✓

FOB is a shipping term that means Free On Board; the purchaser does not pay freight until the point title changes hands.

FOB shipping point means the title to item changes hands at the point of shipping; the purchaser pays the freight charges.

FOB destination means the purchaser takes title when the goods are received; freight charges are paid by the seller.

Recording Shrinkage

Shrinkage refers to any shortages in inventory, or cases where there's less product on hand due to loss, damage, theft, or some other unexplained reason. Companies usually account for shrinkage by writing it off to cost of sales.

Larger firms often set up a contra account known as Inventory Over and Short to record shortfalls in inventory. This account is then credited with the difference between the actual physical count and what was on the books in inventory. Overages, which happen as well due to miscounts or errors in the past, are recorded to this account as debits.

Smaller companies with lower value inventories may find it more efficient to directly expense any shortages to cost of goods sold. At the end of the period, cost of goods sold is deducted from the beginning inventory to arrive at the ending inventory.

SEE ALSO 11.2, "Adjusting Entries"

Estimating Quantities

Physical inventories are taken to verify the quantities of stock still on hand at the end of the period. But a physical count is not always feasible or practical. In these cases, businesses must find other ways to approximate ending inventory, often using gross profit or retail sales as a barometer.

The Gross Profit Method

This method is based on the assumption that over time, a company earns a fairly steady gross profit. Using this ratio as a guide allows you to estimate ending inventory.

As an example, assume Book Universe has a beginning inventory of $450,000. During the period, the company purchased additional stock of $100,000 and sold $300,000 of books at retail. The bookseller has a historical gross profit percentage of 20 percent.

Beginning Inventory	$450,000
Purchases	$100,000
Cost of Goods Available for Sale	$550,000
Sales $300,000	
Less: Gross Profit (20% of $300,000)	$60,000
Cost of Goods Sold	$240,000
Ending Inventory (Estimated)	**$310,000**

SEE ALSO 13.1, "Analysis Methods"

SEE ALSO 13.2, "Assessing Profitability"

The Retail Inventory Method

The second method of estimating ending inventory uses sales price as opposed to cost to compute ending inventory. There's some concern among accountants that it doesn't match costs as well as the gross profit method, so we won't go into detail on this method here.

Basically, instead of computing the cost of each product, the company takes the physical inventory using the retail prices right on the products or merchandise. This gives them the ending inventory at retail. They then deduce inventory value at cost by determining their historical ratio between cost and retail value. The gross profit and retail inventory methods are similar because both use gross profit as the indicator. The methods are most often used by retail stores.

5.2

5.3 Figuring Inventory Costs

Types of Costs

Allocating Overhead

When you've determined your inventory quantities in units, your next step is to apply the appropriate costs to them. In this subchapter, we explain the different kinds of costs that go into inventory and how to allocate them in a way that makes sense for your business.

Types of Costs

Inventory is valued on a cost basis. But what does that mean? Many different costs are related to inventory, but not all of them will become part of its value.

Product Costs

These are costs like freight-in for merchandising companies and labor for a manufacturing firm that makes a specific product. When determining product costs, ask yourself if an expense would disappear if the product had never been purchased or made. If the cost would disappear, it's likely a product cost. Examples include material delivery fees, some supply and repair and maintenance expenses, and some plant electricity charges. Other than the freight, these costs are, of course, overhead.

Period Costs

General and administrative expenses like office worker salaries and business supplies are not dependent on production levels, so these are considered period costs. Even without acquiring or producing the product, these costs would still exist. Examples include salaries of administrative staff, office electricity, and insurance. These costs tend to appear in the expenses section of the chart of accounts. However, at the risk of complicating this issue, even these costs are sometimes required to be in overhead for tax purposes, although using a different formula. If you're uncertain, check with a tax accountant.

SEE ALSO 1.4, "Establishing the Chart of Accounts"

Manufacturing Costs

There are three stages of inventory for a manufacturer:

- Raw materials
- Works in process
- Finished goods

Raw materials costs are generally product and freight costs. Work in process and finished goods also include costs for labor on the actual product as well as overhead (operational costs not directly related to production).

Variable vs. Absorption Costing

In variable costing (also known as direct costing), product and manufacturing costs are further divided into two groups: variable costs and fixed costs. Variable costs are expenses such as fuel or direct labor hours that fluctuate with output. Fixed costs are those that remain constant no matter what you produce. In variable costing, only variable costs are included in determining inventory value. Fixed costs are treated as period expenses.

Proponents of variable costing assert that fixed costs would be incurred anyway even if the production facilities were idle so they shouldn't factor into inventory. It can be useful to management because it isolates those costs truly attributable to the product. However, this method is not acceptable for reporting purposes under GAAP, which requires that revenues and expenses be matched as closely as possible.

SEE ALSO 1.2, "Determining a Form of Entity"

Absorption costing (or *full costing*) includes all costs associated with the production of inventory. The IRS requires that you use a modified version of absorption costing that includes not only direct materials, but also indirect costs, such as utilities, rent, or plant insurance that benefit the product as well.

For the purposes of determining costs to be included in your product, you need to isolate the various expenses, create a schedule so you can see what you have, and allocate costs per unit.

Allocating Overhead

Detailed cost accounting is beyond the scope of this book, but it's worth understanding the basics of computing a unit cost for a product. The following simple illustration outlines how to allocate costs. Assume the total direct costs for every 5,000 mobile home climate control panels made are as follows:

Materials	$1,000
Labor	$1,500
Applied Evenly	$2,500
Cost per Panel (2,500 ÷ 5,000)	**$.50**

Now assume the total indirect costs:

Utilities per Month	$1,000
Indirect Labor to Be Applied	$500
Other	$1,400
Total Indirect Costs	$2,900
Total Indirect Costs per Panel (2,900 ÷ 5,000)	**$.58**
Direct Cost Rate	$.50
Indirect Cost Rate	$.58
Total Direct and Indirect Costs per Panel	**$1.08**

If you produced 26,000 panels during the month:

26,000 × $1.08 = $28,080

So your amount charged to inventory would be $28,080.

Inventory must be valued at cost to comply with accounting rules. But which costs? Companies typically split the costs of doing business into two types: product or period costs. Product costs include any direct or indirect labor, materials, or other expenses associated with making the product or readying it for sale. Period costs are things like office salaries, rent, or utilities that would still be incurred separate from the product. When applying costs to inventory, some companies only use costs directly associated with the product (direct labor and materials) for internal purposes. However, the IRS requires that inventory reflects both direct and indirect costs, which can include everything from materials to office salaries. These costs are allocated on a per unit basis.

5.4 Inventory Valuation Methods

Specific Identification

Average Cost

First In, First Out (FIFO)

Last In, First Out (LIFO)

You've carefully recorded the cost of each purchase or product made for inventory. You've even taken a physical inventory so you know how much you have left in inventory. Now comes the tricky part, especially because your inventory may be composed of similar products that can have different costs. How do you identify which goods, at which costs, have been sold? In other words, what's the best way to value your ending inventory?

This subchapter takes you through the four major methods of applying costs to inventory of like items—specific identification; average cost; first in, first out (FIFO); and last in, first out (LIFO)—and shows how your choice affects not only the value of your inventory, but your company's financial performance as well.

Specific Identification

The specific identification method is only feasible for retail businesses. This method seeks to match specific costs with specific products. When an item is sold, the product cost associated with that item is multiplied by the number of units sold to come up with the cost of goods sold.

In the following example, Miller Home Construction Supply has sold 900 units for the month of July. Using the specific identification method, Miller's accountant computes the cost of goods sold based on their actual unit cost:

SCHEDULE OF INVENTORY PURCHASES

Date	# Units	Unit Cost	Total Cost
7/10	400	$3.00	$1,200
7/14	650	$4.00	$2,600
7/15	425	$4.00	$1,700
7/18	500	$4.50	$2,250
7/30	200	$5.50	$1,100
	2,175		$8,850

The number of units of each product sold are then multiplied by its specific unit cost:

COMPUTATION OF COST OF GOODS SOLD USING THE SPECIFIC IDENTIFICATION METHOD

# Units Sold	Unit Cost	Total Cost
300	$4.00	$1,200
200	$4.50	$900
100	$3.00	$300
300	$5.50	$1,650
Cost of Goods Sold		$4,050

Total cost – Cost of goods sold = Ending inventory

$8,850 – $4,050 = $4,800

For this method, the actual units sold are multiplied by their actual costs to determine the cost of goods sold of $4,050. The company then would make the following journal entry:

	Debit	Credit
7/31 Cost of Goods Sold	$4,050	
Inventory		$4,050
To record cost of goods sold for July.		

To determine its ending inventory, Miller Home Construction Supply deducts the cost of goods sold from total purchases, which in this case is also its beginning inventory. This amount, $4,850, would be shown as inventory on its balance sheet for July. The specific identification method is useful for companies that sell a few high-ticket items and do not have a wide variety of inventory because costing it all out individually can become impractical.

Average Cost

Businesses that sell a wide variety of goods at a range of prices often find it more efficient to value their inventory using an average cost, or what is sometimes called the weighted-average method. The following table shows how Miller Home Construction Supply from our previous example would price its inventory using an average cost basis.

GOODS IN INVENTORY

Date	# Units	Unit Cost	Total Cost
7/10	400	$3.00	$1,200
7/14	650	$4.00	$2,600
7/15	425	$4.00	$1,700
7/18	500	$4.50	$2,250
7/30	200	$5.50	$1,100
	2,175		$8,850

Inventory total cost ÷ Total units = Average cost

$8,850 ÷ 2,175 = $4.07

Units sold × Average cost = Cost of goods sold

900 × $4.07 = $3,663

Total cost inventory – Cost of goods sold = Ending inventory

$8,850 – $3,663 = $5,187

The average cost method saves time because it enables you to compute cost of goods sold using an average cost, as opposed to a number of different costs for the same product. To arrive at ending inventory, you simply subtract cost of goods sold from the total beginning inventory cost.

First In, First Out (FIFO)

This method closely tracks the actual movement of goods in and out of inventory. Using first in, first out, usually referred to as FIFO, the oldest costs should be used first when valuing inventory that's sold. That is, you sell things in the order you bought them.

The following table shows the value of Miller Home Construction Supply total inventory at cost. For simplicity's sake, assume that the inventory is composed of one item, plywood sheets. The unit price has been rising through July as housing starts and, therefore, demand has also picked up.

GOODS IN INVENTORY

Date	# Units	Unit Cost	Total Cost
7/10	400	$3.00	$1,200
7/14	650	$4.00	$2,600
7/15	425	$4.00	$1,700
7/18	500	$4.50	$2,250
7/30	200	$5.50	$1,100
	2,175		$8,850

As before, assume Miller Home Construction Supply sells 900 units. Using FIFO, the company computes the cost of those units as follows:

400 @ $3.00 (7/10 price)	$1,200
500 @ $4.00 (7/14 price)	$2,000
Cost of Goods Sold	$3,200
Ending Inventory	$5,650

Ending inventory is calculated by subtracting cost of goods sold from the total goods in inventory of $8,850.

Last In, First Out (LIFO)

The last in, first out (LIFO) method of costing inventory is the opposite of FIFO. Here, a company uses the most recent inventory unit costs to value inventory as it goes out the door. The rationale is that the current costs are more in line with the costs of items being sold. Generally, the IRS frowns on LIFO, because in a period of rising prices, it results in lower net income. We don't recommend it either, particularly if you're just starting out. If you want to use it, you'll have to file form 970 with the IRS requesting approval.

The following table shows how Miller Home Construction Supply would determine its cost of goods sold using LIFO.

GOODS IN INVENTORY

Date	# Units	Unit Cost	Total Cost
7/10	400	$3.00	$1,200
7/14	650	$4.00	$2,600
7/15	425	$4.00	$1,700
7/18	500	$4.50	$2,250
7/30	200	$5.50	$1,100
	2,175		$8,850

200 @ $5.50 (7/30 "Last" Price)	$1,100
500 @ $4.50 (7/18 Price)	$2,250
200 @ $4.00 (7/15 Price)	$800
Cost of Goods Sold	$4,150
Ending Inventory	$4,700

5.4

Before you start applying costs to inventory and cost of goods sold, you need to decide what cost flow assumption you're going to use. In other words, when you've manufactured or purchased the same goods over a period of time at different prices, which costs will you use to value what you sell? Each method has its advantages and disadvantages, as we outline in the next subchapter. The key is finding the one that best works for your company.

Regardless of the method they choose, most companies with volumes of stock now rely on automated systems to cost and record inventory as doing these calculations manually can be time-consuming and costly. Computerized accounting programs also can use the data to quickly produce reports that can help managers determine which products are selling well, which are not, and how to stock most cost-effectively.

5.5 Cost of Goods Sold

Comparing Cost Flow Assumptions

Factoring in Rising and Falling Prices

Lower of Cost or Market

Cost of goods sold (COGS) is often key in determining whether your business is profitable or it isn't, so making sure this line item on the income statement gives a true picture of your costs is important. As we know from previous subchapters, in computing COGS and ending inventory, companies are given wide berth. This subchapter compares COGS when different inventory flow methods are used and also shows the impact of your choices on the bottom line.

Comparing Cost Flow Assumptions

Cost of goods sold is computed as follows:

Beginning inventory + Purchases − Ending inventory = Cost of goods sold

Your cost of goods sold varies depending on the inventory flow method you choose. A method that uses the most recent costs to value what's left in inventory could give you a lower cost of goods sold, for example, and hence a higher net income than you might get using a different valuation method.

The following table summarizes the effects of different valuation methods for the Miller Home Construction Supply examples discussed earlier:

COMPARISON CHART

	Cost of Goods Sold	Ending Inventory
Specific Identification	$4,050	$4,850
Average Cost	$3,663	$5,187
FIFO	$3,200	$5,650
LIFO	$4,150	$4,700

Note the $950 range between the highest and lowest cost of goods sold and ending inventory estimates. That's a 27 percent difference. This shows that the method you choose can have an impact on your financial results. Accounting rules permit you to choose the method to value cost of goods sold and inventory.

The cost flow method also need not approximate the flow of goods. What's important (and what the IRS looks at) is picking a method that makes sense for your company and your industry and sticking to it. If you decide on making a change, you must disclose this and, in the case of switching to LIFO, obtain permission in advance from the IRS.

Factoring in Rising and Falling Prices

Even if your company has settled on a method, be aware of how a changing economy can affect how accurately it reflects your costs. Rising or falling prices can have a major impact on the suitability of a particular method. For example, let's assume Fun Footwear has an inventory of shoes that breaks down as follows:

Date of Purchase	Quantity (Pairs)	Unit Cost
10/1	400	$2
10/20	500	$4
10/31	400	$7

During the period, Fun Footwear sells 500 shoes at $15 a pair. It has operating expenses of $2,000. In times of rising prices for inventory, if the company uses FIFO, its cost of goods sold will be composed of cheaper inventory (the stuff it bought first when prices were lower). This means Fun Footwear's cost of goods sold could be understated compared with the true cost of the products, resulting in an overstated net income. In addition, it might be overvaluing its remaining inventory.

Cost of Goods Sold:

400 Pairs @ $2	*$800*
100 Pairs @ $4	*$400*
COGS	*$1,200*

Sales: $7,500 (500 × $15/pair) – COGS: $1,200 = $6,300 – Operating expenses: 2,000 = $4,300

With LIFO, Fun Footwear's cost of goods sold is more in line with the current cost of the shoes, but its inventory may be understated in terms of current prices, and income low.

Sales: $7,500 – COGS: $3,200 = $4,300 – Operating expenses: $2,000 = $2,300

In times of falling prices, on the other hand, FIFO is more representative of Fun Footwear's actual cost of goods sold, although perhaps understating its inventory. LIFO would be understating the company's cost of goods sold and perhaps risk overstating inventory.

Lower of Cost or Market

In certain circumstances, companies might want to consider valuing inventory at a lower cost. The lower of cost or market method, or LCM, which is also suitable for tax purposes, could minimize disruption in markets where product costs fluctuate. Under this method, a company values each product by the lower of its cost or market value. For example, Fun Footwear's men's line has three styles of shoes, each with different costs and market values:

	Cost	Market
Men's dress shoes	$60	$50
Men's casual	$30	$45

The LCM method would allow the company to value men's dress shoes at their $50 market price because it's lower than cost and men's casual shoes at the $30 cost. This method can't be used when the costs are computed on a LIFO basis. Even if a company doesn't choose to use LCM, it's allowed to use market value for its cost if it's selling merchandise for less than its cost.

In determining the value of inventory, a company must look at the quantity of goods, the costs, and the flow of goods into the market. Quantities can be tracked, counted, or sometimes estimated. Merchandise inventory is usually costed at purchase price plus any additional charges to ready it for sale. Manufacturing inventory is first divided into stages: raw materials, work in process, and finished goods. Then, materials, labor, and other costs, known as overhead, are applied.

Finally, a business needs to choose an inventory valuation method that identifies which inventory items at which costs have been sold and which remain in stock. The IRS allows a variety of options, as we've outlined in this chapter. Each has different impact depending on the industry, the company, and the economy. Most large retailers use a method that allows inventory to be computed using gross profit and sales price. Small businesses more often choose FIFO, which matches the oldest costs with the first inventory sold, perhaps most accurately reflecting the changing costs of inventory purchased or produced at different times and its flow. The best method for your company depends on your particular situation.

6

Payables and Cash Disbursements

6.1 Accounts Payable

Introducing Accounts Payable

Recording Accounts Payable

Working with Vendor Accounts

Companies that operate on a cash basis pay all their bills within the month, so they don't need to set up accounts payable. All businesses that operate on an accrual basis, however, must set up accounts payable to reflect amounts they owe that have not yet been paid. This subchapter discusses different sources of accounts payable and shows you how to record them.

Introducing Accounts Payable

Accounts payable (or A/P) are your company's unpaid bills. These can be amounts owed for purchases of inventory or to providers of business necessities such as utilities, supplies, or other expenses. An account payable is a verbal agreement to repay an amount owed. The support for and details of this agreement are included on the invoice you receive from the vendor.

INVOICE

ABC, Inc.
PO Box 13
Schaumburg, IL

Billing Address:

Buyer Co.
220 Coast Drive
San Diego, CA

Date	Code	Description		Amount Due
5/07	043	Office desk	#sa1442	$1,100
	047	Desk chair	#s11333	$180
			Total Due	**$1,280**
		Terms: 2/10, n/30		

The preceding invoice from ABC, Inc., to Buyer Co. includes the standard details, date, items and description, prices, and terms at the bottom. This invoice would be placed with other unpaid invoices and filed by due date. Upon payment, it should be stamped paid and filed in the vendor's file.

SEE ALSO 1.3, "Creating a Filing System"

Recording Accounts Payable

If you are in manufacturing or merchandising, inventory purchases bought on trade credit are likely to account for the bulk of your accounts payable. A sample journal entry for a retail clothing store that purchased a line of coats on account from AGM Co. would be:

	Debit	Credit
1/2 Merchandise Inventory	$3,900	
Accounts Payable—AGM Co.		$3,900
To record purchase of inventory on account from AGM Co., terms 2/10, n/30.		

6.1

The next biggest portion of accounts payable goes to providers of supplies and services you need to operate—utilities, rent, insurance, etc. These expenses represent the majority of accounts payable. For example, buying $1,500 of office supplies from Complete Office, Inc., and then paying the invoice right before the end of the month generates the following entries.

SEE ALSO 4.2, "Adjusting and Summarizing Sales"

	Debit	Credit
1/2 Office Supplies	$1,500	
Accounts Payable—Complete Office		$1,500
To record purchase of office supplies on account, 2/10, n/30.		
1/30 Accounts Payable—Complete Office	$1,500	
Cash		$1,500
To record payment of Complete Office—A/P.		

Many larger companies, particularly ones with substantial accounting staffs, keep a purchases journal specifically for recording purchases on credit. Noting all purchases in one place makes it easy to track expenditures.

PURCHASES JOURNAL

Date	Explanation	Reference	Amount
1/2	Complete Office, Inc.	501	$1,500
1/5	Pacific Bell	432	$250

When Hope Company makes a payment on an account payable, the company makes an entry to the cash disbursements journal, as shown in the following simple example.

HOPE COMPANY
CASH DISBURSEMENTS JOURNAL

Date	Payee	Cash Debit	Credit	Accounts Payable Debit	Credit	Purchases Debit	Disc Credit
2/3	Merryvale Corp.		($1,500)			$1,500	
2/9	Pacific G & E		($250)	$250			
2/12	Merryvale Corp.		($1,470)	$1,500			($30)
2/25	TKI Company		($2,350)			$2,350	
			($5,570)	$1,750		$3,850	($30)

All transactions involving accounts payable transactions are initially recorded in journals. Large companies often keep a separate purchases journal to record credit purchases and record payments in a cash disbursements journal. Some companies combine the two. At the end of the month, totals should be checked and posted to the appropriate accounts in the general ledger. In a computerized system, you need only record the transaction once and it will be automatically posted to the appropriate journals, summarized, and carried forward to the financial statements.

SEE ALSO 10.2, "Closing Cash Journals"

SEE ALSO 15.1, "Benefits of Computerized Accounting"

Working with Vendor Accounts

All businesses should set up separate account files for each vendor. Here you'll keep vital data like account information, purchase history, and contacts. This information may be automated, but hard copies of invoices should be kept and filed as backups.

SEE ALSO 1.3, "Creating a Filing System"

In addition, each time you enter a transaction into the purchases register, you also must enter it into the A/P subsidiary ledger, which is kept by customer name. In the subsidiary ledger, open (unpaid) invoices are recorded as debits as this is an asset (accounts receivable) to the vendor. When the bill is paid, the subsidiary ledger is credited with the payment. The following sample ledger for Complete Office Co. offers an illustration.

ACCOUNTS PAYABLE (SUBLEDGER)

Complete Office   011

Date		PR	Debit	Credit	Balance
12/31					$0
1/2	Purchase	P	$1,500		$1,500
1/2	Payment	CD		$1,500	$0

You should keep a separate subsidiary ledger which will include each vendor account. At the end of the month, after you have computed the new balances in each subsidiary ledger, the sum of these should agree with the A/P total in the general ledger, as well as the unpaid invoice file. If they don't, you might need to go back and check your journal entries to be sure they've been recorded to the appropriate accounts, that the debits and credits in the journal balance, and that all transactions recorded in the journal have been posted to the appropriate vendor in the subsidiary ledger.

6.1

6.2 Accounting for Purchases

Documenting Purchases

Recording Purchases

Making Adjustments

Here we focus on documenting and recording purchases. We cover how to record purchases under different accounting systems and how to handle returns and discounts.

Documenting Purchases

All purchases should be supported by a **purchase order.** This document initiates the transaction that ends in the delivery of product and subsequent billing. The following is a purchase order from Simple Simon Toys to The Learning Company. Notice that it is prenumbered so Simple Simon can keep track of outstanding orders. There's also a line for an authorized signature—a safeguard that helps prevent unauthorized orders. The purchase order should also include shipping instructions and a shipping address.

Simple Simon Toys, Inc.
101 Main Street
San Diego, CA
619-555-4300

PURCHASE ORDER
No. **216**

To: The Learning Tree Co.

Ship To: LTC
8 Falling Way
Cassopolis, MI

Terms: 2/10, n/30

Qty.	Units	Description	Unit Price	Total
4	2	Dictionary sets	$21.95	$87.80
10	1	Preschool set	$199.00	$1,990.00
			Subtotal	$2,077.80
			Sales Tax	$143.40
			Shipping and Handling	$15.00
			Other	
			Total Due	**$2,236.20**

Approved: _____

✓

> A **purchase order** is a formal document authorizing the quantity, time, and specifics of an order.

Recording Purchases

It's important to have a system in place to ensure proper recording of all purchases. Lax disbursements policies or procedures could easily result in theft and misappropriation. Misclassification can lead to duplicate purchases, misstated inventory, and other costs and inefficiencies. How you record purchases depends in part on whether you use a perpetual or periodic inventory system, so in this section, we explain each of these separately.

The Perpetual Inventory System

If your business or the company you work for uses a perpetual inventory system, where additions and subtractions are continuously updated, you record purchases directly to inventory. For example, Farm Hand, Inc., an agricultural equipment store that bought $8,000 worth of wheelbarrows on credit at the beginning of the year, would record the following journal entry:

6.2

	Debit	Credit
1/2 Inventory	$8,000	
Accounts Payable—Ryder Co.		$8,000
To record purchase of wheelbarrows from Ryder Co., terms 2/10, n/30.		

SEE ALSO 5.1, "Accounting for Inventory"

The Periodic Inventory System

BK Bike Store uses a periodic inventory system. It would record a $5,000 purchase of bicycle supplies first into a purchases account, because updates to inventory are only made at month end.

	Debit	Credit
1/2 Purchases	$5,000	
Accounts Payable—Racing Form		$5,000
To record purchase of bicycle supplies from Racing Form Company, terms 2/10, n/30.		

Cash flow was tight during the month, so BK didn't get around to paying the Racing Form invoice until the discount period had expired. This means they must pay the full price for the purchase. At that point, they made the following journal entry to record payment:

	Debit	Credit
1/30 Accounts Payable—Racing Form	$5,000	
Cash		$5,000

To record payment of invoice #1412.

SEE ALSO 4.2, "Adjusting and Summarizing Sales"

Freight Charges

Depending on the contract, either the seller or the buyer may be responsible for shipping charges. If you, as purchaser, bear the cost of freight, this amount is included in a separate account that becomes part of net purchases. For example, assume shipping charges for the bicycle parts BK Bike Store purchased came to $150. This amount is recorded to the following account:

	Debit	Credit
1/2 Freight-In	$150	
Cash*		$150

*To record paying of freight charges for invoice #1412. (*Assumes charges paid in cash on delivery.)*

Regardless of which system you use, your purchases ultimately end up in inventory. If you use a perpetual system, this happens immediately. Under a periodic system, inventory purchases go first to a purchases account and are updated to inventory at the end of the month. It's up to you to decide which system works best for your company.

Making Adjustments

Just because you've recorded a purchase and its accompanying account payable for the same amount doesn't mean that's what you'll ultimately pay. In fact, if you're running your business in the most cost-effective way, you'll be paying a discount price, which will require adjusting your books. If you return any of the merchandise, you'll also have to adjust your accounts for the return. We address both of these adjustments separately.

Purchase Discounts

Purchase discounts are handled in much the same way as discounts on sales. Trade discounts are reflected in the purchase price and do not require any special accounting treatment. Cash discounts for paying within the discount period (e.g., payment for an invoice with terms, 2/10, n/30, within 10 days) are credited to an income account cash discounts earned. Many businesses try to pay the bills early to get the discount. Farm Hand, Inc., from our earlier example had a similar policy and paid within 10 days to avoid losing the discount on its wheelbarrows. Here's what the corresponding journal entry would look like:

	Debit	Credit
1/11 Accounts Payable—Ryder Co.	$8,000	
Cash		$7,840
Discount Earned		$160
To record payment of invoice #132.		

SEE ALSO 1.4, "Establishing the Chart of Accounts"

SEE ALSO 4.2, "Adjusting and Summarizing Sales"

The discount taken represents income to Farm Hand, Inc. For this reason, some companies record purchases at price net of discount and record a discount lost when they don't pay early. This way management can see how effective the company is at managing timely payments. If Farm Hand had chosen that method, it would have recorded the original purchase and accounts payable as $7,840. Then if the company was late paying the bill, the following entry would be required:

	Debit	Credit
1/20 Accounts Payable—Ryder Co.	$7,840	
Discounts Lost	$160	
Cash		$8,000
To record payment of accounts payable with discount surrendered.		

SEE ALSO 1.4, "Establishing the Chart of Accounts"

Either way is acceptable, although most companies choose the gross purchases method and record the discount, if appropriate, at payment.

Purchase Returns and Allowances

In certain instances, you might need to return some or all of an order because the merchandise is damaged, defective, or otherwise unacceptable. In this case, the resulting adjustment would be made directly to purchases or to an account for **purchase returns and allowances.** This is a temporary account that serves as a deduction from net purchases to arrive at cost of goods sold on the income statement. Determining the remedy is up to you and the seller. In instances where part of a shipment is damaged or parts are defective, a partial or total return with an accompanying credit is usually the answer. In other cases, where the customer is not completely satisfied, the seller might give an "allowance" by reducing the price to be paid.

✓

Purchase returns and allowances represents credits for goods returned to vendor or additional amounts discounted by vendor because of problems with goods.

Say BK Bike Store opens its shipment of bicycle parts and discovers that approximately half of them have been crushed or broken because of mishandling during shipping. BK contacts the seller, Racing Form, and is instructed to return the damaged parts for a full refund. When the credit memorandum has been issued, BK could record the following entry:

		Debit	Credit
1/5	Accounts Payable—Racing Form	$2,500	
	Purchase Returns and Allowances (or Purchases)		$2,500

To record return of defective merchandise.

Many businesses do not use a separate account, but merely charge or credit the inventory or purchases accounts. Particularly with small businesses, the information gleaned from a separate account is meaningless.

Computing Net Purchases

When you're preparing your financial statements at the end of the period, all the components we've detailed in this subchapter (with the exception of discounts if handled separately) go into computing net purchases and cost of merchandise purchased:

Purchases	$15,000
Less: Purchase Returns and Allowances	$2,500
Net Purchases	$12,500
Add in: Freight	$1,300
Cost of Merchandise Purchased	$13,800

This amount can then be used to compute ending inventory for and cost of goods sold.

SEE ALSO 5.1, "Accounting for Inventory"

What you owe for a purchase may be adjusted after the fact—either for discounts or returns and allowances. These adjustments will be made to separate accounts and reduce your liability (accounts payable). At the end of the period, both discounts and returns and allowances must be deducted from total purchases and freight costs you pay added in to determine the total cost of the merchandise purchased.

6.2

6.3 Notes Payable

Interest-Bearing Notes Payable

Non-Interest-Bearing Notes Payable

In addition to accounts payable, other expenses and liability accounts are paid through your cash disbursements system. The most common of these are wage-related accounts and **notes payable.** Notes payable typically represents amounts a company has taken in short-term loans from a bank or to finance a purchasing transaction in lieu of the vendor offering trade credit. Notes payable might be issued, for example, if you're a new customer or considered a credit risk.

✓

> A **notes payable** is a written promise to repay a company a certain amount by a specified time at a stated interest rate.

Notes payable may be classified as short-term or long-term depending on when they're due. Short-term payables are due in less than 1 year, whereas long-term payables are payable beyond 1 year. They may have a stated interest rate, or the borrower may have to pay more than face value for them when they are issued.

SEE ALSO 8.5, "Recording Payroll"

Interest-Bearing Notes Payable

Interest-bearing notes payable come with a stated interest rate. A company can make a purchase with a $5,000 note payable at 12 percent due in 90 days. The interest rate generally depends on what the entity accepting the note charges as interest. For interest-bearing notes, monthly interest is computed by multiplying interest rate by the amount due and dividing by 12.

Let's say on May 1, Gopher Corp., a yard-care equipment manufacturer, signs a note for $10,000 at 10 percent interest, due in 60 days. Gopher makes the following entry to record the note on its books:

	Debit	Credit
5/1 Cash	$10,000	
Notes Payable		$10,000
To record notes payable, 60 days, 10 percent.		

Gopher Corp. generates financial statements monthly. At the end of May, its accountants would make this journal entry to record accrued interest on the note:

	Debit	Credit
5/31 Interest Expense	$83	
Interest Payable		$83
To accrue interest for 1 month.		

When Gopher pays off the note in June, the company will pay an additional $83 interest charge for the total interest payment of $166 for the note.

Non-Interest-Bearing Notes Payable

Non-interest-bearing notes payable, or zero-interest notes payable, don't have a stated interest charge, but they still have a cost because you as borrower have to pay more than face value for them when they're issued. The difference is called a discount on the note and is a deduction from the proceeds available to the borrower. The note has an "imputed" or implied interest rate.

6.3

For example, if Gopher Co. was able to issue a $10,000 non-interest-bearing notes payable for 60 days to purchase inventory, it would account for the note as follows:

	Debit	Credit
5/1 Inventory	$9,850	
Discount on Notes Payable	$150	
Notes Payable		$10,000
To record purchase of inventory with notes payable.		

The "discount" on the notes payable is actually the imputed interest charge of 9 percent on the note. Gopher's inventory purchase was for $9,850, but the company was required to issue a note (borrow) $10,000.

Notes payable is a written agreement to pay a company a certain amount by a certain time in the future. There's usually some cost in using a notes payable, either in terms of a stated interest rate or an imputed one, for the privilege of the additional financing. These notes are often required by businesses just starting out and trying to establish credit as added insurance that a debt will be paid.

6.4 Cash Disbursements

Timing of Payments

Employing Internal Controls

The Voucher System

The Cash Disbursements Journal

In this subchapter, we examine the cash disbursements cycle and look at procedures to help ensure cash is safeguarded and transactions are properly recorded.

Timing of Payments

Careful records must be kept of billing and account payment information so payments are made in a timely manner. Most companies make it a policy of paying early to get the discount, as forfeiting it adds additional costs to the purchase.

SEE ALSO 4.2, "Adjusting and Summarizing Sales"

To keep on top of payments and see how well you're meeting obligations, prepare an A/P aging schedule, which enables you to break down individual accounts by due dates. A similar schedule is used to track accounts receivable.

SEE ALSO 4.3, "Accounts Receivable"

Most computerized accounting systems automatically generate an aging schedule of accounts payable whenever you need it, but you can also prepare one manually without too much trouble. Simply separate accounts by due date:

FARM HAND, INC.
A/P AGING SCHEDULE
DECEMBER 31

Vendor	Amount Due	Current	31 to 60 Days	61 to 90 Days	91 to 120 Days
Eagle Company	$3,510	$1,510	$900	$1,100	
Ryder, Inc.	$5,000	$5,000			
Snowy Corp.	$4,600	$4,100	$500		
KTL Play	$3,500	$3,500			
Freeman PLC	$1,500				$1,500
Totals	$18,110	$14,110	$1,400	$1,100	$1,500

As we can see, while some of the accounts appear to be current, there are older amounts that bear investigation. For example, is the amount owed Freedman PLC, which is older than 60 days, in dispute? Eagle Company also has a balance over 60 days. Further inquiry would definitely be warranted to determine whether these were isolated account difficulties or a bigger cash flow issue—particularly because Farm Hand's stated policy is to take all discounts.

Employing Internal Controls

As we mentioned in an earlier chapter, all businesses need to have strong internal controls over cash disbursements to minimize the opportunity for misappropriation. It's worth going over a few of the more important internal controls here:

- Use a voucher system to authorize and control cash disbursements. Prenumbered vouchers provide a way to track each bill to be paid and make sure it has been properly approved.

- Be sure the same people don't handle checks and record them.

- Stamp all invoices paid so they can't be resubmitted for payment.

- Ensure that the signature stamp is properly safeguarded.

6.4

Solid procedures around the timing and payment of accounts payable help ensure that cash disbursements are proper and appropriately recorded. To keep payments on track and stay on top of what's coming due, it's useful to keep good files of unpaid invoicing and prepare periodic aging of accounts payable if time and staffing levels permit.

SEE ALSO 3.3, "Implementing Internal Controls Over Cash"

The Voucher System

Most medium and large companies opt for a voucher system as a means of controlling cash disbursements. A voucher is an authorization form that must be approved before payment of any bill. Upon receipt of an invoice, a prenumbered voucher is stapled to the bill and filled in with payment and account information. The voucher is then recorded in the **voucher register** and filed by date, along with supporting documentation, in the unpaid voucher file. (With a computerized accounting system, this is done automatically.)

SEE ALSO 1.3, "Creating a Filing System"

✓

> A **voucher register** is the journal for recording all vouchers as bills are received and approved.

Shortly before the due date, the voucher/invoice packet is sent out for approval, typically to a manager and someone separate from the person who records the invoice or prepares it for payment. The approved voucher is then forwarded to the treasury office so a check can be cut and sent to the vendor. The check is recorded in the check register.

It's worth noting that when a voucher system is used, the journal of first entry is the voucher register to recognize the liability and the check register for payment. For example, TerraMax Systems, a maker of computer components, uses a voucher system to handle all its payables. On March 13 TerraMax bought $5,200 worth of wiring and computer boards for its upcoming production line. The vendor, The Insider Co., billed TerraMax the same day. TerraMax recorded the accounts payable in its voucher register as shown on the next page.

Then TerraMax moved the voucher to its unpaid voucher file. In a voucher system, this replaces the subsidiary ledgers that separate invoices by account. When the voucher is paid, TerraMax will move it to the paid voucher file. On March 25 TerraMax paid The Insider Co., as reflected in the following journal entry:

	Debit	Credit
3/25 Vouchers Payable	$5,200	
Cash		$5,200
To record payment with check #373.		

TERRAMAX SYSTEMS
VOUCHER REGISTER

Date	Payee	Voucher #	Date Paid	Check #	Vouchers Payable (Credit)	Purchases Debit	Supplies Debit	Salaries Expense Debit	Advertising Expense Debit	General Accounts Debited	PR	Amount
3/2	Pacific G & E	1611	3/2	369	$859					Utilities		$859
3/4	Twilight Display	1612			$2,300				$2,300			
3/6	Payroll	1613	3/6	370	$1,590			$1,590				
3/9	Staples	1614	3/10	371	$550		$550					
3/10	Green Landscaping	1615	3/12	372	$4,200					Land improvements		$4,200
3/13	Insider Co.	1616	3/13	373	$5,200	$5,200						
3/17	J. Lewis	1617	3/18	374	$2,120					Notes payable		$2,000
										Interest expense		$120
3/31	Total				$16,819	$5,200	$550	$1,590	$2,300			$7,179

A posting reference (PR) column can be included after the payee column to note the account number.

6.4

TerraMax also recorded to the check register:

CHECK REGISTER

Date	Payee	Voucher #	Check #	Vouchers Payable Debit	Purchases Discount (Credit)	Cash (Credit)
3/17	Insider Co.	1616	373	$5,200		$5,200

The Cash Disbursements Journal

Transactions related to accounts payable and cash disbursements should be recorded on a daily basis to the appropriate journal. We've already covered the purchases journal, where companies enter all purchases on credit. Payments of bills and all other cash outlays are recorded in the cash disbursements journal.

SEE ALSO 2.4, "Recording in Journals"

Many companies use a cash disbursements journal similar to the one shown in the following example. Here both cash and credit transactions can be recorded in addition to purchases and a number of additional expenses. Farm Hand's purchases are primarily inventory with some freight and utilities expenses.

Other businesses might include payroll in the combined cash disbursements/purchases journal. This can be useful in a small company where many accounting functions fall to the same person and maintaining separate journals is too time-consuming. The Farm Hand, Inc., Cash Disbursements Journal on the next page puts it all together.

In the second table, notice how the cash disbursements journal for Adams Company includes separate columns for each type of payroll tax. Again, this makes it simple to total the column and post the total to the general ledger. As we've seen, there are no hard-and-fast rules about how to set up ledgers for purchases and cash disbursements. You can create separate journals or combine them. What's important in the end is that the format you choose works for your company.

FARM HAND, INC.
CASH DISBURSEMENTS JOURNAL

Date	Description	Posting Reference	General Account Debit	Accounts Payable Debit	Accounts Payable (Credit)	Purchases Debit	Purchases (Credit)	Discounts Earned (Credit)	Cash (Credit)
1/2	Freight	A/C 455	$150						($150)
1/5	A/P—Ryder Co.			$5,000				($100)	($4,900)
1/14	A/P—Eagle Co.			$2,000					($2,000)
1/15	A/P—Snowy Corp.			$500					($500)
1/18	A/P—Ryder				($4,200)	$4,200			
1/22	A/P—KTL Play				($1,000)	$1,000			
1/31	A/P—Freeman			$1,500			($1,500)		
1/31	Boise Gas and Electric	A/C 430	$1,200						($1,200)
			$1,350	($9,000)	($5,200)	$5,200	($1,500)	($100)	($8,750)
				{210}			{401}	{402}	{102}

Numbers in ( ) are credit balances. Numbers in { } are account numbers.

6.4

ADAMS COMPANY
CASH DISBURSEMENTS JOURNAL

Date	Payee	Check #	Cash (CR) Amount	FICA Withheld	Federal Tax Withheld	State Tax Withheld	Payroll	Accounts Payable	Purchases	Maintenance	Cash Discounts Earned	Misc.	Acct. #	Other Debit	Other Credit
2/2	Wells Paper	303	$1,860					$2,000			($40)				
2/7	Payroll	304–320	$9,880	($1,224)	($3,990)	($906)	$16,000								
2/10	EF Stationers	321	$150									Supplies	501	$150	
2/13	Rent	322	$5,000									Rent	429	$5,000	
2/25	Utilities	323	$1,760									Utilities	430	$1,760	
2/27	Repairs	324	$2,490							$2,490					
2/27	Payroll	325–342	$9,880	($1,224)	($3,990)	($906)	$16,000								
	Total		$31,020	$2,448	$7,980	$1,812	$32,000	$2,000		$2,490	($40)			$6,910	
			{102}	{230}	{231}	{232}	{410}	{210}		{435}	{402}				

Total = numbers to be posted to the general ledger.

Numbers in ( ) are credit balances. Numbers in { } are account numbers.

6.5 Reconciling Accounts Payable

Journal to General Ledger

Reconciling with Vendor Accounts

This subchapter is devoted to ensuring that all accounts paid are properly and accurately recorded. It shows you how to reconcile accounts payable with the individual vendor accounts (subledgers) as well as the amounts paid in cash disbursements.

At the end of the period, the totals from the cash disbursements journal are **footed** and **cross-footed** to be sure all entries have been recorded. Next, you add up the columns in the cash disbursements journal and post the totals to the general ledger by account. For example, the totals from the accounts payable column are posted to accounts payable in the general ledger. You total up debits and credits to compute the general ledger balance for accounts payable, which is then compared with the combined total of the customer accounts in the subsidiary ledger. Such checking and double-checking helps you catch errors early as opposed to later down the line. In a computerized system there is no need to manually calculate the totals, as this is automatically done for you.

6.5

✓

To **foot** is to sum a *column* of numbers, such as the totals in the purchases journal.

To **cross-foot** is to sum a *row* of numbers, making sure debits equal credits.

Journal to the General Ledger

At the end of the month, account totals are posted from journals to the general ledger. For Farm Hand, Inc., this means posting from the cash disbursements journal. Our totals there again were as follows.

FARM HAND, INC.
CASH DISBURSEMENTS JOURNAL

Date	Description	Posting Reference	General Account Debit	Accounts Payable Debit	Accounts Payable (Credit)	Purchases Debit	Purchases (Credit)	Discounts Earned (Credit)	Cash (Credit)
	Totals		$1,350	$9,000	($5,200)	$5,200	($1,500)	($100)	($8,750)
				{210}		{401}		{402}	{102}

The first thing the company needs to do is cross-foot the totals to be sure debits equal credits. Fortunately, this journal is in balance.

For purposes of this example, we'll focus on account 210, which is accounts payable. Farm Hand needs to take the debit and credit totals and post them to the general ledger. This is usually done as a net (combined) entry; however, we will show both the debit and credit to better illustrate the account changes.

Here's the accounts payable account in the general ledger:

FARM HAND, INC.
GENERAL LEDGER

Acct. 210   ACCOUNTS PAYABLE

Date	Reference	Debit	Credit	Balance
12/31	Balance			$17,610
1/31	CD	$9,000		
	CD		$5,200	$13,810

Farm Hand began the period with a balance of $17,610 in accounts payable. In a summary posting from the cash disbursements register, accounts payable is debited $9,000 from account payments and credited $5,200 in new bills. The new balance at 1/31 is $13,810.

Reconciling with Vendor Accounts

A final check now needs to be done to ensure that all account activity has been recorded. To do this, Farm Hand will reconcile its subsidiary ledgers for each vendor account with the general ledger. The total of the individual ledger balances should equal the balance in the accounts payable general ledger.

Following is the subsidiary ledger (sometimes called subledger) for Farm Hand. The debits and credits will be the opposite of how they appear in the general ledger (a payment will be a credit, for example) because these accounts represent assets for the vendors.

FARM HAND, INC.
ACCOUNTS PAYABLE (SUBLEDGER)

Eagle Co.   011

Date		PR	Debit	Credit	Balance
12/31					$3,510
1/14		CD		$2,000	$1,510

Ryder Co.   013

Date		PR	Debit	Credit	Balance
12/31					$5,000
1/5		CD		$5,000	$0
1/18		P	$4,200	$4,200	$4,200

Snowy Corp.   014

Date		PR	Debit	Credit	Balance
12/31					$4,100
1/15				$500	$3,600

KTL Play   022

Date		PR	Debit	Credit	Balance
12/31					$3,500
1/22		PJ	$1,000		$4,500

Freeman PLC   039

Date		PR	Debit	Credit	Balance
12/31					$1,500
1/31	Purchase Returns	GJ		$1,500	$0

Total Balance Subledger   **$13,810**

6.5

Adding the balances, Farm Hand arrives at a total of $13,810, which does agree with the general ledger amount at 1/31. This indicates that all accounts payable transactions entered into the subsidiary ledgers when invoices were recorded or paid were appropriately summarized and posted to the general ledger. This doesn't mean a transaction couldn't have fallen through the cracks, but combined with the journals balancing and internal controls it lessens that possibility. If the numbers hadn't balanced, Farm Hand would have had to go over the numbers in both the ledger and the subledger again to try to identify the error.

SEE ALSO 1.1, "Accounting Basics"

SEE ALSO 10.2, "Closing Cash Journals"

All companies incur bills that must be paid in the course of their operations. In this chapter, we've attempted to outline how to record purchases and accounts payable as well as how to develop the necessary procedures and controls to ensure that payments are made promptly and cash disbursements are properly handled and recorded.

7

Depreciable Assets and Intangibles

7.1 Property, Plant, and Equipment

Classification and Valuation

Additions and Improvements

Keeping Records

Some of the most valuable assets your company owns are those it never intends to sell. Your **property, plant, and equipment** assets are those such as the building you work in, the fleet of delivery trucks, or the computers and office equipment you use to provide your services. This subchapter helps you identify these assets and properly value them on your books.

✓

Property, plant, and equipment (PP&E) are the tangible assets you need to operate your business. You might also hear them called *plant* or *fixed assets.* They're typically big-ticket items you plan on holding indefinitely.

Classification and Valuation

Fixed assets are valued at **cost,** which is purchase price plus any additional charges required to ready the property for use.

✓

Cost is the purchase price of an asset plus the charges to put it in service. This is also referred to as the *cost basis.*

On the balance sheet, plant assets are divided into categories such as land, buildings, machinery and equipment, and office equipment. These categories might vary slightly based on the type of business or industry, but these are typical account designations found in PP&E.

Land

Land refers to property used to produce income for your business, such as the site of your factory. Land held purely for speculation is considered an investment and listed separately. Unlike other fixed assets, land is not depreciated because its usefulness does not decline over time. In fact, land is more likely to go up in value, due to scarcity and location. Unfortunately, you're not allowed to book any such increases until you sell the property.

Natural resources on land, however, may be written off in a process known as **depletion.** Also, improvements to land, such as a parking lot, may be depreciated.

✓

> **Depletion** is the write-off of a natural resource like timber, oil, or gas as it's extracted or used.

Like all fixed assets, land is valued at cost. This means the amount you record in the land account—the cost basis—is the purchase price of the land, plus any additional charges paid to make it ready for its intended use. These could include title insurance and attorney's fees, real estate commissions, and any other costs of preparing the land to build.

On May 29, for example, Lucy Song purchased land to build a new music store and teaching center for $120,000. She also paid $1,300 in attorney's fees and $5,000 to demolish and remove an old building from the site. Here's how Lucy computed the land's value to record in the books:

Cash Price of Property	$120,000
Demolition and Removal Costs	$5,000
Attorney's Fees	$1,300
Cost of Land	**$126,300**

7.1

To record the acquisition of this land, Lucy debited the land account $126,300.

Buildings

The buildings account is where you record your factory or office if you own it. If you purchase your building, its value on the books includes costs similar to those for land—closing costs, attorney's fees, and so on, plus any repair or remodeling costs.

If you construct your building, its cost is the contract price plus items such as architecture fees, building permits, excavation costs, and interest costs incurred during the construction period. Again, the rule of thumb is that any costs associated with construction or readying the building for use are depreciable. Repairs and maintenance and other costs incurred subsequent to moving into the building are considered expenses and not added to the value of the asset.

Let's say Otto VanDorn and his partner, Randy Crook, both artists, started building a design studio on a piece of property Otto inherited from his grandmother. They applied for the appropriate permits, hired an architect and contractor, and now, a year later, they're ready to open their new gallery. They incurred the following costs and want to know how to value the building for business purposes:

Permits Fees	$1,500
Construction and Materials	$235,000
Architect's Fees	$8,500
Advertising Expenses (to publicize the building and the move to the new place)	$2,400

Otto and Randy have a cost basis for the building of $245,000, which includes construction and materials and architect's and permit fees. Advertising expenses are not to be included. Instead, they are expensed in the period.

Machinery and Equipment

Items in the machinery and equipment account typically consist of productive machinery used in a plant or factory. Any machines, robotics, forklift trucks, or product testing equipment used to make the product fall into this category.

For example, Cozy Copy, Inc., imports a new molding machine from China for $200,000. In addition, Cozy pays $5,000 for shipping as well as $1,570 for customs and tariffs—charges management is willing to swallow because comparable machines made at home cost twice as much. When the machine is in the United States, Cozy forks over another $12,000 for delivery and installation.

Under the cost basis, all these charges are included in the book value of the machine, so Cozy Copy, Inc., makes the following entry to put the new machine on its books:

		Debit	Credit
4/1	Equipment—Machinery	$218,570	
	Cash		$218,570
	To record cost basis of new machinery.		

Some companies include automobiles or delivery trucks in this account. Others choose to put vehicles in a separate account—automobiles—for ease of calculating depreciation. Either classification is acceptable.

Office Equipment

The office equipment category contains the company computers, desks and chairs, copiers, printers, scanners, shredders, and so on, used in the course of the business. Paper, pens, notebooks, printer cartridges, and other smaller, frequently replaced items are not considered equipment. Instead, these are categorized as office supplies and expensed as they're incurred.

As with other fixed assets, office equipment is valued at the cost of the machine plus any charges to ready it for use. In the case of office cubicles, for example, delivery costs and labor to assemble the cubicle are capitalized as part of the asset. Regular maintenance, on the other hand, is considered an expense and is not included in the asset value.

Sometimes furniture, including desks and chairs, is put in a furniture and fixtures account. This is an older designation that's not used much anymore unless the company is talking about nice or expensive office furniture, fixtures in the bathrooms, lights, and perhaps artwork. In practice, office equipment is usually the preferred designation.

Additions and Improvements

7.1

Additions and improvements to any of the fixed asset accounts are also capitalized, as they usually prolong the life of the asset. Examples include putting a new roof on an office building, replacing the motor in plant machinery with an updated version that is longer-lasting, or adding a new driveway into the factory. These amounts would be added to the asset totals and depreciated over their useful lives.

Repairs, for the most part, are not considered additions or improvements and are directly expensed. This is the case even if they involve the purchase of replacement parts that are required to maintain the asset. Unless the new part extends the useful life of the asset, it is not capitalized.

SEE ALSO 1.4, "Establishing the Chart of Accounts"

Treatment

Fixed asset records must be updated for any major repairs, additions, or improvements. The amounts should be entered into the accounting records on the fixed asset schedule, showing the cost of the addition, the date, and a description of the addition or improvement. If you have a computerized accounting system, you will only need to input this data once in order to update all the appropriate accounting records.

SEE ALSO 15.4, "Converting to an Automated System"

For example, say Richards and Sons Lumber, Inc., needs to extend its loading dock to accommodate larger vehicles at a cost of $7,000. In addition to updating its fixed asset schedule with the costs of the construction, the company would also need to make the following journal entry to its building account.

	Debit	Credit
12/31 Building	$7,000	
Cash (or Accounts Payable)		$7,000
To record the costs of building extension.		

Meanwhile, the supporting documentation—invoices, purchase order, etc.— should be put together in the file for that fixed asset and retained. These records are necessary for providing required information in the event of a sale or other disposition. See the next section for discussion of depreciation of additions and improvements.

Land Improvements

The land improvements account holds any changes made to the property that substantially add to its value, such as paving a driveway, installing a new drainage system, or adding a parking lot. Such alterations are subject to wear and tear and decrease in value over time, so they're depreciable. Land improvements are valued at cost.

Leasehold Improvements

Similar to land improvements, the leasehold improvement account holds the costs of any upgrades made to the property you're leasing. New paneling or remodeling that will have value to the owner at the end of the lease term are considered leasehold improvements. Sometimes, leasehold improvements are classified as intangibles and **amortized** over their useful life, as required by the IRS. This is covered in more detail in the "Intangible Assets" section later in this chapter.

SEE ALSO 7.4, "Leases"

✓

Amortization is the gradual reduction of an asset or expense account over the time you benefit from its use. Accounts such as intangibles and deferred charges are amortized.

Keeping Records

All documents—invoices, receipts, purchase orders, bills, or memos supporting the initial purchase of a fixed asset and its related charges—should be filed in a separate folder for each asset. By opening one of these files and tallying the charges on the supporting documents, you should be able to determine the cost basis for the fixed asset. And indeed, if you are ever audited, these documents serve as evidence of the asset value.

For each asset, you should keep a schedule listing the charges that support its original cost basis, plus any additions or improvements that have been made over the years. Also include a schedule of repairs and maintenance so you can track expenses by asset and better predict when items might need to be replaced. Retain these records for as long as you have the asset and for at least 3 years after its disposal or retirement.

7.1

SEE ALSO 1.3, "Creating a Filing System"

SEE ALSO 11.6, "Additional Reports"

7.2 Depreciation

Depreciation Basics

Computing Depreciation

Revising Depreciation Estimates

Recording Depreciation

Depreciation for Tax Considerations

This subchapter explains the rationale behind depreciation and demonstrates methods of calculating depreciation on your fixed assets and recording the expense on your books or on the tax return.

Depreciation Basics

Over time, all PP&E assets, with the exception of land, experience a decrease in usefulness. Buildings and autos suffer wear and tear; machinery becomes obsolete; and land improvements erode with age. To reflect this decline in value, accountants use depreciation, which is essentially a way to allocate the cost of an asset to expenses over its years of service.

To depreciate an asset, you must know three things about it:

- The cost
- Its **useful life**
- Its **salvage value**

✓

Useful life is an estimate of the asset's expected productive life.

Salvage value (or *residual value*) is the estimated value at the end of an asset's useful life. Salvage value is not used in depreciation for income tax purposes.

Useful life is usually expressed in years, but you can also use machine hours, units of production, mileage, or whatever gauge seems the most accurate to measure decline. Useful life may be based on the experience you've had with a similar asset in the past or management's expectations for the future. Here are some general guidelines; you also might look at the estimates contained in the IRS Publication 946 on its website:

- Autos are typically depreciated over 3 to 5 years.

- Most other equipment is depreciated from 5 to 10 years.

- New buildings can be depreciated 30 to 50 years.

The salvage or residual value is the amount you would expect to be able to sell the asset for as scrap at the end of its service. The cost basis of an asset less the salvage value becomes its depreciable basis.

Computing Depreciation

You have a number of choices when it comes to computing depreciation. The method you choose depends on the asset you're depreciating and how quickly you expect its value to decline. For tax purposes, all fixed assets purchased after 1986 must be depreciated using a special method called the *Modified Accelerated Cost Recovery System* or MACRS (pronounced *mackers*). For the sake of simplicity, many businesses, particularly small ones, use this method to compute depreciation for both financial reporting and tax reporting purposes. Either way is acceptable. What's important, if you choose to use a different method for bookkeeping or "book" purposes, is consistency. Once you've selected a method, retain it from year to year. Businesses with a large volume of fixed assets will likely find that an automated system is a more cost-effective and time-efficient way of computing depreciation and valuing fixed assets.

7.2

SEE ALSO 15.1, "Benefits of Computerized Accounting"

The Straight-Line Method

The straight-line method is the most popular method of determining depreciation. It enables you to expense an equal amount each period, using the following formula:

Cost – Salvage value = Depreciable cost

Depreciable cost ÷ Useful life = Annual depreciation expense

As an example, let's say Eat Well Corp. purchased a line of refrigerated cases for their grocery store that cost $22,500 after installation. The freezers are expected to have a useful life of about 10 years, after which wear and tear becomes a factor and the company will be lucky to sell them for $2,000 to a parts dealer. Eat Well should compute depreciation as follows:

Cost – Salvage value = Depreciable cost

$22,500 – $2,000 = $20,500

$20,500 ÷ 10 = $2,050

Your annual depreciation expense would be $2,050, as shown in the following schedule:

EAT WELL CORP.

Year	Accumulated Depreciation	Annual Depreciation	Book Value
			$22,500
1	$2,050	$2,050	$20,450
2	$4,100	$2,050	$18,400
3	$6,150	$2,050	$16,350
4	$8,200	$2,050	$14,300
5	$10,250	$2,050	$12,250
6	$12,300	$2,050	$10,200
7	$14,350	$2,050	$8,150
8	$16,400	$2,050	$6,100
9	$18,450	$2,050	$4,050
10	$20,500	$2,050	$2,000

For simplicity's sake, Eat Well management has decided to record depreciation annually, so for the first year, it would make the following entry (assuming it bought the equipment in January):

		Debit	Credit
12/31	Depreciation Expense	$2,050	
	Accumulated Depreciation—Equipment		$2,050
	To record annual depreciation expense on freezers.		

The Units-of-Production Method

This method is used when it makes more sense to determine an asset's useful life based on some measure of output, as opposed to years in operation. If you have a press, for example, that stamps a million buttons and then falls out of service or is no longer good, the units-of-production method is the best to use. This method is also sometimes used with vehicles on a per-mile basis.

For example, let's say you bought a new delivery truck for $28,000. It has an estimated salvage value of $3,000. You plan to retire the truck after it's been driven 200,000 miles. Under the units-of-production method, you compute depreciation as follows:

(Cost – Salvage value) ÷ Estimated output (miles) = Cost per mile

($28,000 – 3,000) ÷ 200,000 = $0.125 per mile

Annual depreciation for the truck, using actual miles driven, is shown in the following schedule.

DEPRECIATION SCHEDULE

Year	Miles Used	Depreciation Amount/Unit	Annual Depreciation	Accumulated Depreciation	Book Value
					$28,000
1	40,000	.125	$5,000	$5,000	$23,000
2	30,000	.125	$3,750	$8,750	$19,250
3	32,000	.125	$4,000	$12,750	$15,250
4	28,000	.125	$3,500	$16,250	$11,750
5	25,000	.125	$3,125	$19,375	$8,625
6	20,000	.125	$2,500	$21,875	$6,125
7	16,000	.125	$2,000	$23,875	$4,125
8	9,000	.125	$1,125	$25,000	$3,000

7.2

You record depreciation annually, so you would debit depreciation expense $5,000 and credit accumulated depreciation—vehicles $5,000 in the first year, $3,750 in the second year, and so on.

But what if you finish depreciating an asset using this method and then find the asset is still usable? You have two options: you can keep depreciating the asset until you write off the residual value to depreciation expense:

	Debit	Credit
12/31 Depreciation Expense	$3,000	
Accumulated Depreciation—Truck		$3,000

To record write-off of salvage value of truck fully depreciated.

Or you can keep the asset on the books at the residual value and record a loss at the time of sale or disposal. The option you choose depends on whether you want the income reduction now or later.

Double-Declining Balance

This form of depreciation is what's called an accelerated method. It's particularly useful with assets that experience their biggest declines in productivity in the early years—computers or automobiles, for example. To use it, first compute the straight-line rate and then double it. Next, multiply the doubled rate by the book value each year. Unlike the straight-line method, you needn't deduct salvage value at the beginning, but this should be the stopping point when you're depreciating.

Consider this: M&L Cleaners bought four trucks for $125,000, which they expect to have in service for 5 years. Using double-declining balance method, we can compute their rate as follows:

Book value ÷ Useful life = Annual depreciation

$125,000 ÷ 5 = $25,000

Straight-line rate = 20%; Doubled = 40%

Year	Depreciation Rate	Annual	Accumulated	Book Value
				$125,000
1	40%	$50,000	$50,000	$75,000
2	40%	$30,000	$80,000	$45,000
3	40%	$18,000	$98,000	$27,000
4	40%	$10,800	$108,800	$16,200
5	40%	$6,480	$115,280	$9,720

Depreciation expense in the first year is the highest at $50,000, declining precipitously to $30,000 by the second year, and so on. Because the residual value is $10,000, assets need not be depreciated beyond this point.

Revising Depreciation Estimates

Depreciation is at best an estimate, so you should review it periodically to be sure it isn't inadequate or excessive based on wear and tear or obsolescence issues. If you determine your depreciation calculations are off the mark, you can make a change. You needn't go back and make changes, but going forward, you can take the remaining book value and extend or shorten the useful life as necessary.

Let's imagine, that after 5 years, Eat Well Corp. managers from our earlier example decided their freezers were in better shape than expected. Good enough condition, in fact, to give them 10 more years as opposed to 5. It would be perfectly reasonable in this case to make the following revision:

Book value at end of year 5 ÷ Estimated years left = Depreciation expense

$12,250 ÷ 10 = $1,225

So instead of a depreciation expense of $2,050 per year for the next 5 years, Eat Well deducts $1,225 for the next 10 years, reflecting the extended useful life of its equipment.

An entry to reflect the change isn't required. At the next period, however, Eat Well would book the new amount. It would also have to disclose the change in the financial statements if it was what accountants consider a "material" or significant amount (that is, a change that would have an impact on the company's revenues, which $625 for a year is unlikely to do).

Recording Depreciation

7.2

When you've completed your depreciation schedule, you can use it to figure out your journal entry. Some companies enter depreciation once a year; others make monthly entries. Either way is acceptable, as long as you remain consistent.

SEE ALSO 10.5, "Adjusting Entries"

Because the depreciation schedule computes depreciation on an annual basis, to determine your monthly cost, divide by 12. To record a portion of a year, prorate the annual expense. For example, borrowing from the schedule in the previous section:

Year	Depreciation Rate	Annual	Accumulated	Book Value
				$125,000
1	40%	$50,000	$50,000	$75,000

If this company records depreciation monthly, it would divide the annual expense ($50,000) by 12 months to get a depreciation charge of $4,167 for each period.

Note that depreciation is recorded to a contra asset account, accumulated depreciation. The fixed asset—trucks in the preceding case—is carried on the books, at cost, to most accurately reflect cost and usage. The asset value less accumulated depreciation is known as the book value of the asset.

	Debit	Credit
12/31 Depreciation Expense	$4,167	
Accumulated Depreciation—Trucks		$4,167
To record depreciation expense for the period.		

Depreciation for Tax Considerations

Depreciation can be recorded differently for book and tax purposes, and any of the previous methods are acceptable for your books. At tax time, the IRS requires that you use the Modified Accelerated Cost Recovery System (MACRS) for computing depreciation of most assets put into service after 1986. For simplicity's sake, many companies used this method for both book and tax depreciation. This method divides assets into classes based on estimated useful lives, as shown in the following table:

MACRS TABLE BY PROPERTY CLASS

Class	Items Included
3-year property	Tractors, race horses (2 years), horses (12 years), when placed in service
5-year property	Autos, taxis, buses, trucks, computers and peripherals, office machines (faxes, copiers calculators, etc.), property used in research or experiments, cattle, certain energy property (geothermal, solar, wind)
7-year property	Office furniture and fixtures, any property not yet designated to another class
10-year property	Vessels, barges, tugs, similar water transport equipment, single-purpose agricultural structures, trees or vines bearing fruits or nuts
15-year property	Land improvements—shrubs, fences, roads, bridges, restaurant property
20-year property	Farm buildings
25-year property	Water utility property such as water treatment plants, municipal sewers put into use after 1996, residential rental property—building in which 80% or more of its income is from rental units (usually depreciated over 27.5 years), nonresidential real property, business property (such as an office, store, or warehouse) that is nonresidential and has a recovery period of more than 27.5 years (typically depreciated over 39 years)

Source: IRS Publication 946.

The following table shows the annual depreciation rate for fixed assets with varying useful lives, or recovery periods, as they are called for tax purposes.

MACRS TABLE FOR PROPERTY AT HALF-YEAR CONVENTION

Year	Depreciation Rate for Recovery Period					
	3-Year	5-Year	7-Year	10-Year	15-Year	20-Year
1	33.33%	20.00%	14.29%	10.00%	5.00%	3.750%
2	44.45	32.00	24.49	18.00	9.50	7.219
3	14.81	19.20	17.49	14.40	8.55	6.677
4	7.41	11.52	12.49	11.52	7.70	6.177
5		11.52	8.93	9.22	6.93	5.713
6		5.76	8.92	7.37	6.23	5.285
7			8.93	6.55	5.90	4.888
8			4.46	6.55	5.90	4.522
9				6.56	5.91	4.462
10				6.55	5.90	4.461
11				3.28	5.91	4.462
12					5.90	4.461
13					5.91	4.462
14					5.90	4.461
15					5.91	4.462
16					2.95	4.461
17						4.462
18						4.461
19						4.462
20						4.461
21						2.231

Source: IRS Publication 946, Appendix Table A-1.

Computing depreciation using MACRS is easier than the tables might suggest. In the first table (MACRS Table by Property Class), locate the property class for the asset. Then, in the second table (MACRS Table for Property at Half-Year Convention), find the factor for the year of use you're depreciating. The formula is as follows:

Asset cost × Factor = Annual depreciation

For example, if you're depreciating office furniture worth $70,000, you would make the following computation:

$70,000 × 14.29% = $10,000 annual (full-year) depreciation

161

Half-year convention is the principle that treats property as if it were acquired midyear—hence, in the first year only half of the annual depreciation or $5,000 would be deducted. The balance would be deducted in the final year of the depreciation schedule or when the item was sold.

Another important reminder: salvage value is not deducted to determine depreciation for tax purposes.

7.3 Disposal of Fixed Assets

Retiring an Asset

Selling an Asset

Trading in an Asset

Even though depreciation is used to offset the carrying value of a fixed asset, you won't make an adjustment to the cost value of the actual asset until you actually remove the asset from your books by retiring, selling, or trading it in. This sub-chapter shows how to handle each of these situations and guides you through the journal entries to record these events.

Retiring an Asset

To retire an asset, you close out both the asset and the accumulated depreciation accounts. If you have fully depreciated $14,000 of copiers, for example, and no residual value remains, make the following entry:

	Debit	Credit
4/31 Accumulated Depreciation—Copiers	$14,000	
Equipment—Copiers		$14,000
To record the retirement of copy machines.		

This entry reduces the equipment—copiers account by $14,000 and eliminates the offsetting accumulated depreciation contra account.

On the other hand, what if you retired the same copiers 2 years earlier? Even though only $10,000 of their value had been depreciated, they had worn out more quickly than you anticipated. In this case, you need to record a loss as follows:

	Debit	Credit
4/31 Accumulated Depreciation—Copiers	$10,000	
Loss on Disposal	$4,000	
Equipment—Copiers		$14,000
To record loss on disposal of copiers.		

So whether you retire an asset when it's fully depreciated or sometime before then, its entire value must be removed from the books. If you retire it at the end of its useful life, the fixed asset and accumulated depreciation accounts are netted out against each other. If you retire it early, you record a loss, which will be a charge against income.

Selling an Asset

To record the sale of a fixed asset, you first need to compute the gain or loss by deducting the book value (asset cost less accumulated depreciation) from the sales price. Once you have done this, the transaction will be handled in one of two ways, as we describe in the following sections.

Selling at a Loss

If you sell an asset at a loss, this amount is a deduction on your income statement. For example, say you were forced to sell your delivery fleet of three trucks for $29,000. The trucks were originally purchased for $95,000 and have accumulated depreciation at $18,000 a year for the past 3 years. At the time of the sale, the accounts are as follows:

Equipment—Trucks	Accumulated Depreciation—Trucks
$95,000	$18,000
	$18,000
	$18,000
	$54,000

Therefore:

Cost of Equipment	$95,000
Less: Accumulated Depreciation	$54,000
Book Value	$41,000
Proceeds from Sale	$29,000
Loss on Sale	$12,000

The entry to record the sale would be as follows:

	Debit	Credit
6/9 Cash	$29,000	
Accumulated Depreciation—Trucks	$54,000	
Loss on Sale	$12,000	
Equipment—Trucks		$95,000
To record the loss on sale of company delivery trucks.		

A loss on the sale of a fixed asset is recorded as a debit or a charge against income. But before computing the loss, you must be sure you have accounted for accumulated depreciation. If you sell the asset midyear, for example, and only record depreciation annually, you must prorate the depreciation to date of sale before calculating the book value.

Selling at a Gain

A gain on the sale of a fixed asset is added to income. Using our previous example, if the trucks had been sold for $43,000 instead of $29,000, you would have recorded a gain instead of $2,000:

7.3

	Debit	Credit
6/9 Cash	$43,000	
Accumulated Depreciation—Trucks	$54,000	
Equipment—Trucks		$95,000
Gain on Sale		$2,000
To record a gain on the sale of company delivery trucks.		

A gain on the sale of fixed assets is considered income for tax purposes. When computing the book value of the asset, the same rules for depreciation apply, so again it is important to ensure that depreciation expense is up to date, as this could affect the size of your gain or loss.

Trading in an Asset

To record the trade-in of old equipment for new equipment, you first have to compute the depreciable basis of the trade-in. When you have done that and determined whether you have a gain or a loss, you will handle the transaction in one of the ways described in the following sections.

Trading In for a Loss

A loss on trade-in is not recognized in the same way as a loss on a sale of an asset. Instead, the loss merely reduces the base value of the new asset. As an example, say you traded in two trucks for $4,000 less than they were worth. Then you purchased two new trucks for $30,000 each. The value of the new trucks would be $56,000 ($60,000 – $4,000). The transaction would be recorded as follows:

		Debit	Credit
6/9	Cash	$43,000	
9/31	Delivery Equipment—New	$56,000	
	Accumulated Depreciation—Delivery Equipment	$36,000	
	Delivery Equipment—Old		$45,000
	Cash		$47,000

To record purchase of two trucks and the trade in of older trucks.

You could also make the entry combining the debit and credits for delivery equipment on one line ($56,000 debit, $45,000 credit), or by netting the two amounts for a debit of $9,000, but an entry such as the previous one makes it easier to understand the transaction.

Trading In for a Gain

A gain on a trade-in of similar assets is also not booked as a gain. Instead, the new equipment is valued at the difference between fair market value and the book value of the asset given up.

		Debit	Credit
12/31	Office Equipment—New	$30,000*	
	Accumulated Depreciation—Old	$40,000	
	Office—Old		$50,000
	Cash		$20,000

*To record trade-in with gain deferred and purchase of new office equipment. (*50,000 – $20,000 = $30,000 new fair market value with gain on trade taken into account.)*

In summary, gains and losses can be recorded on the sale of fixed assets. On trade-ins, however, there is no such thing as a "gain" or a "loss." Instead, the difference in purchase price and trade-in value merely affects the cost basis of the new asset. The new cost basis will equal the cash difference plus the undepreciated value (book value) of the trade-ins.

7.4 Leases

Operating Leases

Capital Leases

Leaseholds

Sometimes it makes more economic sense to lease property than own it. This subchapter aims to help you differentiate between **lease** types and learn how to account for them properly. How you account for a lease on your books depends on what type of lease it is. The two main categories of leases are operating leases and capital leases.

✓

A **lease** is an agreement with which one person or entity (the lessee) is guaranteed rights to use a piece of property or land belonging to another (the lessor) for a specific period of time in return for payment of a rental charge.

Operating Leases

An operating lease is an agreement to rent a piece of property, like an office or an automobile, for a defined period of time. It is considered an expense of doing business, as the use of the property reverts from the lessee to the lessor at the end of the lease term.

Recording an operating lease is fairly straightforward. The costs are expensed monthly when rental payments are made, as shown in the following journal entry:

		Debit	Credit
2/1	Rent Expense	$2,200	
	Cash		$2,200

To pay monthly rent on office space.

At the end of the year, a footnote summarizing outstanding lease payments should be included on the balance sheet.

SEE ALSO 11.4, "Generating Financial Statements"

Capital Leases

A capital lease is an agreement that, although not technically a purchase, gives the lessee substantial ownership rights. For this reason, it's treated as an asset on the balance sheet. To qualify as a capital lease for accounting purposes, a lease must meet one of the following four criteria:

- The lease transfers ownership of the asset to you at the end of the term.

- It contains an option for a bargain purchase—if you want it, you get a deal.

- The lease term equals 75 percent or more of the estimated economic life of the leased property.

- The rental payments approximate the fair market value of the property.

So how do you value a capital lease on the balance sheet? By using the following calculation, which might seem complicated, but basically is just an estimate of the combined lease payments:

Lease payment × Present value (# pay periods, interest rate) = Lease value

7.4

Let's say Howard Corp. needed some office equipment but couldn't afford to purchase it outright. Instead, the company leased the equipment for 18 months at 8 percent. At the end of that period, the company would own the equipment. The journal entry to record the lease as an asset and its accompanying liability would be as follows:

	Debit	Credit
7/1 Leased Equipment	$18,400	
Lease Payment Obligation (Liability)		$18,400

To record acquisition of office equipment through capital lease. (Terms: 18 months, 8 percent.)

To record the first month's payment, Howard Corp. makes this entry:

	Debit	Credit
7/1 Lease Payment Obligation	$632	
Interest Expense	$368	
Cash		$1,000

To record monthly lease payment. (Interest expense calculated at 2 percent of $18,400 = $368.)

SEE ALSO 9.5, "Capital Leases"

There are two kinds of leases: operating and capital. Rental payments on ordinary operating leases are classified as expenses. But both the IRS and accounting rules require the capitalization of leases when such agreements meet certain criteria. This includes leases that confer ownership of the asset at the end of the term or offer you a deal on purchasing it, where the lease term is 75 percent of the useful life of the asset, or where lease payments approximate the fair market value of the asset.

Leaseholds

Leaseholds are lease agreements that are related to property as opposed to equipment. You will usually have leaseholds for buildings or other facilities.

✓

A **leasehold** is the right to use a given real estate property for a specific time period at an agreed-upon rent payment. Typically, you might have a leasehold for your building or company office.

Leaseholds can be accounted for in three ways, depending on the terms of the lease:

- *As an expense.* If rent payments are due monthly, you would record the following entry at the time rent is paid:

	Debit	Credit
2/1 Rent Expense	$2,000	
Cash		$2,000

To record payment or rent on office.

- *As a prepaid expense.* If rent is paid in advance, a prepaid rent account must be converted to expense over the lease period. For example:

	Debit	Credit
2/1 Prepaid Rent	$24,000	
Cash		$24,000
To record annual building rental.		

- Then, each month you would expense a portion of the rent:

	Debit	Credit
2/28 Interest Expense	$2,000	
Prepaid Rent		$2,000
To record building rental for February.		

- As a prepayment on a long-term lease:

	Debit	Credit
5/9 Deferred Charges—Prepaid Rent	$96,000	
Cash		$96,000
To record a long-term lease.		
6/31 Rent Expense	$2,000	
Deferred Charges—Prepaid Rent		$2,000
To record monthly rent expense on a prepaid lease.		

7.4

As with leases, leasehold contracts specify rental payments for a certain term. These rental payments may be treated in different ways, depending on whether they are required in advance (as prepayments) or paid periodically as they become due.

7.5 Intangible Assets

Understanding Intangibles

Types of Intangibles

Amortizing Intangibles

Tax Considerations for Intangibles

In this subchapter, we take you through the various kinds of intangible assets and show you how to account for them and amortize their values.

Understanding Intangibles

Intangibles are assets that lack physical substance, but have value such as a brand name or goodwill. When working with intangibles, an important first step is establishing some supportable cost basis. Accounting for intangibles is similar in some ways to what you do with fixed assets. Intangibles are classified as long-term assets on the balance sheet, but their costs must be allocated over the periods benefited. Instead of using depreciation and an offsetting contra account (accumulated depreciation), however, intangibles are amortized, and this **amortization** expense is deducted directly from the asset's value.

✓

An **intangible** is an asset that lacks physical substance, but has value.

Amortization is the gradual reduction of the value of an asset or expense account over the time you benefit from its use. Accounts such as intangible assets and deferred charges are amortized.

Types of Intangibles

Intangibles can range from rights granted by the government—such as a patent, trademark, or license—to franchise fees or certain lease payments. These are the main types of intangibles:

- Trademarks
- Patents
- Copyrights
- Franchises
- Goodwill

In the following sections, we show how to determine the value of each of these intangible assets.

Trademarks

A trademark or trade name is a word, phrase, song, or symbol that identifies a particular company or product and is registered with the U.S. Patent Office. This registration protects a trademark for 20 years and is renewable. Trademarks and trade names are valued in one of two ways:

- If you purchase your trade name from another company, you value it on your books at the purchase price. For example, if you paid $5,000 to buy the name Katie's Kitchen from the previous owner, you record the trademark at $5,000 on your books.

- If your company creates its own trademark, the cost includes any related design costs, attorneys' fees, registration fees, and other costs related to securing the trademark. You could also add in any legal costs for successfully defending it against infringement, if incurred.

You're legally entitled to amortize a trademark over its useful life or 40 years, whichever is shorter. Typically, trademarks are amortized over much shorter periods.

7.5

Patents

A patent is an exclusive right given by the U.S. government allowing a company to sell, produce, manufacture, or control an invention or process for a period of 20 years without infringement. Patents are not renewable. The cost of a patent also includes any legal fees to set it up and defend it successfully. Patents can be amortized over 20 years or the useful life, whichever is shorter.

Copyrights

A copyright gives the owner of artistic or published work sole right to copy and sell that work. Copyrights are good for the life of the creator and extend 70 years after his or her death. The cost value of a copyright is determined by how much you spend in securing it, which can be as little as the registration fee. Copyrights can be amortized by as much as 40 years but are typically written off over 2 or 3 years.

Franchises

Franchises are contractual agreements to sell, market, or distribute a company's products; render certain services in its name; and use trademarks and trade names for a specified period of time and usually in a particular geographical area. The cost of securing the franchise or license becomes the basis for the asset's value. But franchise fees are considered operating expenses and expensed as incurred.

Goodwill

Goodwill is often the largest intangible asset. It's the value of the company's reputation, contacts, location, and any other positive attributes that result in a premium being paid over the market value of its assets.

Unlike other intangibles or fixed assets, goodwill cannot be sold. The only way to value it is through a sales transaction in which goodwill would equal the excess of the purchase price over the value of the net assets purchased. As an example, let's say you bought Annie's Bakery Shop located in the center of Pleasanton for $200,000. At the time of sale, Annie's had assets of $340,000 and liabilities of $180,000. Your goodwill is the difference between the purchase price of $200,000 and net assets of $160,000 ($340,000 – $180,000), which equals $40,000, and you record the purchase on the books as follows:

		Debit	Credit
6/2	Assets	$340,000	
	Goodwill	$40,000	
	Liabilities		$180,000
	Cash		$200,000
To record purchase of Annie's Bakery Shop.			

Amortizing Intangibles

All intangibles were once believed to have finite useful lives, so it was the practice to reduce or (amortize) their value over the period benefited. The amortization amount of an intangible is computed using the following formula:

Cost ÷ Useful life = Annual amortization

Marvel Medicines, Inc., holds a patent purchased from a competitor for $50,000 for a new pain reliever it believes will cure cancer. Although the patent is for 20 years, Marvel suspects with the pace of research they'll be lucky to get 6 years out of the drug. So the annual amortization is:

$50,000 ÷ 6 = $8,333

Marvel records this on the books as follows:

	Debit	Credit
12/31 Amortization Expense—Patents	$8,333	
Patents		$8,333
To record patent amortization.		

Note that unlike depreciation, which is credited first to a contra account, amortization directly reduces the asset. Amortization expense, meanwhile, is an operating expense.

Different types of intangibles have different useful lives, as noted in the following table. The general rule used to be that intangibles like patents, trademarks, and goodwill could be amortized over their useful life up to a ceiling of 40 years. But with intangible assets becoming an ever-increasing part of a company's value in the information age, this standard has been relaxed somewhat. Some assets can now be amortized over longer periods. In addition, goodwill needn't be amortized at all if you can demonstrate that its value to the company is not decreasing over time. However, you must demonstrate this each year. Because of the complexity and rapid change in the area of intangibles, we recommend checking with the IRS for the most current information on treatment.

7.5

Intangible	Legal Life	Amortization Period
Patents	20 years	Usually between 5 and 40 years, or whichever is shorter
Trade names	40 years	Up to 40 years
Franchise	Varies	Varies
Copyright	70 years after death	2 or 3 years
Goodwill	40 years	Up to 40 years*

In 2001, law relaxed so this period was extended and amortization was not always necessary.

Tax Considerations for Intangibles

The IRS has special requirements for intangible assets that you purchased from another company. In addition, you can also capitalize and amortize certain start-up expenses for a business, as we explain in the following sections.

Section 197, Intangibles

For tax purposes, most intangible assets that you acquired after August 10, 1993, are termed 197 intangibles (for the code section) and are usually amortized over 15 years—with the exception of certain types of software, including the following:

- Goodwill
- Patents
- Trademarks
- Business books, training manuals, operating systems, customer lists
- Franchises
- Covenants not to Compete by former employees of the company

This rule applies to intangibles you acquired, not those your company developed. The only exception would be if the intangible was created using assets you acquired that were a substantial part of a trade or business. For a full listing and more details on Section 197 assets, check out Publication 535 on the IRS website at irs.gov/publications/p535/index.html.

Capitalizing Business Start-Up Costs

The IRS also permits businesses to capitalize certain start-up costs if they meet two criteria:

- They would be valid business expenses if the start-up were in operation.
- They were incurred before the business began operations.

Items such as interest and research and development costs are *not* included. Qualifying expenses include the following:

- Costs of analyzing potential markets
- Costs for training employees
- Cost for advertising opening
- Costs incurred securing suppliers, distributors, and customers
- Salaries and fees for executives and consultants
- Organizational costs for setting up partnerships and corporations, such as accountant's and attorney's fees

You can capitalize these amounts and amortize them over 60 months if you started business before October 24, 2004. If your business began after that date, you can deduct a limited amount of start-up and organization costs and amortize the rest over 180 months.

Property, plant, and equipment (PP&E), or fixed assets, are the physical assets—land, buildings, and equipment—you need to operate your business. Because most of these assets are held indefinitely, they're carried on the books at cost and depreciated over their useful lives.

Intangible assets, on the other hand, are assets that have value—often great value, but no physical substance. These are things like copyrights, trademarks, and patents. Intangible assets can be written down over their useful lives via amortization. Tax treatment for depreciating and amortizing fixed assets and intangibles may be different from how you do it for your books. This is another area where a computerized system, which usually can quickly compute the value of assets under a variety of scenarios (and according to GAAP and IRS rules), can be beneficial.

SEE ALSO 15.2, "Evaluating Computerized Systems"

7.5

Salaries, Wages, and Benefits

8.1 Setting Up Payroll

Obtaining a Federal ID Number

Authorizing New Employees

Employee or Independent Contractor?

Implementing System Safeguards

Outsourcing Payroll Services

Determining Pay Periods

Here we take you through the basics of setting up a payroll system. You learn what you need to do to comply with federal and state laws and how to set up safeguards to minimize the possibility of errors or misappropriation.

Obtaining a Federal ID Number

Before you hire your first employee, you're going to need to obtain a federal employer identification number (EIN). If you haven't already done this to open your business bank account, don't sweat it. It's a fairly simple process. Just log on to the IRS website (www.irs.gov) and download form SS-4. You can fill it out online and then fax, email, or mail it into the IRS.

The purpose of this number is to identify you as an employer and to provide a reference number for the tax payments you are required to remit to the government. Every employer only needs one ID. If you operate more than one business, you use a separate number for each company. If you purchase the assets of a business from someone else, you must also apply for a new EIN, as you are not allowed to use the previous owner's number.

While you're on the IRS website you'll also want to make sure to download a copy of Circular E, which is the Employers Tax Guide. All businesses are required to have this publication on hand as it contains the latest news, changes, and tax rates.

Most states require employers to have a separate state ID number as well. Check with officials in your area to determine the requirements in your state.

Authorizing New Employees

Every business needs a method for authorizing new employees and adding them to the payroll. In large companies, this is done by turning over the hiring process to a separate human resources department. In a smaller business, it's usually enough to require proper documentation for all employees and institute policies about who can approve a new hire.

Necessary Data and Forms

When authorizing a new employee, you need to obtain his or her Social Security number for government tax reporting purposes, so a space for this number should be provided somewhere on the employee application.

In addition, any new employees are required by law to fill out a W-4 tax withholding form. This form lists such things as an employee's marital status and number of dependents. It is used to determine how many exemptions an employee claims to reduce the amount withheld for federal income taxes.

You also need to fill out an I-9 form for each new employee to verify his or her legal status to work in the United States. You can obtain this form from the U.S. Customs and Immigration Service through its website, www.uscis.gov.

Keep in mind if you're a small business owner, you may also find it beneficial to be an employee, too. That way your wages and taxes are paid through the company payroll account in a timely manner.

New-Hire Procedures

All new hires need to be authorized. The person doing this should preferably be someone senior, who is not involved in computing or preparing payroll to prevent a check being cut for a "phantom" or nonexistent employee. Some companies require a signed form before a new name is added to payroll. For legal reasons, this is also the time to fully explain employee responsibilities, rights, and benefits, to avert costly problems down the road should the hire not work out.

8.1

All documentation supporting the hiring—applications, approvals, tax documents, etc.—should be filed individually in a personnel file set up for the employee. These records should be updated with wage data, performance evaluations and increases, pension payments, change of address, fringe benefits, payroll deduction authorization forms, and anything else affecting the status of the employee.

Employee or Independent Contractor?

Just because you're going to have someone work for you doesn't automatically make them an employee, nor require that they become part of your payroll. Some individuals who work for a company are not considered employees, but **independent contractors.** These persons might be paid on a per project basis or by contract, and their remuneration is handled differently. This is important to know, because misclassifying a contractor as an employee can get you in trouble with the IRS.

✓
_____

An **independent contractor** is an individual who performs work for a company and has substantial control over what he or she is doing in terms of where, when, and how it's done.

Companies that hire independent contractors do not have to handle withholding their federal and state income taxes, nor pay Medicare or Social Security. This is handled by the independent contractor, who for legal purposes is considered a separate business. Further, independent contractors do not fill out W-4s, or receive W-2 forms detailing annual wages. Instead, the employer is required to get their Social Security number and prepare a 1099-MISC at the end of the year to any contractor paid more than $600 for that year.

SEE ALSO 12.4, "Income Taxes"

The IRS is leery of companies calling employees independent contractors as a way to avoid paying taxes and other benefits, so it has set up very stringent guidelines as to who qualifies and who doesn't. The most important factor in determining whether someone is an independent contractor or an employee is the degree of control she has over the work she has been asked to do, not only in terms of how it is done, but where and when.

Here are some general tests to determine if someone is an independent contractor or an employee:

An independent contractor ...

- Often has a written contract.
- Has a significant investment in his or her business.
- Can realize a profit or loss on the work he or she has taken on.
- Can decide how, when, and where to do the work.
- Does not receive training or excessive instructions on the project.
- Is not reimbursed for expenses.

An employee ...

- Must do the work at a specific place and time.
- Collects revenue for the company.

- Receives specialized training.

- Must do the project in a certain way.

- Receives benefits from the company.

Still can't decide? You might want to take a look at Form SS-8, Determination of Worker Status for Purposes of Federal Employment Taxes and Income Tax Withholding, on the IRS website or publication 1779, Employee Independent Contractor Brochure, to avoid problems later. Not only can the IRS come after you, but independent contractors who feel they are being denied benefits to work as employees on the cheap can file an SS-8 with the IRS.

Implementing System Safeguards

Because the payroll system involves the distribution of cash, establishing appropriate internal controls over it is very important. There are myriad ways to tamper with the payroll system, including …

- Overstating hours to make higher paychecks.

- Issuing unauthorized paychecks or checks to nonexistent employees.

- Manipulating the system to generate duplicate payroll checks.

The most effective way to prevent payroll funds from being misappropriated is to put safeguards in place and monitor them. The following procedures should provide a good start:

8.1

- If payroll is processed in house, have the computations checked by someone separate from the preparer.

- Make supervisors verify hours on time cards.

- Number and account for all paychecks.

- Some businesses find it beneficial to have a separate bank account just for payroll rather than running it through the company's operating account. This can make it easier to reconcile the account at the end of the period, minimize confusion with other business expenses, and allay concerns about overdrafts. With a separate account you automatically deposit the funds for payroll before the checks go out. A separate account, though it usually comes at a fee, also has the advantage of limiting access to your primary checking account number, which some business owners prefer—particularly when using a third party to process their payroll.

SEE ALSO 1.1, "Accounting Basics"

SEE ALSO 3.2, "The Business Bank Account"

Remember, establishing sound procedures at the outset helps you avoid problems with payroll down the road. It also ensures that the whole payroll process runs efficiently.

Outsourcing Payroll Services

Many businesses, particularly those with small staffs, send their payroll data to outside firms like Automated Data Processing, Inc. (ADP), and Paychex to be processed. This adds another level of protection, by separating the people preparing the data from those actually cutting the checks.

For as little as $3 a check, you can submit employee hours, deductions, and salary amounts, and these services will compute the payroll for you. In addition, these payroll services can also handle employee retirement programs, direct deposit paychecks, compute taxes, and generate W-2 forms of employee annual earnings and payroll tax returns.

When picking an outside payroll service, keep in mind the availability and capability of your own staff versus the cost of paying an outside service. You should know going in precisely what services are provided in what time frame and at what cost.

Also look at the reputation, cost, and location of the outside service. Your payroll service needs to be professional, cost-effective, and fairly accessible to your office, particularly if documents are to be picked up or delivered.

If you're outsourcing payroll headaches, you could go ahead and outsource all of them. At the very least, your payroll service should provide a payroll summary, quarterly payroll and tax withholding, tell you what your deposits should be, and prepare payroll tax returns and annual W-2 forms.

SEE ALSO 12.2, "Payroll Taxes"

Another alternative is automating payroll by using accounting software or an online system. Assuming that you enter employee data correctly, this can be a nice middle ground; employee pay and deductions are computed automatically, cutting down on your work. But keep in mind that computerizing payroll is not a panacea. Between generating the payroll and ensuring that the myriad payments are made to the IRS and benefits providers, there is ample room for error, and penalties (especially for late tax deposits) can be unforgiving.

SEE ALSO 15.4, "Converting to an Automated System"

Determining Pay Periods

The pay period is the interval in which you choose to pay your employees. Some employers pay their employees weekly; others pay semimonthly, monthly, quarterly, or annually. The pay period you choose is important because that's the date that determines when your tax payments need to be made. When you have established a pay period, you should plan to stick with it.

Pay periods stay the same, even if employees work only part of the period. Generally, payroll checks are drawn 2 or 3 days after the end of the designated payroll period. For example, payroll checks would be drawn on January 10 for the pay period ending on January 7, or on a Tuesday for the 2 weeks ending on the preceding Saturday.

8.1

8.2 Computing Wages

Establishing Pay Rates
Wage Components

This subchapter goes over the components involved in computing payroll. We demonstrate how to use wage guidelines and show you how to calculate regular pay and overtime. In addition, we cover basic deductions and computing net pay.

Establishing Pay Rates

For a small company just starting out, establishing a pay rate for a new employee might be a rather informal process. You figure out what the going rate is, say, for a secretary, and make an offer. But as a company grows in size and employees, more structured wage guidelines should be developed. Payroll taxes and benefits costs also obviously need to be factored into the equation. The following chart shows the guidelines for Smith's Warehouse Company, a newly opened storage and delivery business.

SEE ALSO 12.2, "Payroll Taxes"

SMITH'S WAREHOUSE COMPANY
WAGE GUIDELINES
UPDATED: 6/5

	Starting	Yearly Raise	Upper Limit
Nonexempt (Hourly)			
Warehouse Clerk	$9.00	10%	$11.00
Shipping Clerk	$9.25	10%	$11.50
Receiving Clerk	$9.50	10%	$12.00
Custodian	$9.00	10%	$11.70
Exempt (Salaried)			
Assistant Supervisor	$45,000	5% to 10%	$52,000
Supervisor	$60,000	Tied to performance	$66,000

Notice that the first four employee categories (the **nonexempt** employees) offer hourly rates—these are hourly employees and earn wages. The supervisors' pay is quoted in an annual figure because they are salaried (**exempt**) employees.

✓

Nonexempt employees are not exempted from overtime pay so they are required to be paid a premium if they work more than 40 hours in a week. This is governed by the wage and hour laws, for which booklets are available from the federal government. Nonexempt employees are typically hourly workers, but not always. Some salaried workers, particularly in jobs covered by union contracts, are nonexempt.

Exempt employees are not required to be paid overtime under the Federal Wage and Hours law. No matter how many hours they work, their pay is at quoted rates. Exempt employees are usually, but not always, salaried workers.

Salary is usually stated as an annual rate, but it may be prorated monthly, biweekly, or weekly, depending on the length of the pay period.

Wage Components

Wages are derived from two components, rate of pay and hours worked. For hourly workers, the base rate is multiplied by number of hours worked. For salaried workers who are exempt from overtime, use either a rate or divide their annual salary evenly over the number of pay periods in a year. This gives you gross pay, which is earnings before taxes and other deductions. In the following section, we illustrate how to compute **gross pay.**

8.2

✓

Gross pay is the total pay earned before taxes and other deductions.

Gross Pay

Gross pay is computed by multiplying hours worked by an employee's pay rate, taking into account adjustments for overtime. For salaried workers, you can take the annual salary and divide it evenly among pay periods. So if the shipping clerk at Smith's Warehouse Company worked 38 hours the first week and 30 hours the second week, his gross pay for the 2-week period would be:

Rate of pay × Hours worked

$9.25 × 68 = $629

If he had worked 45 hours the first week and 23 hours the second week, his total hours worked would have also been 68, but he would have qualified for overtime pay, so his gross pay would be different. Overtime pay is typically time and a half

($9.25 + $4.63 = $10.88). His gross pay would be computed as follows:

40 hours + 23 hours = 63 hours × $7.25 =	$582.75
5 hours × $13.88 =	$69.40
Gross Pay	**$721.55**

In the same 2-week period, the assistant supervisor would earn gross pay of:

(Annual rate ÷ # weeks in year) × Weeks in pay period

45,000 ÷ 52 = $865.38 × 2 = $1,730.76

Net Pay

Net pay is what an employee takes home after various state and federal taxes, Social Security, Medicare, and any other voluntary amounts, such as a contribution to a charity or health plan, are deducted from gross wages. Employees should always receive a check stub or direct deposit advice itemizing the deductions from their gross pay.

Smith's Warehouse's assistant supervisor's paycheck lists a gross pay of $1,730.76. The check stub lists a further breakdown of deductions:

Gross Pay	$1,730.76
FICA	($97.79)
Federal Withholding	($238.73)
State Withholding	($66.97)
Health Plan	($100.00)
Net Pay	**$1,227.27**

✓

Net pay, also known as take-home pay, is your pay after (net of) deductions for taxes and benefits.

FICA refers to Social Security and Medicare taxes companies must withhold from employee wages and as mandated by the Federal Income Contribution Act (FICA) of 1933. Employers must also match this contribution.

8.3 Making Payroll Deductions

Mandatory Deductions

Voluntary Deductions

A number of deductions serve to reduce gross pay to the amount an employee ultimately takes home. This subchapter explains the different types of deductions and shows you how to account for them.

Mandatory Deductions

By law, employers are required to make a number of payroll deductions. For most businesses these are FICA taxes (Social Security and Medicare), federal income taxes, and state income taxes. Employers deduct these taxes from all employee paychecks and then remit the money to the appropriate tax authority.

In certain states, a deduction for state disability insurance is also required, as explained later in this section. In addition, if an employee is under union contract, deducting union dues may also be mandatory.

FICA

FICA stands for the Federal Insurance Contributions Act, better known as the law that established Social Security. Medicare taxes also fall under FICA. (Medicare was separated from Social Security in 1991 so some companies classify them in separate accounts. Many businesses, however, put both into one account such as Payroll Taxes or FICA Taxes. Either way is acceptable, so long as it is consistent.)

8.3

Social Security is the deduction from workers' pay that goes into the federal pension system for retired, disabled, and survivors. It is a nonprogressive tax, so the 6.2 percent rate* is the same for everyone, no matter how much they earn. Social Security is charged on all income up to a ceiling of $106,800 in 2011. (These ceilings are adjusted periodically by the government.) Money earned over this amount is not taxed for FICA purposes.

*Historically, the Social Security rate has been 6.2 percent, with employers paying a matching amount. In 2011, the employee rate was lowered to 4.2 percent by the federal government. Currently, the lower rate remains in effect through February 2012, and it is unclear whether it will be extended beyond that. For the most up-to-date information, check with the IRS.

If you're an employer, you must make matching payments of this tax to the federal government. For an employee paid $4,000 every 2 weeks, for example, Social Security would be computed as follows:

$$\$4,000 \times 6.2\% = \$248$$

The total amount the employer owes the government for that employee in that period is $496—the $248 deducted from the employee's paycheck, plus the additional $248 matching amount from the employer.

Medicare is the federal government–sponsored health insurance program for the people over 65. The Medicare deduction rate is now 1.45 percent, and, unlike with Social Security, there is no income ceiling. The Medicare deducted on $4,000 of income is $58 ($4,000 × 1.45%). Similar to Social Security, the employer has to match this amount.

Federal Income Taxes

Federal income taxes must be paid as income is earned. The amounts employers withhold from each paycheck are based on employee marital status, income, and what he or she claimed on their W-4 form. You can determine the amount of the deductions by looking at IRS tax tables. The idea is for the withholding to approximate the actual taxes owed that year. When the employee files her tax return on April 15, if the amount withheld from her paycheck is more than she owes, she will get a refund. If it is less, she must send a check to the IRS for the additional taxes.

As employer, you act as a tax collector in the sense of deducting and remitting these withheld income taxes to the government. You do not have to match these amounts.

State Income Taxes

In most states and some cities and counties, businesses may also be responsible for deducting state and local taxes. In New York, for example, employers withhold both state and city income taxes. Check with your state for specific requirements and procedures.

SEE ALSO 12.2, "Payroll Taxes"

State disability insurance pays benefits for employees who become disabled. Currently, it's a requirement in only five states (California, Hawaii, New Jersey, New York, and Rhode Island) and Puerto Rico, with rates ranging from .3 percent to

1.4 percent of gross wages. Some states also have disability programs that require employer contributions. Companies are charged rates based on risk factors and their overall safety records.

Voluntary Deductions

In addition to the mandatory deductions taken from each paycheck, employees can also choose voluntary deductions, such as deductions for:

- Health plans
- Insurance and retirement benefits
- Charitable giving

These deductions may be individual, as in the case of a regular pledge to United Way, or group plans, like insurance. They all require written authorization— typically a standard form signed by the employee. Generally, there are two kinds of benefits, tax-exempt and those that are not.

Tax-Exempt Benefits

The important thing to remember about tax-exempt benefits is that they are deducted *before* taxes are computed. So for example, a deduction for a health savings plan, which allows workers to deduct a certain amount of money for un-covered medical expenses, reduces taxable income. So if an employee earning $2,000 a week decides to put $50 of that in a health savings account, his or her federal taxes are computed based on $1,950.

Pretax deductions reduce your taxable income and, hence, your tax burden. The reduction applies to your Social Security and Medicare taxes as well. In other words, you may be paying health costs out of your pocket, but you're also saving a little money that would normally go to taxes.

These deductions must be authorized in writing. There are also certain deadlines for when these forms must be completed for employees to be eligible for the tax break.

Other Benefits

This category includes such benefits as profit-sharing, participation in group in-surance, or charitable giving. These benefits must be authorized in writing by the employee, usually on a standard preprinted form for each benefit. The employee must complete and sign the form before any deductions can be taken from his or her paycheck.

8.3

These benefits are taken after taxes, which means that FICA, federal, and state tax withholding must first be deducted, so there's no tax break for the employee, and the employer must still pay its full share of FICA taxes.

In addition to tax payments, employees may choose to have other amounts deducted from their gross pay—for charity, savings, or an employee health plan, for example. In deducting these amounts gross pay, employers must take care to distinguish between tax-exempt benefits, which are taken before taxes, and non-tax exempt deductions. All deductions should also be authorized in writing by the employee with these forms kept on file.

8.4 Employer Payroll Taxes

Taxes

Deposits

In addition to deducting taxes from employee paychecks, employers must also match certain payments and make regular deposits of those funds to the government. This subchapter tells you how.

Taxes

As an employer, you are required to match certain employee contributions— Social Security, Medicare, and state disability insurance. Another tax, the Federal Unemployment Tax (FUTA), is paid solely by employers. There is also a state unemployment tax (SUTA). These taxes pay for temporary benefits to unemployed workers.

The unemployment tax rate is 6.2 percent. Currently, employers pay it on the first $7,000 of each employee's wages. FUTA tax deposits are computed quarterly and due by the end of the next month. You can report the tax annually by filling out IRS Form 940.

Businesses are often subject to state unemployment compensation insurance as well. Your federal payment will be credited by 5.4 percent for what you pay in state unemployment compensation insurance. State unemployment taxes vary by state, but all payments are credited to the federal employment tax, so the net unemployment tax would amount to .8 percent of the first $7,000 of taxable wages for each employee.

Once you start filing payroll tax returns, you'll find out just how costly these taxes are, particularly Social Security and Medicare, where you must chip in your own matching share. Keep in mind when establishing your wage rates, that you'll be paying an additional 7.65 percent (6.2% Social Security + 1.45% Medicare) of each employee's total wages (up to $106,800) for their health care and retirement, although you probably won't be able to convince your employees of this fact. So when you set an hourly rate of $10, this does not translate to $20,800 for a year (52 weeks = 2,080 hours). Rather, you pay $22,391.20 for that year. This extra expense is significant when you have more than a few employees.

Deposits

Tax payments deducted from employee paychecks and employer matching contributions—including FICA (Social Security and Medicare), federal, and state withholding—must be deposited periodically with the IRS. Failure to do so on a timely basis could result in a penalty. Since 2011, all deposits must be made through the Electronic Federal Tax Payment System (EFTPS). These deposits can be made online or by phone, 24 hours a day, 7 days a week. More information on how to enroll in the system can be found at eftps.gov.

For state withholding, quarterly payments are only required if it is above a certain amount, which varies by state. Usually when you register to do business, your state will send you all this information. Federal and state unemployment insurance contributions paid by employers must also be remitted.

The schedule for these deposits is as follows; note the return varies according to total amounts of wages paid:

WHEN TO FILE

Taxes	Deposits	Return
FICA	At least monthly	Quarterly
Medicare	At least monthly	Quarterly
Federal	At least monthly	Quarterly and annually
State	Monthly or quarterly	Quarterly and annually
Disability	Usually monthly	Varies by state
FUTA	Quarterly, month after quarter ends, or annually	Annually

SEE ALSO 12.2, "Payroll Taxes"

The journal entry to record payroll would be as follows:

	Debit	Credit
7/31 Office Salaries Expense	$35,000	
Wages Expense	$25,000	
FICA Taxes Payable		$4,590
Federal Withholding Taxes Payable		$16,000
State Withholding Taxes Payable		$8,000
Cash		$31,410
To record payroll for the week ending 7/31.		

When you remit taxes withheld and pay the employer's share of FICA in the next pay period, you would record the following journal entry:

	Debit	Credit
8/14 Payroll Tax Expense	$4,590	
Federal Withholding Taxes Payable	$16,000	
State Withholding Taxes Payable	$8,000	
FICA Taxes Withheld	$4,590	
Cash		$33,180
To record payroll tax remittance to the IRS.		

8.4

Don't be confused by the two FICA debits for the same amount in this journal entry. The first, Payroll Tax Expense, represents the employer's share of FICA. Further down, FICA Taxes Withheld (or FICA Taxes Payable at some companies) is a reversal of the liability recognized with employee payroll in the 7/31 entry. Both must be remitted to the government.

Businesses are responsible for collecting and paying a number of payroll taxes. Federal and state income taxes and FICA contributions must be withheld from employee paychecks and remitted to the IRS by a specific date. In certain states, employers must also deduct disability insurance payments. Employers are also required to pay their own share of FICA taxes (Social Security and Medicare) by a certain date.

8.5 Recording Payroll

Recording Employee Earnings

The Payroll Register

Making Payments

Properly accounting for payroll means keeping accurate records and summarizing and recording all payroll transactions and payments, as we demonstrate in this subchapter.

Recording Employee Earnings

Businesses are required by law to keep a year-to-date record of each employee's gross and net pay and deductions. This is called the employee earnings record. It is updated for each employee after every pay period.

A typical employee earnings record might look like this:

EMPLOYEE EARNINGS RECORD

Name: _____ Social Security #: _____

Address: _____

Phone: _____ Date of Birth: _____ No. Exemptions: 1

Pay Period Ending	Date Paid	Total Regular Hours	Over-time	Pay Rate	Total Pay	Social Security	Medi-care	Federal Income Tax	State Income Tax	Net Pay

Your company is likely to use the employee earnings records for at least three things:

- To determine when employees have reached the maximum earnings subject to FICA

- To file state and federal tax returns

- To determine total earnings, deductions, etc., for the year to put on the W-2 statement you are required to give each employee shortly after the end of the year

By law, you are required to keep payroll tax records for at least 6 years. Depending on your storage capacity, you may choose to keep them longer.

SEE ALSO 10.3, "Closing Employee Accounts"

The Payroll Register

The payroll register lists earnings for all employees by pay period. The register has gross and net earnings, plus deductions by type. The payroll register for HGB Company is shown on the following page.

The totals for the pay period can be used as the basis for the journal entry recording the payroll. For HGB Company, the journal entry to record payroll would be as follows:

	Debit	Credit
7/31 Salaries Expense	$10,000	
Wages Expense	$25,000	
Social Security Taxes Payable		$2,170
Medicare Taxes Payable		$506
Federal Income Taxes Payable		$7,000
State Income Taxes Payable		$900
CARE Payable		$1,500
Health Plan Payable		$3,000
Salaries Payable		$5,335
Wages Payable		$14,589
To record payroll for the period ending 7/31.		

8.5

The amount of wages and salaries expense should equal the total amount of checks paid plus deductions. In the following sample payroll register, S. Nam is the manager and only salaried worker, so his take-home pay becomes salaries payable. Wages payable is the total of the net pay from the remaining employees. Individual deductions should add up as well. Also note how this company splits FICA taxes into separate liability accounts for Social Security taxes and Medicare taxes.

Making Payments

Managers can distribute paychecks, or these can be mailed to employees. You can also have the funds electronically transferred directly to the employee's bank account (direct deposit). For this you'll need to get a written authorization from the employee.

HGB COMPANY
PAYROLL REGISTER
FOR THE MONTHLY PAY PERIOD ENDING 4/30

Employee Name	Gross Pay	FICA Tax	Medicare Tax	Federal Withholding Tax	State Withholding Tax	Other Deductions Item	Amount	Total Deductions	Net Pay
Rosa, K.	$7,000	$434	$101	$1,400	$120	Care	$500	$2,555	$4,445
Jennings, D.	$7,000	$434	$101	$1,400	$150	Care	$500	$2,585	$4,415
Nam, S.	$10,000	$620	$145	$2,500	$400	Pension	$1,000	$4,665	$5,335
Mayorga, D.	$7,000	$434	$101	$1,400	$150	Pension	$600	$2,685	$4,315
Hershon, T.	$2,000	$124	$29	$150	$40	Pension	$900	$1,243	$757
Panah, Y.	$2,000	$124	$29	$150	$40	Pension	$500	$1,343	$657
						Care	$500		
Totals	$35,000	$2,170	$506	$7,000	$900		$4,500	$15,076	$19,924

Note: If this were an actual payroll, employee checks would have dollars and cents, but we have rounded for brevity.

Employee checks are printed with detachable stubs, which show gross and net earnings and deductions by type. The stubs also list year-to-date totals in these categories. For paychecks directly deposited, the advice, or remittance summary, also carries this information.

No matter how you make the payroll payments, the net effect of the journal entry to record payment of payroll is as follows:

	Debit	Credit
7/31 Salaries Payable	$5,335	
Wages Payable	$14,589	
Cash		$19,924

To record payment of payroll for period ending 7/31.

SEE ALSO 6.4, "Cash Disbursements"

This journal entry is usually made to the payroll or cash journals, depending on how your company's system is set up. Payroll isn't complete until it's recorded. This starts individually with employee earnings records that keep track of employee wages and deductions by pay period for the year. The payroll register is the record of earnings and deductions for all employees each pay period. Its totals can be used as the basis for the journal entry to record payroll. When employees are paid and checks are cut, this journal entry is often made to a cash or cash disbursements journal, although some companies keep a separate journal just for payroll.

8.5

Time Value of Money

9.1 Time Value Basics

Understanding Time Value

Computing Interest

Annuities

The value of certain assets and liabilities depends on how long you hold them and at what price. This subchapter explains the **time value of money** concept and demonstrates the basics of computing interest and determining values for these accounts.

✓

Time value of money is the concept that there's a difference between $1 today and $1 sometime in the future.

Understanding Time Value

Most of us are comfortable with the concept that $1 today is worth more than $1 will be worth 5 years from now if you invest that $1 and presumably earn a return. Businesses must similarly consider the effects of timing and returns when valuing assets and liabilities. Investments, bond purchases, mortgages, long-term loans, leases, and pension liabilities are just a few of the areas where looking at the **present value (PV)** versus the **future value (FV)** comes into play.

✓

Present value (PV) is the amount you'd have to put in now to get a future sum or sums assuming compound interest. **Future value (FV)** is the amount you'll have at some future date if you invest a sum or sums of money at compound interest. This can also be called the future amount.

Time value of money computations are also useful in analyzing costs and benefits to make business decisions. For example:

How much will we have to invest now to have saved $30,000 in 3 years?

What is the value of a capital lease?

What will our company's monthly mortgage payment be if we buy that new building?

In each of these scenarios, computing the present or future value gives you the answer because it takes the impact of interest charges into account in determining the amounts involved. We demonstrate how to solve these kinds of problems and others in the upcoming sections.

Computing Interest

When you borrow money, you pay a cost. The amount depends on the **interest** rate on the loan. You pay this interest in addition to the **principal,** or the amount you borrowed. In the same way, if you invest funds or make a loan, you also earn a return, which depends on the interest you're able to earn or charge.

✓

> **Interest** is the extra amount to be paid for the use of money.
>
> **Principal** is the original amount of money you borrowed.

There are two kinds of interest—simple and compound. Simple interest is computed on the original balance each period. Compound interest is added back into the balance so the base it is charged on (and hence the return) keeps getting bigger. We look at each type of interest separately.

Simple Interest

Simple interest is charged or earned on funds over one time period and is used for shorter-duration loans and investments. For a loan, simple interest is computed only on the principal, using the following formula:

Principal × Interest rate × Time (number of periods) = Simple interest

Using this formula, if you took out a 4-year loan of $20,000 at 12 percent, you would compute simple interest as follows:

$20,000 × .12 × 4 = $9,600

If you borrowed the same amount for 6 months rather than 4 years, the time would now be a fraction of a year. The computation would change to:

$20,000 × .12 × .5 = $1,200

To compute simple interest, you need to know three things: the principal amount, the rate of interest, and the time or the number of periods over which interest is computed or paid.

9.1

Compound Interest

Compound interest is computed on principal *and* any interest earned or owed that has not been paid or withdrawn. Investors love compound interest because it increases the value of the asset exponentially as time and the return grow.

Compound interest is computed on two or more time periods, as its benefits only start accumulating after the first interest return or payment is received. Because compound interest is calculated on an ever-increasing balance, a straight computation using the interest rate for several periods can be cumbersome, so take advantage of compound interest tables, which take the compounding effect into consideration. Or you can use a calculator with PV and FV factors built in.

The following excerpts are from one the most common compound interest tables. This table is often used to determine how much you need to invest now at a particular return to get a certain future amount:

PRESENT VALUE OF $1

Period	Interest Rate									
	1%	2%	3%	4%	5%	6%	7%	8%	9%	10%
1	0.990	0.980	0.971	0.962	0.952	0.943	0.935	0.926	0.917	0.909
2	0.980	0.961	0.943	0.925	0.907	0.890	0.873	0.857	0.842	0.826
3	0.971	0.942	0.915	0.889	0.864	0.840	0.816	**0.794**	0.772	0.751
4	0.961	0.924	0.888	0.855	0.823	0.792	0.763	0.735	0.708	0.683
5	0.951	0.906	0.863	0.822	0.784	0.747	0.713	0.681	0.650	0.621

Period	Interest Rate									
	11%	12%	13%	14%	15%	16%	17%	18%	19%	20%
1	0.901	0.893	0.885	0.877	0.870	0.862	0.855	0.847	0.840	0.833
2	0.812	0.797	0.783	0.769	0.756	0.743	0.731	0.718	0.706	0.694
3	0.731	0.712	0.693	0.675	0.658	0.641	0.624	0.609	0.593	0.579
4	0.659	0.636	0.613	0.592	0.572	0.552	0.534	0.516	0.499	0.482
5	0.593	0.567	0.543	0.519	0.497	0.476	0.456	0.437	0.419	0.402

The percentages across the top represent the expected rate of return, while the numbers along the left side show the number of periods. Using this table, it's easy to figure out how much an investment now would be worth in the future given different interest rates. For example, let's say you have $10,000 to invest and you know you can earn an interest rate of 8 percent. If you want to do things the long way, you can compute interest each year and add it to the new base as follows:

Year 1:	$10,000 × .08 = $800
Year 2:	$10,800 × .08 = $864
Year 3:	$11,664 × .08 = $933.12
Total After 3 Years:	*$11,664 + $933.12 = $12,597.12*

Now for the easy way: instead of going year by year and adding the returns back in for each new period, you can get the same amount by using a factor from the preceding table. For example, you can deduce how much a $10,000 investment earning 8 percent for 3 years would grow to, using the following equation:

Present value (PV) ÷ Factor = Future value (FV)

You know the (PV) present value is $10,000. To find the factor in the PV of $1 interest table, you would go to the row for the number of periods—3 in this case. Next, find the interest rate column for 8 percent. The point where the two columns intersect is your factor: .794.

PV ÷ Factor = Investment after 3 years

$10,000 ÷ .794 = $12,594

Note the $3 difference from $12,597 is due to rounding of .794 from .7938 and is not considered significant.

9.1

Annuities

In accounting, you'll often encounter instances where you want to value not just one but a series of payments or receipts compounded periodically, as with life insurance contracts, notes on installment sales of equipment, or loan repayments, for example. Such transactions involving a series of equal payments made at regular intervals where interest is compounded are called **annuities.**

✓
___

An **annuity** is a series of equal payments made at equal intervals.

A simple annuity problem might involve figuring how much an investment will grow over the years if each year you invest $1,000 and are earning 12 percent interest compounded. How much will you have after 5 years? To solve this problem we'll use this formula, locating the factor in the following compound interest table for ordinary annuities excerpt:

Periodic payment × Factor = Future value

$1,000 × 6.353 = $6,353

FUTURE VALUE FOR AN ORDINARY ANNUITY (EXCERPT)

Period	6%	7%	8%	9%	10%	11%	12%
1	1.000	1.000	1.000	1.000	1.000	1.000	1.000
2	2.060	2.070	2.080	2.090	2.100	2.110	2.120
3	3.184	3.215	3.246	3.278	3.310	3.342	3.374
4	4.374	4.439	4.506	4.573	4.641	4.709	4.779
5	5.637	5.750	5.867	5.985	6.105	6.228	**6.353**

For purposes of this book, we've compiled these tables, rounding to the nearest $1/1000$. Complete versions of present value and future value tables for single amounts and annuities can easily be found on the web; just search for "present value of $1" or "present or future value of an ordinary annuity."

Present and future value of an annuity computations are very common in accounting. They are used to value instruments like leases and mortgages that involve a number of periodic payments. They can also be used to calculate how much needs to be invested annually to earn a certain amount by a certain time.

9.2 Applying Time Value of Money

Computing Required Investments

Evaluating Investments

Time value of money computations are essential in certain business situations. This subchapter shows you how to use present value (PV) and future value (FV) to determine investment amounts and evaluate returns.

Computing Required Investments

A common way to use the time value of money concept is to determine how much money you'll need to invest to earn a certain return sometime in the future. You can use PV and FV to compute a one-time investment or periodic payments.

Determining Initial Investments

If you want to have a certain amount of money after a period of years and you know the interest rate, you can compute how much money you have to invest now (present value) by using a variation of the following formula:

Present value × Factor = Future value

For example, if you want to know how much you would have to invest now at 10 percent interest to have $50,000 in 5 years, you would solve for the present value as follows:

Future value ÷ Factor = Present value

9.2

To complete the equation, you must first locate the correct factor on the compound interest table. For this problem, you would use the following Future Value table excerpt, which shows how much a single amount invested would grow for different amounts and periods. The factor for 5 years at 10 percent is 1.611.

FUTURE VALUE FOR A SINGLE PRESENT AMOUNT

	Interest Rate									
Period	**1%**	**2%**	**3%**	**4%**	**5%**	**6%**	**7%**	**8%**	**9%**	**10%**
1	1.010	1.020	1.030	1.040	1.050	1.060	1.070	1.080	1.090	1.100
2	1.020	1.040	1.061	1.081	1.103	1.124	1.145	1.166	1.188	1.210
3	1.030	1.061	1.093	1.125	1.157	1.191	1.123	1.126	1.130	1.133
4	1.041	1.082	1.126	1.170	1.216	1.263	1.311	1.361	1.412	1.464
5	1.051	1.104	1.159	1.217	1.276	1.338	1.403	1.469	1.539	**1.611**

So you put that factor into your equation (Future value ÷ Factor = Present value) and solve as follows:

$50,000 ÷ 1.611 = $31,037

You would have to invest $31,037 today to let compounding do its magic so you would have $50,000 in 5 years.

Determining Periodic Payments

Often instead of a single investment, you'll be making periodic investments or payments to attain a certain end amount. For example, if in the previous problem you needed to make annual payments that would grow to $50,000 in 5 years, you would use this annuity formula:

Periodic payment × Factor = Future amount

Or to convert this formula so you're solving for the periodic payment:

Future amount ÷ Factor = Periodic payment

$50,000 ÷ Factor (6.1051) = $8,189.87*

**Factor from the following table: 5 years, 10%*

FUTURE VALUE FOR AN ORDINARY ANNUITY (EXCERPT)

	Interest Rate						
Period	**6%**	**7%**	**8%**	**9%**	**10%**	**11%**	**12%**
1	1.000	1.000	1.000	1.000	1.000	1.000	1.000
2	2.060	2.070	2.080	2.090	2.100	2.110	2.120
3	3.184	3.215	3.246	3.278	3.310	3.342	3.374
4	4.374	4.439	4.506	4.573	4.641	4.709	4.779
5	5.637	5.750	5.867	5.985	**6.105**	6.228	6.353

If you want to accumulate a certain amount by a certain time, present and future value computations can be used to compute either the lump sum investment or periodic deposits you'll need to make. Compound interest tables can also assist in determining periodic payments on loans and dividing these payments into interest and principal.

Evaluating Investments

You can also use PV calculations to find out how much money you'll have or to look at whether the cash flow generated from an investment will be worthwhile.

Projecting Returns

To see how much an investment today would be worth in the future, you can use the following formula:

Present value × Factor = Future value/amount

Or in real-life terms: if you put $15,000 in an investment earning 10 percent for the next 4 years with interest compounding annually, you'll have:

$15,000 × 1.464 = $21,960

You can find the factor from the following future value table excerpt—in this case, the future value of $1 after 4 years (or periods).

FUTURE VALUE FOR A SINGLE PRESENT AMOUNT

Period	Interest Rate									
	1%	2%	3%	4%	5%	6%	7%	8%	9%	10%
1	1.010	1.020	1.030	1.040	1.050	1.060	1.070	1.080	1.090	1.100
2	1.020	1.040	1.061	1.081	1.103	1.124	1.145	1.166	1.188	1.210
3	1.030	1.061	1.093	1.125	1.157	1.191	1.123	1.126	1.130	1.133
4	1.041	1.082	1.126	1.170	1.216	1.263	1.311	1.361	1.412	**1.464**
5	1.051	1.104	1.159	1.217	1.276	1.338	1.403	1.469	1.539	1.611

Evaluating Cash Flow

If a company is considering an investment that's expected to provide not a single lump sum, but a series of annual cash flows, you can evaluate it by using this formula:

Expected net cash flows × Factor = Present value flows

Say we expect a 10 percent return on our investments and want to buy new finishing equipment that's expected to save $25,000 a year for the next 5 years. We know our expected cash flows are $25,000 per year. Then we go to the present value compound interest table for annuities (excerpted here), or punch the interest and period data into our calculator, if we have one that does PV computations, and find our factor is 2.991.

PRESENT VALUE OF ANNUITY VALUE OF $1

Period	Interest Rate									
	1%	2%	3%	4%	5%	6%	7%	8%	9%	10%
1	0.901	0.893	0.885	0.877	0.870	0.862	0.855	0.847	0.840	0.833
2	1.713	1.690	1.668	1.647	1.626	1.605	1.585	1.566	1.547	1.528
3	2.444	2.402	2.361	2.322	2.283	2.246	2.210	2.174	2.140	2.106
4	3.102	3.037	2.974	2.914	2.855	2.798	2.743	2.690	2.639	2.589
5	3.696	3.605	3.517	3.433	3.352	3.274	3.199	3.127	3.058	**2.991**

Putting these numbers into our equation, we find:

Expected net cash flows × *Factor* = *Present value of net cash flows*

$25,000 × 2.991 = $74,775

This means we shouldn't pay any more than $74,775 for our new equipment.

SEE ALSO 13.5, "Making Decisions"

As we've seen in this subchapter, time value of money concepts can be very useful in determining investment amounts to earn a certain return. This is true whether you plan on a single lump sum or a periodic payment. Present value and future value calculations can also help you evaluate potential investments before you take the plunge. Once you've determined what problem you'd like to solve, you can identify the compound interest table you need and using your interest rate and number of periods, find the factor that will help you compute your answer.

9.3 Investments

Short-Term Securities

Equity Investments

Debt Securities

Even small companies sometimes find themselves with more cash than they need to operate their business and want to put the excess to good use. In this subchapter, we cover different types of investments and give information on how to classify and value them.

Short-Term Securities

Short-term securities are perhaps the most common investment a small company would make. They include the following:

- Marketable securities
- Certificates of deposit
- U.S. Treasury securities

These typically have maturities of less than a year and lower risk levels. They are considered cash equivalents and classified as cash in the current assets section of the balance sheet.

SEE ALSO 3.1, "Classifying Cash"

Short-term securities are valued at cost and classified in the cash account. Interest is treated as interest income on the income statement. Annual interest of 8 percent on $5,000 in marketable securities would be recorded as follows:

	Debit	Credit
12/31 Cash	$400	
Interest Income		$400
To record interest on marketable securities.		

Equity Investments

Equities are investments in shares of stock of another company. They are typically valued at cost, which would include any brokerage fees or commissions, although the financial statements should disclose market value in the footnotes. How you classify them depends on how long your company intends to hold them. If you plan to sell stock investments soon after you buy them, they should be classified as **trading securities** and listed in the current assets section of the balance sheet.

✓

Trading securities are shares of stock or bonds purchased for resale in the near future.

As you sell these securities, you record any gains and losses in a valuation or trading account. For example, if the Rhodes Company, a financial services firm, bought $10,000 worth of stock (including broker commissions and fees) in May and sold the shares for $9,000 in July, they would need to make the following entries:

		Debit	Credit
5/2	Trading Securities	$10,000	
	Cash		$10,000
To record purchase of stock for investment.			
7/31	Cash	$9,000	
	Valuation Account	$1,000	
	Trading Securities		$10,000
To record loss on sale of stock.			

In the second journal entry, we omitted the transaction costs, which would have reduced the cash proceeds further and would be included if this were an actual transaction.

Stocks you intend to hold for a longer period are classified as investments or equity investments on the balance sheet in the noncurrent assets section. They are typically valued at cost unless your company has significant influence or control over the other company. Market value is noted in the footnotes to your financial statements. Gains or losses in the market value of the stock are not recorded until you actually sell the shares.

For example, if Rhodes Company bought the same $10,000 of stock and sold after 3 years for $9,500, it would enter the sale in its books as follows:

	Debit	Credit
6/31 Cash	$9,500	
Loss on Sale of Investment	$500	
Equity Investments		$10,000
To record loss on sale of stock investment.		

Any dividends received, which are periodic distributions made on shares of common stock, are recorded to dividend income or dividend revenue.

Debt Securities

Debt securities are bonds or long-term debt issued by the government or another company. These are mostly an issue for larger companies.

Valuing and Recording

Bonds are valued at cost plus any brokerage fees and commissions and put in a debt investments account on the balance sheet. Whether you should qualify them as current or long-term depends on how soon you expect to resell them.

For example, if Rhodes Company purchased one 12 percent $10,000 bond for $10,200 plus $100 in fees, it would record the transaction as follows:

	Debit	Credit
1/01 Debt Investments	$10,300	
Cash		$10,300
To record purchase of bonds.		

Recording Interest Payments

Because bonds pay interest, you would also need to record these payments. The 12 percent $10,000 bond the Rhodes Company purchased pays interest annually, which would be recorded to the journal at 12/31 as follows.

9.3

	Debit	Credit
12/31 Cash	$1,200	
Interest Income		$1,200
To record interest income on bonds.		

Investments, which are typically valued at cost plus any brokerage fees, are classified as current or long-term assets on the balance sheet, depending on how long the company intends to hold them. Any interest earned should be recorded separately in an interest income account. Changes in market value of investments should be disclosed in notes to the financial statements.

9.4 Long-Term Receivables

Computing Future Cash Payments

Computing Interest

Long-term receivables include items such as notes receivable not due within the year. In this subchapter, we explain how you can use present value (PV) and future value (FV) calculations to measure interest income and proceeds on long-term receivables.

Computing Future Cash Payments

Long-term notes are written agreements to pay a certain amount of money to your company. What qualifies them as "long term" is the fact that they are not due within the year. If your company receives a note, you record it at its present value. The amount you ultimately receive, thanks to interest and compounding, will be much larger.

For example, if Rhodes Company is holding a 5-year note for $100,000 at 10 percent, you could compute what they expect to be paid as follows:

Note amount × Interest rate × Duration of note = Total proceeds

$100,000 × .10 × 5 years = $50,000

The total proceeds would be $50,000 (interest and compounding) + $100,000 (original note amount) = $150,000.

SEE ALSO 4.5, "Notes Receivable"

9.4

Computing Interest

Sometimes, a long-term note won't have an interest rate. In these cases you must value it using the following computation:

Rate × Time = Present value of the payments

Let's say Rhodes Company sold a building for $100,000 cash and a 4-year note for $200,000, payable in annual installments of $50,000. No interest rate is listed on the note, but a reasonable rate for financing the building would be 7 percent. Because both the IRS and Generally Accepted Accounting Principles (GAAP) require that loan proceeds and interest be recorded separately, Rhodes would have to first figure out how to divide the note value between these to accounts.

To do this, the company would have to value the note by computing the present value of the note payments ($50,000 for 4 periods at 7 percent). Using the following table, we can identify the PV factor as 3.387.

PRESENT VALUE OF AN ORDINARY ANNUITY OF $1

Period	1%	2%	3%	4%	5%	6%	7%	8%	9%	10%
1	0.990	0.980	0.971	0.962	0.952	0.943	0.935	0.926	0.917	0.909
2	1.970	1.942	1.913	1.886	1.859	1.833	1.808	1.783	1.759	1.736
3	2.941	2.884	2.829	2.775	2.723	2.673	2.624	2.577	2.531	2.487
4	3.902	3.808	3.717	3.630	3.546	3.465	**3.387**	3.312	3.240	3.170
5	4.853	4.713	4.580	4.452	4.329	4.212	4.100	3.993	3.890	3.791

So to determine the value for the note:

$50,000 × 3.387 = $169,350

The difference between this and $200,000 would be interest income:

$200,000 − $169,350 = $30,650

Rhodes would then have to amortize (or allocate) the interest over the different periods:

AMORTIZATION TABLE

Balance Period	Unpaid Date Paid	Annual Payment	Interest Expense*	Reduced	Balance
					$169,350
1	12/31	$50,000	$11,855	$38,145	$131,205
2	12/31	$50,000	$9,184	$40,816	$90,389
3	12/31	$50,000	$6,327	$43,673	$46,716
4	12/31	$50,000	$3,284	$46,716	$0

*7 percent × unpaid balance.

In the final period: Interest = Payment − Unpaid balance due to rounding errors.

For long-term receivables, present value calculations can be used to determine future cash payments you can expect as well as interest income. You will often prepare an amortization table to allocate interest to periods and determine expected payments.

9.5 Capital Leases

Capital leases are leases that confer most of the benefits of ownership to the lessee, as we noted in Chapter 7. In this subchapter, we expand on how to value these leases using present value calculations.

SEE ALSO 7.4, "Leases"

A capital lease is valued by taking the present value of future lease payments. This can be done using an annuity (present value) computation like the ones we discussed back in subchapter 9.1. To the lessee, it is considered an asset; to the lessor, a sale. For example, if the Rhodes Company leased some manufacturing equipment for 3 years with annual payments of $12,000 and a 5 percent interest rate, you could compute the value of the lease by using the following formula:

Annual payment × PV factor = Lease value

$12,000 × 2.723 = $32,676

PRESENT VALUE OF AN ORDINARY ANNUITY OF $1

Period	1%	2%	3%	4%	5%	6%	7%	8%	9%	10%
1	0.990	0.980	0.971	0.962	0.952	0.943	0.935	0.926	0.917	0.909
2	1.970	1.942	1.913	1.886	1.859	1.833	1.808	1.783	1.759	1.736
3	2.941	2.884	2.829	2.775	**2.723**	2.673	2.624	2.577	2.531	2.487
4	3.902	3.808	3.717	3.630	3.546	3.465	3.387	3.312	3.240	3.170
5	4.853	4.713	4.580	4.452	4.329	4.212	4.100	3.993	3.890	3.791

9.5

Rhodes would record the lease as follows:

		Debit	Credit
1/1	Leased Equipment	$32,676	
	Lease Payment Obligation		$32,676
To record equipment acquisition through a capital lease.			
12/31	Interest Expense	$1,634	
	Lease Payment Obligation	$10,366	
	Cash		$12,000
To record annual payment and interest expense for equipment lease for year 1.			

Present value calculations are used to determine the value of capital leases. This involves taking the present value of the future lease payments, which depend on the number of years in the lease and the interest rate. Present value also enables you to set up an amortization schedule showing how to divide annual payments between interest and principal.

9.6 Long-Term Liabilities

Mortgages

Bonds

Pensions

Time value of money calculations frequently come up when dealing with long-term liabilities. In this subchapter, we show you how present value (PV) and future value (FV) can be used in the valuation of mortgages, long-term notes and bonds, and pensions.

Mortgages

Mortgage notes payable, like other long-term notes, represent noncurrent amounts due but unpaid. Both large and small companies often use mortgages or installment notes to purchase plant assets, such as buildings or expensive machinery. Notes payable are recorded at face value.

PV and FV calculations can help you weigh different mortgage options or financing options, as well as determine what monthly payments would be. For example, say the Rhodes Company is considering purchasing a new office building for $400,000. The company has reviewed financing options, and it's looking at a 10-year 9 percent mortgage. The company is currently renting space in another building for $5,000 a month.

This time we'll use T-Value, an amortization software program commonly used by companies and accountants, to compute the monthly payment and interest and set up an amortization schedule for the mortgage. This involves keying into the computer program the loan amount of 400,000 over 10 years (or 120 periods) at 4 percent interest. Using PV/FV computations, T-Value computes Rhodes's monthly payment as:

Present value ÷ Factor = Annual payment

$400,000 ÷ 98.77* = $4,049.81

*Factor for 120 periods (12 monthly payments for 10 years) compounded at 4%.

So Rhodes Company would be able to buy the building with little effect on its costs, and ultimately eliminate rent expense.

T-Value also prepares an amortization chart for the entire period of the lease so you can easily pull off payments and interest for journal entries. A partial amortization schedule showing Rhodes Company's first few 2012 mortgage payments would look like this:

AMORTIZATION SCHEDULE—NORMAL AMORTIZATION

	Date Paid	Payment	Interest	Principal	Balance
Loan 12/27/2011				$400,000	
2012 Totals	$0.00	$0.00	$0.00		
1	01/27/12	$4,049.81	$1,333.33	$2,716.48	$395,950.19
2	02/27/12	$4,049.81	$1,319.83	$2,729.98	$391,900.38
3	03/27/12	$4,049.81	$1,306.34	$2,743.47	$387,850.57

If Rhodes decides to go with the purchase, company officials would make the following entry when the mortgage loan is received:

	Debit	Credit
12/27 Cash	$400,000	
Mortgage Notes Payable		$400,000
To record mortgage loan.		

When Rhodes makes its first mortgage payment, the company would record the following entry:

	Debit	Credit
1/27 Mortgage Notes Payable	$2,716.48	
Interest Expense	$1,333.33	
Cash		$4,049.81
To record first monthly mortgage payment.		

Bonds

Bonds are interest-paying debt issued by a company or the government. Small companies don't issue bonds, so you're unlikely to encounter bonds unless you work for a larger organization. Bonds are classified as bonds payable in the long-term liabilities section of the balance sheet. Bonds are valued at issue price, which could be the **face value** or the face value at a **premium** or **discount.** Bond interest for the year is classified as a current liability, bond interest accrued, or interest accrued.

✓

Bonds are debt instruments issued by the government or a company that can be sold to raise money.

Face value is the amount of principal a bond issuer must pay. For example, with a $100,000 12 percent bond, $100,000 would be the face value. When the rate of interest paid on a bond exceeds the market rate, we say a bond is bought at a **premium.** When the rate of interest paid on a bond is less than the market rate, that bond was acquired at a **discount.**

If you issued $10,000 of 9 percent bonds at face value, you would make the following entry:

	Debit	Credit
1/2 Cash	$10,000	
Bonds Payable		$10,000
To record the issuance of bonds.		

Now assume you have to pay interest twice a year, or semiannually. You would compute interest as follows:

9.6

$10,000 \times .09 \times \frac{6}{12}$ *(6 months, the first semiannual payment)* = $450

This amount would be recorded in June as shown in the following journal entry:

	Debit	Credit
6/31 Bond Interest Expense	$450	
Cash		$450
To record payment of bond interest expense.		

Pensions

Recent changes in accounting rules now require that all companies list the cost of future pension liabilities as a liability on the balance sheet. Previously, these amounts were disclosed as footnotes so they didn't affect a company's net worth.

This is primarily an issue for larger companies with traditional defined benefit pension plans.

SEE ALSO 8.3, "Making Payroll Deductions"

Funding pensions is a matter of investing the right amount of money to get a certain return. So computing pension liabilities is essentially a matter of determining the present value of the initial investment. For example, let's say you wanted to make a lump sum investment now to have a pension fund worth $10 million for your employees in 10 years. You figure you can safely project a 10 percent return. You can determine how much you would have to invest now by using the following formula:

Future value ÷ Factor = Present value (investment needed today)

$10,000,000 ÷ 2.594 = $3,855,050

Note that the factor for 10 periods at 10 percent would be taken from the following table:

FUTURE VALUE OF A $1 AFTER *N* PERIODS

Period	Interest Rate									
	1%	2%	3%	4%	5%	6%	7%	8%	9%	10%
6	1.062	1.126	1.340	1.419	1.501	1.587	1.677	1.772	1.870	1.974
7	1.072	1.149	1.230	1.316	1.407	1.504	1.606	1.714	1.828	1.949
8	1.083	1.172	1.267	1.369	1.478	1.594	1.718	1.851	1.993	2.144
9	1.094	1.195	1.305	1.423	1.551	1.689	1.838	1.999	2.172	2.358
10	1.105	1.209	1.344	1.480	1.629	1.791	1.967	2.216	2.237	**2.594**

As this chapter illustrates, time value of money computations have many uses in accounting. Present and future values can be used to make business decisions, compute payments or investment returns, and help set up amortization schedules for interest. In addition, these computations help you value investments and other assets such as leases as well as liabilities such as long-term bonds. Despite the complex-looking tables, the calculations are relatively simple; software programs are also available to do the work for you.

Monthly Closing Procedures

10.1 The Closing Process

Accounts and Operations

Financial Statements

This subchapter provides an overview of the monthly closing process and walks you through the steps involved. We summarize standard monthly closing procedures for accounts and operations as well as how to process interim (monthly) financial reports.

Accounts and Operations

Chances are, the end of the month at your business is a fairly busy time. Even if your company doesn't produce monthly financial statements, certain bookkeeping tasks must be performed every 30 days or so, including:

- Sending customer statements
- Reviewing and paying bills as necessary
- Making tax payments

SEE ALSO 12.1, "Advanced Planning"

SEE ALSO 12.2, "Payroll Taxes"

- Processing employee expense reports
- Updating employee records
- Reconciling your bank accounts

SEE ALSO 3.4, "Preparing a Bank Reconciliation"

Some of these procedures are covered in separate chapters, as noted. The rest, and how to coordinate them with your closing duties, are detailed in the sections that follow.

Financial Statements

All organizations have to produce financial statements at least once a year for many purposes. Large public companies must file quarterly as well. And in practice, many businesses choose to generate monthly financial reports to keep tabs on how they're doing.

Procedures vary from firm to firm, but the steps you use to summarize data from transactions into financial statements are fairly standard:

1. Summarize and total journals. **Reconcile** to supporting accounts or ledgers.

2. Post reconciled totals to the general ledger. Compute general ledger balances for each account.

3. Compile a **trial balance** using general ledger balances. Be sure debits equal credits. If they don't, go back and check postings to locate source of imbalance.

4. Prepare **adjusting entries** to ensure all costs and revenues are recorded in the proper period. Record to general journal, and post to general ledger.

5. Use revised general ledger balances to prepare the **adjusted trial balance.**

6. If you're preparing interim financial statements (those for periods prior to the end of the year), you can take the numbers directly from the trial balance and plug them into the balance sheet and income statement.

✓

To **reconcile** means to verify that account totals agree with supporting data or calculations.

The **trial balance** is a listing of the general ledger accounts to see if total debits and credits are equal.

Adjusting entries are journal entries typically made at the end of the period to be sure costs and revenue match and are recorded in the proper period and correct any errors in the general ledger accounts.

The **adjusted trial balance** is a listing of general ledger accounts that have been adjusted and corrected to see if they balance.

10.1

In the rest of this chapter, we take you through these steps in detail. But feel free to flip back to our list at any time if you want to know where you are in the process.

10.2 Closing Cash Journals

Cash Receipts and Sales

Cash Disbursements and Purchases

This subchapter focuses on closing the books and making sure all activity is properly summarized and posted. We discuss sending monthly statements, paying bills, and recording credit card costs. In addition, you learn how to close cash journals, post to the general ledger, and reconcile account totals with supporting data.

Cash Receipts and Sales

The totals from your cash receipts and sales journal need to be reconciled and posted to the general ledger at the end of the month. But before you get to that point, you need to perform other bookkeeping duties first.

Generating Monthly Statements

Although it's not required, it's good business practice to compile a monthly accounts receivable aging schedule to check on the status of outstanding customer accounts. This not only enables you to keep tabs on how well customers are paying their bills, but it can be converted into statement information for your monthly billing. (Most accounting software programs automatically generate statements from aged balances.)

SEE ALSO 4.3, "Accounts Receivable"

The Hobby Company doesn't have a lot of open accounts, so management probably has a pretty good handle on who is behind on payment. But we've included an aging schedule for 10/31 as an example:

THE HOBBY COMPANY
A/R AGING SCHEDULE
OCTOBER 31

Customer	Balance 10/31	Current	31 to 60	61 to 90	Over 90
				Days Past Due	
Smith	$1,000	$1,000			
Fun, Inc.	$2,410	$1,830			$580
Total	$3,410	$2,830			$580

The Hobby Company should talk to Fun, Inc., about why they haven't paid their bill for $580. It is already over 90 days old, which is too old to let pass and could suggest a problem. The end of the month is a good time to analyze accounts to determine where to concentrate your collection efforts and who might need to be cut off. At the end of this process, you'd be ready for billing. The monthly statement for Fun, Inc., generated from this data would look like this:

INVOICE/STATEMENT

Visual Arts Limited
PO Box 4119
Carlsbad, CA

Billing Address:

MLM Services
1948 Main Street
San Diego, CA

Date	Code	Description	Amount Due
12/7	043	Graphic services	$1,100
		Previous balance	
10/14	156	Signage	$2,300
9/8	041	Graphics and consulting	$1,500
		Total Outstanding Balance Due	**$4,900**
		Note: Your account is over 60 days past due. Please pay now to avoid late charges.	

SEE ALSO 4.3, "Accounts Receivable"

Recording Credit Card Fees

If your business accepts credit cards, you will have an additional fee to record at the end of the month. Credit card companies can charge a variety of fees, from a monthly percentage of sales, to charges for customer support, securing internet transactions, and handling disputed accounts. This is why it's so important to shop around initially when pricing credit cards, and be sure you're aware of all monthly charges upfront.

You'll find the fee amount listed as a charge on the monthly statement you receive from the bank processing your transactions. If, for example, you had credit card sales of $5,500 and a 5 percent fee, your monthly charge would be $275, which you would record with the following entry:

	Debit	Credit
10/31 Credit Card Fees	$275	
Cash		$275
To record credit card fees for October.		

If your bank statement isn't available at closing time, you might be able to make an entry based on total credit sales. This is called an accrual.

SEE ALSO 10.5, "Adjusting Entries"

Summarizing the Cash and Sales Journal

Throughout the month, you've been recording cash taken in from sales, customer payments, and other transactions in either a cash receipts journal or cash and sales journal.

SEE ALSO 4.1, "Recording Sales"

Unless you sell only a few high-ticket items—say luxury goods or specialized machinery or vehicles—it's unlikely that you'll journalize sales individually. Not only is it impractical, it's also inefficient. Most retailers, for example, record sales on a daily basis after totaling cash register tapes. Manufacturers compile a daily sales summary. As an example, let's look at the October cash and sales journal for The Hobby Company. The Hobby Company sells gaming systems and records sales on a twice-weekly basis.

At the end of the month, Hobby totals each of these columns and then cross-foots (adds the column totals together) to be sure the debits equal credits. (Note: In the case of the Miscellaneous column, these items are added for balancing purposes only. The individual amounts are recorded to the accounts listed in the posting reference column.)

THE HOBBY COMPANY
CASH AND SALES JOURNAL

Date	Description	PR	Misc. Account	Sales	Accounts Receivable Debit	Accounts Receivable (Credit)	Sales Discounts	Cash
10/2	Sale			($15,140)				$15,140
10/5	Sale			($6,140)				$6,140
10/8	A/R TR Crow Co			($3,200)		($3,200)	$320	$2,880
10/15	Sale			($1,450)				$1,450
10/20	Sale			($2,130)				$2,130
10/27	Equipment Sale	180	($1,570)					$1,570
10/28	A/R Smith			($1,000)	$1,000			
10/29	Notes Receivable	230	($2,000)					$2,000
10/30	A/R Fun Co			($1,830)	$1,830			
Totals			($3,570)	($27,690)	$2,830	($3,200)	$320	$31,310
				{301}	{140}	{140}	{310}	{102}

Numbers in ( ) are credit balances. Numbers in { } are account numbers.

10.2

Debits	Credits
$31,310 + $320 + $2,830 = $34,460 = $27,690 + $3,200 + $1,570 + $2,000	

Because the totals balance, we know Hobby's accountant recorded the appropriate amounts of debits and credits. If the totals hadn't agreed, Hobby would have had to go back to the original transactions to find the mistake. An automated system would automatically reconcile these totals, but if there were an error you would still likely have to review the initial transactions.

SEE ALSO 15.1, "Benefits of Computerized Accounting"

At 10/31, Hobby will post the following to the general ledger:

	Debit	Credit
10/31 Cash	$31,310	
Cash Discounts Earned	$320	
Accounts Receivable	$2,830	
Accounts Receivable		$3,200
Notes Receivable		$2,000
Equipment		$1,570
Sales		$27,690
To record cash receipts and sales for October.		

Reconciling Accounts

You've determined that Hobby's cash receipts journal columns cross-foot and have posted the monthly sales to the general ledger. Next you'll want to be sure the company's accounts receivable balance in the general ledger reconciles with the accounts receivable subledgers. The subledger contains the individual records for each customer's account, so all you need to do is add them up.

SEE ALSO 4.3, "Accounts Receivable"

For example, the general ledger account for accounts receivable appears as follows at the end of the month:

ACCT. 140   ACCOUNTS RECEIVABLE

Date	Reference	Debit	Credit	Balance
10/1	Balance	$3,780		
10/31	CR	$2,830		
10/31	CR		$3,200	$3,400

Now we would have to go to the subledger and tally the individual customer account balances to see if they agree. (Again, in a computerized system this would be done automatically.) For the sake of simplicity, we'll assume The Hobby Company only has three open customer accounts:

ACCT. 121   ACCOUNTS RECEIVABLE—SMITH

Date	Reference	Debit	Credit	Balance
10/1	Balance			$0
10/31	Invoice #113		$1,000	($1,000)

ACCT. 123   ACCOUNTS RECEIVABLE—FUN, INC.

Date	Reference	Debit	Credit	Balance
10/1	Balance			($580)
10/31	Inv. 114		$1,830	($2,410)

ACCT. 124   ACCOUNTS RECEIVABLE—TR CROW CO.

Date	Reference	Debit	Credit	Balance
10/01	Balance			($3,200)
10/31	Inv. 114	$3,200		$0

10.2

Account 124, TR Crow Co., has been paid off, so the only subsidiary ledger balances carried forward are from accounts 121 and 123. When added, these amounts should agree with total accounts receivable per the general ledger if the entries have been posted correctly.

Acct.#	Customer	Balance
121	Smith	$1,000
123	Fun, Inc.	$2,410
	Total Subsidiary A/R Ledger	$3,410
	Total A/R per G/L	$3,410

The accounts receivable ledger and subsidiary ledgers are in balance, so we can move on. If there had been a difference, we would have checked the math and made sure each transaction was entered properly.

Cash Disbursements and Purchases

Just as with cash receipts, you'll keep track of cash payments made to purchase inventory or fixed assets or to pay various expenses in a specialized journal called the cash disbursements journal. The totals from this record will be posted to the general ledger at the end of the month, after certain bookkeeping duties are taken care of.

Reviewing Accounts Payable

The end of the month is a good time to review your accounts and be sure you're paying all bills in a timely manner. Some companies find it useful to prepare an aging schedule, which shows how much you owe and for how long. If your company uses a voucher system, you can compare vouchers paid to checks that have been written.

SEE ALSO 6.4, "Cash Disbursements"

You should also review both paid and unpaid bills to determine that all have been recorded in the appropriate period. Any amounts owed but not yet paid, which are known as accruals, need to be recorded in this month's accounts.

SEE ALSO 10.4, "Developing a Trial Balance"

Temporary Holding Accounts

Sometimes you have to pay a bill before knowing how the costs are going to be allocated. For example, if you use an outside payroll service, you are often required to remit the amount to them for total payroll, before they've sent you the detail of how it breaks down. In this case, you might post the disbursement to a holding account until you have the full details. This is often called a suspense account or a temporary distribution account.

	Debit	Credit
10/15 Suspense	$10,180	
Cash		$10,180
To record payroll funds remitted.		

When you've received the proper documentation, you're able to reverse the amount in this account and debit it to the proper expenses. At the end of the month, you should review this account to determine adjusting entries that need to be made. List the remainder on the income statement as miscellaneous expenses.

Summarizing the Cash Disbursements Journal

During the month, The Hobby Company records all purchases and cash outlays in the cash disbursements journal as shown on the next page.

Just as with the cash and sales journal, at the end of the month, the columns are tallied and the totals are posted to the general ledger. Some companies do not include payroll in their cash disbursements ledger, choosing to make biweekly journal entries as it is paid out, and post to the general ledger separately. But for the purposes of this example, we recorded all disbursements into the cash disbursements journal and summarized them into the following journal entry.

	Debit	Credit
10/31 Staff Salaries	$10,200	
Commissions	$200	
Rent Expense	$1,500	
Utilities Expense	$720	
Accounts Payable	$2,000	
Purchases	$2,940	
Cash		$13,520
Discounts		$40
FICA Payable		$760
Fed Withheld Payable		$2,600
State Withheld Payable		$640
To record cash disbursements for October.		

10.2

Whether The Hobby Company uses the preceding entry or records payroll separately, as we do in the next section, the net result will be the same.

THE HOBBY COMPANY
CASH DISBURSEMENTS JOURNAL

Date	Payee	Check #	Cash (Credit)	FICA Withheld	Federal Tax Withheld	State Tax Withheld	Payroll	Accounts Payable	Purchases	Main-tenance	Cash Discounts Earned	Misc.	Acct. #	Other Debit	Credit
10/2	Lincoln Computers	221	($1,960)					$2,000			($40)				
10/4	Payroll	222–226	($3,200)	($380)	($1,300)	($320)	$5,200								
10/13	Rent	227	($1,500)									Rent	429	$1,500	
1025	Utilities	228	($720)									Utilities	430	$720	
10/27	Visual Arts	229	($2,940)						$2,940						
10/27	Payroll	230–234	($3,200)	($380)	($1,300)	($320)	$5,000					Commissions	448	$200	
Total			($13,520)	($760)	($2,600)	($640)	$10,200	$2,000	$2,940		($40)			$2,420	
			{102}	{230}	{231}	{232}	{410}	{210}	{401}	{435}	{402}				

Numbers in ( ) are credit balances. Numbers in { } are account numbers.

Total = numbers to be posted to the general ledger.

Reconciling Accounts Payable

You also need to reconcile the balance in accounts payable in the general ledger with the amounts in the accounts payable subledger (or voucher register if you use that system). This is similar to what you did with accounts receivable earlier.

The balance in accounts payable for The Hobby Company at 10/31 was $2,960. The subsidiary ledgers carried balances of $1,100, $700, $1,050, and $110, which total $2,960. So the accounts reconcile. If they had not, you would have checked your math first and then made sure all transactions were recorded properly.

10.2

10.3 Closing Employee Accounts

Reviewing Employee Expense Accounts

Updating Employee Records

Posting Payroll

At the end of the month you will perform certain activities related to payroll. Employee expense accounts must be filed and approved for payment, payroll should be posted, and employee accounts need to be updated for wages and benefits. This subchapter takes you through these tasks and shows you how to prepare the monthly adjusting entry for payroll.

Reviewing Employee Expense Accounts

If employees at your company incur expenses in the course of business, they need to file expense reports for reimbursement. Each business has its own criteria for determining what a business expense is, but standard business expenses include the following:

- Travel

- Entertainment

- Auto (for mileage or gasoline on company business)

- Supplies

Not coincidentally, these are also the items the IRS considers business expenses for tax purposes.

SEE ALSO Chapter 12, "Taxes"

SEE ALSO 14.4, "The Operating Expenses Budget"

Your company should have a system in place so employees can file for reimbursement. Standard procedure is to require employees to itemize expenses on an expense report and attach receipts. These reports are then forwarded to a supervisor for review and approval.

Many companies process reports close to the end of the month, for purposes of efficiency and comparing different employees' expenses. This process also makes it easier for accounting to prepare a summary journal entry allocating these expenses to their various accounts. For example, in October, assume The

Hobby Company had employees submit expense reports for a total of $1,250. This included travel and entertainment of $900, auto expenses of $250, and supplies expenses of $100. After noting the supervisor's approval on the report, Hobby's accountant approves the reports for payment. The company would need to record the following entry at 10/31:

	Debit	Credit
10/31 Travel and Entertainment	$900	
Auto Expenses	$250	
Supplies Expense	$100	
Cash		$1,250
To reimburse employees for October expenses.		

Large companies might break down the expenses even further into travel, lodging, meals, and entertainment. But because Hobby only has about 20 employees, 3 of whom incur expenses, fewer accounts are used for simplicity.

Updating Employee Records

The end of the month is also a good time to update employee records. This includes …

- Making necessary postings to the employee earnings reports from the payroll register.
- Updating benefits to reflect new vacation time earned, days taken, absences, etc.
- Making changes or alterations to benefits as allowed from written employee request. This includes, for example, updates to health-care allowance accounts.

10.3

Part of closing payroll involves processing employee expense reports. You'll want to be sure you've laid out clear guidelines for allowed expenses and supporting documentation and then have someone in a supervisory position review and approve all reports filed. The end of the month is also a good time to update payroll records on pay rates, benefits, and so on.

Posting Payroll

There are a couple ways to close payroll, depending on how your system is set up. You can do it the way The Hobby Company did in the previous section. After posting payroll biweekly to the cash disbursements journal, payroll and the rest of cash disbursements for the month are summarized to the general ledger. Other companies handle payroll separately and post monthly to the general ledger from the payroll register.

SEE ALSO 8.2, "Computing Wages"

SEE ALSO 8.5, "Recording Payroll"

If The Hobby Company recorded payroll separately in the payroll register, it would use the following alternative entry to record payroll for the month:

		Debit	Credit
10/31	Staff Salaries	$10,200	
	Commissions	$200	
	FICA Taxes Payable		$760
	Federal Withholding Taxes Payable		$2,600
	State Withholding Taxes Payable		$640
	Cash		$6,400
To record payroll for October.			

Companies also need to ensure that any payroll taxes for the previous period have been remitted and paid by the end of the month. Federal and state withholding taxes and FICA taxes must be deposited at least monthly, which means a company should be making a minimum of one payment each month. This payment includes both the federal and state withholding and FICA taxes deducted from employee paychecks as well as the company's share of FICA taxes.

SEE ALSO 8.4, "Employer Payroll Taxes"

Let's assume The Hobby Company had the same payroll taxes payable in September that it did in October. The entry to record the tax payment for September, which it would make at the end of October when its taxes were due, would be as follows:

		Debit	Credit
10/31	Payroll Tax Expense	$760	
	FICA Taxes Payable	$760	
	Federal Withholding Taxes Payable	$2,600	
	State Withholding Taxes Payable	$640	
	Cash		$4,760

To record payment of payroll taxes for September.

Note that the entry is essentially a reversal of the tax liabilities in the initial journal entry. In addition, The Hobby Company records the payroll tax expense for its share of FICA and deducts the total amount of tax paid from cash. As a final step, because the last pay period ended on October 24, it's necessary to make an accrual for the wages to be paid on November 2.

SEE ALSO 10.5, "Adjusting Entries"

10.3

10.4 Developing a Trial Balance

After you've reconciled the journal balances and made sure all monthly activity is correctly posted to the general ledger, it's time to do what is called a trial balance. This trial balance isn't a public document. Rather, it's a tool to help you determine if the accounts are in balance before you adjust them and prepare financial statements.

To compile the trial balance, list the ending balances from each of the general ledger accounts. The initials near the entries indicate the journal that the entry was posted from. CD is cash disbursements journal, CR is cash and sales journal, GJ is general journal.

ACCT. 102   CASH IN BANK

Date	Reference	Debit	Credit	Balance
10/1				$5,080
10/31	CR	$31,310		
10/31	CD		$13,240	
10/31	GJ		$225	
10/31				$22,925

ACCT. 105   PETTY CASH

Date	Reference	Debit	Credit	Balance
10/1	Balance			$200

ACCT. 130   NOTES RECEIVABLE

Date	Reference	Debit	Credit	Balance
10/1	Balance			$3,000
			$2,000	$1,000

ACCT. 140   ACCOUNTS RECEIVABLE

Date	Reference	Debit	Credit	Balance
10/1	Balance			$3,780
10/31	CR	$2,830		
10/31	CR		$3,200	$3,410

ACCT. 150   INVENTORY

Date	Reference	Debit	Credit	Balance
10/1	Balance			$2,510
10/31	CD	$2,940		
10/31	CR		$2,050	$3,400

ACCT. 160   PREPAID EXPENSES

Date	Reference	Debit	Credit	Balance
10/1	Balance			$2,100

ACCT. 170   LAND

Date	Reference	Debit	Credit	Balance
10/1	Balance			$90,000

ACCT. 175   BUILDING

Date	Reference	Debit	Credit	Balance
10/1	Balance			$60,000

ACCT. 176   ACCUMULATED DEPRECIATION—BUILDING

Date	Reference	Debit	Credit	Balance
10/1	Balance			($12,000)

ACCT. 180   MACHINERY AND EQUIPMENT

Date	Reference	Debit	Credit	Balance
10/1	Balance			$25,000

10.4

ACCT. 181   ACCUMULATED DEPRECIATION—MACHINERY AND EQUIPMENT

Date	Reference	Debit	Credit	Balance
10/1	Balance			($10,000)

ACCT. 185   OFFICE EQUIPMENT

Date	Reference	Debit	Credit	Balance
10/1	Balance			$4,570
10/31	CR		$1,570	$3,000

ACCT. 186   ACCUMULATED DEPRECIATION—OFFICE EQUIPMENT

Date	Reference	Debit	Credit	Balance
10/1	Balance			($3,000)

ACCT. 190   AUTOMOTIVE

Date	Reference	Debit	Credit	Balance
10/1	Balance			$15,000

ACCT. 191   ACCUMULATED DEPRECIATION—AUTOMOTIVE

Date	Reference	Debit	Credit	Balance
10/1	Balance			($6,000)

ACCT. 210   ACCOUNTS PAYABLE

Date	Reference	Debit	Credit	Balance
10/1	Balance			($4,960)
10/31	CD	$2,000		($2,960)

ACCT. 230   FICA WITHHELD

Date	Reference	Debit	Credit	Balance
10/1	Balance			($760)
10/31	CD		$760	($1,520)

ACCT. 231   FEDERAL INCOME TAX WITHHELD

Date	Reference	Debit	Credit	Balance
10/1	Balance			($2,600)
10/31	CD		$2,600	($5,200)

ACCT. 232   STATE AND COUNTY INCOME TAX WITHHELD

Date	Reference	Debit	Credit	Balance
10/1	Balance			($640)
10/31	CD		$640	($1,280)

ACCT. 240   OTHER ACCRUED LIABILITIES

Date	Reference	Debit	Credit	Balance
10/1	Balance			$0

ACCT. 270   LONG-TERM NOTES PAYABLE

Date	Reference	Debit	Credit	Balance
10/1	Balance			($40,000)

ACCT. 290   PROPRIETOR'S CAPITAL

Date	Reference	Debit	Credit	Balance
10/1				($139,075)

ACCT. 291   PROPRIETOR'S DRAWING

Date	Reference	Debit	Credit	Balance
10/1	Balance			$5,000

ACCT. 299   PROFIT AND LOSS

Date	Reference	Debit	Credit	Balance
10/1	Balance			$0

10.4

ACCT. 301   SALES

Date	Reference	Debit	Credit	Balance
10/1	Balance			$0
10/31	CR		$27,690	($27,690)

ACCT. 310 CASH DISCOUNTS ALLOWED

Date	Reference	Debit	Credit	Balance
10/1	Balance			$0
10/31	CR	$320		$320

ACCT. 401 PURCHASES

Date	Reference	Debit	Credit	Balance
10/1	Balance			$0
10/31	CD	$2,940		$2,940

ACCT. 402 CASH DISCOUNTS EARNED

Date	Reference	Debit	Credit	Balance
10/1	Balance			$0
10/31	CD		$40	($40)

ACCT. 410 STAFF SALARIES

Date	Reference	Debit	Credit	Balance
10/1	Balance			$0
10/31	CD	$10,200		$10,200

ACCT. 415 PAYROLL TAX EXPENSE

Date	Reference	Debit	Credit	Balance
10/1	Balance			$0

ACCT. 420 AUTOMOTIVE EXPENSES

Date	Reference	Debit	Credit	Balance
10/1	Balance			$0
10/31	GJ	$250		$250

ACCT. 425 INSURANCE EXPENSES

Date	Reference	Debit	Credit	Balance
10/1	Balance			$0

ACCT. 427   RENT EXPENSE

Date	Reference	Debit	Credit	Balance
10/1	Balance			$0
10/31	CD	$1,500		$1,500

ACCT. 430   UTILITIES EXPENSE

Date	Reference	Debit	Credit	Balance
10/1	Balance			$0
10/31	CD	$720		$720

ACCT. 440   ADVERTISING EXPENSE

Date	Reference	Debit	Credit	Balance
10/1	Balance			$0

ACCT. 448   COMMISSIONS EXPENSE

Date	Reference	Debit	Credit	Balance
10/1	Balance			$0
10/31	CD	$200		$200

ACCT. 450   TRAVEL AND ENTERTAINMENT EXPENSE

Date	Reference	Debit	Credit	Balance
10/1	Balance			$0
10/31	GJ	$900		$900

ACCT. 501   OFFICE SUPPLIES AND EXPENSE

Date	Reference	Debit	Credit	Balance
10/1	Balance			$600
10/31	GJ	$100		$700

ACCT. 505   DEPRECIATION EXPENSE

Date	Reference	Debit	Credit	Balance
10/1	Balance			$0

10.4

The balances from each general ledger account are carried forward to the trial balance. Accounts here are set up in order: balance sheet first and then income statement. Some accounts such as depreciation have zero balances at this point because adjusting entries have not yet been made. We cover how to make adjusting entries in the next subchapter.

The important thing at this point is that the general ledger balances are properly computed and transferred to the correct accounts in the trial balance. A computerized system will do this automatically for you.

THE HOBBY COMPANY TRIAL BALANCE AS OF 10/31

Account Title	Account #	Debit	Credit
Cash in Bank	102	$22,925	
Petty Cash	105	$200	
Notes Receivable	130	$1,000	
Accounts Receivable	140	$3,410	
Inventory	150	$3,400	
Prepaid Expenses	160	$2,100	
Land	170	$90,000	
Building	175	$60,000	
Accumulated Depreciation—Building	176		$12,000
Machinery and Equipment	180	$25,000	
Accumulated Depreciation—Machinery and Equipment	181		$10,000
Office Equipment	185	$3,000	
Accumulated Depreciation—Office Equipment	186		$3,000
Automotive	190	$15,000	
Accumulated Depreciation—Automotive	191		$6,000
Accounts Payable	210		$2,960
FICA Withheld	230		$1,520
Federal Income Tax Withheld	231		$5,200
State and County Income Tax Withheld	232		$1,280
Other Accrued Liabilities	240		
Long-Term Notes Payable	270		$40,000
Proprietor's Capital	290		$139,075
Proprietor's Drawing	295	$5,000	

Account Title	Account #	Debit	Credit
Profit and Loss	299		
Sales	301		$27,690
Cash Discounts Allowed	310	$320	
Purchases	401	$2,940	
Cash Discounts Earned	402		$40
Staff Salaries	410	$10,200	
Payroll Tax Expense	415		
Automotive Expenses	420	$250	
Insurance Expenses	425		
Rent Expense	427	$1,500	
Utilities Expense	430	$720	
Advertising Expense	440		
Commission Expense	448	$200	
Travel and Entertainment	450	$900	
Office Supplies and Expense	501	$700	
Depreciation Expense	505		
Total		**$248,765**	**$248,765**

We are fortunate that in this trial balance the Debit and Credit columns equal. If they had not been—as is often the case—we would have had to troubleshoot to find the source of the error before we moved on.

Some common ways accountants check for errors include …

- Checking to see if the difference is divisible by 9. If it is, two digits in one of the numbers might have been reversed.

10.4

- Verifying that if the difference is 10 or 100, a 0 wasn't added where it shouldn't be.

- Dividing the difference in half. If the answer is a number on the trial balance, perhaps a debit or a credit has been misclassified.

By the time you're putting together the trial balance, you've come pretty far along the accounting cycle. You've recorded your transactions, summarized them for the period (a month in this case), and posted them to the general ledger. Once you transfer these numbers to the trial balance, you can start to see your company's financial situation and how you've performed. Now you're ready to make your final adjustments.

10.5 Adjusting Entries

Identifying Adjusting Entries

Recording Accruals

Working with Deferrals

The purpose of adjusting entries is to ensure that all transactions are recognized in the proper period. In this subchapter, we cover the various types of adjusting entries and how to make them.

Identifying Adjusting Entries

At the end of each month, you will need to adjust accounts that have had activity that's not yet been recorded. Some adjustments such as depreciation, amortization, and interest are made regularly. These are usually a set amount, so the entries should be fairly straightforward. In fact, in computerized accounting systems they are typically referred to as recurring entries and can often be set up to be made automatically each month. Others, such as expenses incurred, but not paid and unearned revenues, will require some digging. You will need to look at unpaid bills, for example, to see if any are due. Or consider prepayments made on service contracts that won't finish for months.

Over time, you will develop a list or special journal of entries you commonly need to adjust, and the monthly process should become routine.

Recording Accruals

Accruals—which affect revenue and expense accounts—are among the most common adjusting entries. Unless you're using the cash method of accounting, you most likely need to record accruals at the end of the month. You will use these records to adjust the books for expenses that have been incurred but not paid and revenues that have been earned but payment is not yet due from a customer.

SEE ALSO 2.2, "Timing"

For example, if The Hobby Company has telephone charges of $150 for October but does not receive the bill until early November, an accrual must be set up as follows to recognize the expense in the October financial statements:

	Debit	Credit
10/31 Telephone Expense	$150	
Accounts Payable		$150
To accrue telephone charges for October.		

Most likely, The Hobby Company would have discovered the need for this entry by reviewing monthly expenses and noting that you hadn't paid October phone expenses. Remember, they're doing the closing after the period has ended, in November, so bills for the previous month or portions of it are starting to come in as other companies close their own books. In the interest of matching revenues and expenses, you want to record as much in the period realized or incurred as you can. In other cases, you might uncover potential accruals by going through the unpaid bill file and noting those for which payment is due.

Accrued Expenses

Accrued expenses are fairly common and usually result from one of these reasons:

- You are not yet obligated to pay an expense.
- You have not been billed for an expense.
- You have incurred a liability but not paid it for whatever reason.

Common accrued expenses include the following:

- Salaries
- Payroll taxes
- Income tax expense

For example, if Hobby incurred $1,000 in advertising services but did not receive the bill until the first week in November, they would still need to record the expense for October as follows:

	Debit	Credit
10/31 Advertising Expense	$1,000	
Accrued Advertising		$1,000
To accrue advertising expenses for October.		

When Hobby ultimately makes the payment in November, instead of debiting advertising expense—because they'd properly recognized the expense as a liability the month before—the company makes this entry:

	Debit	Credit
11/20 Accrued Advertising	$1,000	
Cash		$1,000

To record payment for October on advertising contract.

A second type of accrued expense involves assets that are converted to expenses as they're used up. Supplies, for example, often receive this treatment. If you have $600 of supplies at the beginning of the month, purchase $100, and only have $250 left at the end, you would make the following entry to adjust the balance and reflect the cost of supplies used:

	Debit	Credit
1/31 Supplies Expense	$450	
Office Supplies		$450

To record supplies used during January.

Accrued Revenue

Just as you can incur expenses that aren't yet due to be paid, you can also earn revenue for services for which your customer isn't yet required to pay. This includes unbilled revenue and interest income.

Interest charged on notes or loans accumulates monthly but you won't receive it until the debt is paid off. So if you have a note receivable from a customer with a face value of $1,200 and 10 percent interest payable in 3 months when the note is due, you'll likely be required to make an adjusting entry to record interest monthly as you earn it.

First you would need to compute the monthly interest:

Amount × Interest ÷ 12 = Monthly interest earned

$1,200 × .10 = $120 ÷ 12 = $10

At the end of the first month, you would make the following adjusting entry to record earned income not received:

	Debit	Credit
3/31 Interest Receivable	$10	
Interest Income		$10

To record interest earned on 90-day notes receivable.

Two months later when the note is due, you would record the following entry:

	Debit	Credit
5/31 Cash	$1,230	
Interest Receivable		$20
Interest Income		$10
Notes Receivable		$1,200

To record payment of note with interest.

Working with Deferrals

Deferrals are expenses or revenues incurred or earned in the current period but not recognized because they benefit future periods. Common examples are amounts prepaid in full for annual expenses like insurance or advance payments on contracts. Deferrals are set up as either assets or liabilities, with expenses and revenues recorded as they are incurred or earned, as explained in the following sections.

Deferred Expenses

Deferred expenses are sometimes called prepaid expenses because they often result from contracts for services that must be paid at the offset, but may benefit many periods in the future.

10.5

A good way to locate deferred expenses is to review any contracts or policies for which you pay an annual fee. Insurance, advertising, or rental agreements, which require payment up front, are often accounted for as deferred or prepaid expenses. Note that these amounts are classified as assets to reflect the purchase of something of value that has not yet been used. At the end of the period, the prepaid asset or deferral is credited to reflect the portion used or expired, as follows.

	Debit	Credit
10/31 Insurance Expense	$100	
Prepaid Insurance		$100
To record insurance expense for October.		

Note that some accountants also consider depreciation of fixed assets and amortization on intangibles and other types of assets a deferral. Basically, depreciation is a long-term, period-by-period recognition of asset usage. For the purposes of this book we cover depreciation in our chapter on fixed assets.

SEE ALSO 7.2, "Depreciation"

Deferred Revenue

Deferred revenue (also called deferred income) is revenue that's been received but not yet earned. For this reason, it's often called unearned revenue. Deferred revenue is recorded as a liability on the balance sheet, because the services or products for this revenue are still owed in future periods. The most common type of deferral here is a customer deposit on merchandise not yet delivered.

For example, if a company receives $1,200 in advance payment in June for a corporate training session in December, the following would need to be recorded:

	Debit	Credit
6/1 Cash	$1,200	
Unearned Income		$1,200
To record deferred income for training session.		

The purpose of making adjusting entries is to help ensure that transactions are recorded in the correct period to properly match revenues and expenses. These entries are often for accruals and out-of-period items (inventory or services received but not yet recorded and expense items generally prorated to the period end, such as wages, interest, payroll taxes, or unbilled revenues). Other adjusting entries are deferrals—prepaid expenses or advance payments for goods or services of some kind.

10.6 The Adjusted Trial Balance

Posting Adjusting Entries

Preparing the Adjusted Trial Balance

This subchapter covers the posting of adjusting entries to the general ledger and preparation of the adjusted trial balance.

Posting Adjusting Entries

Adjusting entries are recorded first in the general journal. Then they're posted to the general ledger and the adjusted balances are recalculated. The adjusted balances are then transferred to the adjusted trial balance, which becomes the basis for the financial statements.

THE HOBBY COMPANY
GENERAL JOURNAL

Date	Account #	Description	Debit	Credit
10/31	432	Telephone Expense	$150	
	210	Accounts Payable		$150
To record telephone bill charges for October.				
	440	Advertising Expense	$1,000	
	240	Accrued Liabilities		$1,000
To record advertising bill for October.				
	425	Insurance Expense	$100	
	160	Prepaid Insurance		$100
To write off expired portion of insurance.				
	505	Depreciation Expense	$1,400	
	176	Accumulated Depreciation—Building		$500
	181	Accumulated Depreciation—Machinery and Equipment		$600
	191	Accumulated Depreciation—Automotive		$300
To record depreciation expense for October.				
	410	Staff Salaries	$2,750	
	240	Accrued Liabilities		$2,750
To record accrued payroll for October.				
	401	Purchases	$1,500	
	150	Inventory		$1,500
To adjust inventory to physical.				

10.6

Going through the records, Hobby's accounts discovered they had never entered the 10/31 payroll tax payment. (September taxes are due to be deposited in the next month.) So they added this journal entry as well:

Date	Account #	Description	Debit	Credit
	415	Payroll Tax Expense	$760	
	230	FICA Taxes Withheld	$760	
	231	Federal Withholding Taxes Payable	$2,600	
	232	State Withholding Taxes Payable	$640	
	102	Cash		$4,760

To record payment of payroll taxes for September.

Following are the general ledger accounts. The initials are posting references: CR is the cash receipts journal (cash and sales journal) and sales journal, GJ is the general journal, and CD is the cash disbursements journal.

ACCT. 102   CASH IN BANK

Date	Reference	Debit	Credit	Balance
10/1	Balance			$5,080
10/31	CR	$31,310		
10/31	CD		$13,240	
10/31	GJ		$225	
10/31	GJ Adjusting Entry		$4,760	**$18,165**

ACCT. 105   PETTY CASH

Date	Reference	Debit	Credit	Balance
10/1	Balance			$200

ACCT. 130   NOTES RECEIVABLE

Date	Reference	Debit	Credit	Balance
10/1	Balance			$3,000
10/31	CR		$2,000	**$1,000**

ACCT. 140   ACCOUNTS RECEIVABLE

Date	Reference	Debit	Credit	Balance
10/1	Balance			$3,780
10/31	CR	$2,830		
10/31	CR		$3,200	**$3,410**

ACCT. 150   INVENTORY

Date	Reference	Debit	Credit	Balance
10/1	Balance			$2,510
10/31	CR	$2,940		
10/31	CD		$2,050	
10/31	GJ Adjusting Entry		$1,500	**$1,900**

ACCT. 160   PREPAID EXPENSES

Date	Reference	Debit	Credit	Balance
10/1	Balance			$2,100
10/31	GJ Adjusting Entry		$100	**$2,000**

ACCT. 170   LAND

Date	Reference	Debit	Credit	Balance
10/1	Balance			$90,000

ACCT. 175   BUILDING

Date	Reference	Debit	Credit	Balance
10/1	Balance			$60,000

ACCT. 176   ACCUMULATED DEPRECIATION – BUILDING

Date	Reference	Debit	Credit	Balance
10/1	Balance			($12,000)
10/31	GJ Adjusting Entry		$500	**($12,500)**

ACCT. 180   MACHINERY AND EQUIPMENT

Date	Reference	Debit	Credit	Balance
10/1	Balance			$25,000

ACCT. 181   ACCUMULATED DEPRECIATION—MACHINERY AND EQUIPMENT

Date	Reference	Debit	Credit	Balance
10/1	Balance			($10,000)
10/31	GJ Adjusting Entry		$600	**($10,600)**

ACCT. 185   OFFICE EQUIPMENT

Date	Reference	Debit	Credit	Balance
10/1	Balance			$4,570
10/31	CR		$1,570	$3,000*

ACCT. 186   ACCUMULATED DEPRECIATION—OFFICE EQUIPMENT

Date	Reference	Debit	Credit	Balance
10/1	Balance			($3,000)*

No balance carries forward, as assets have been sold.

ACCT. 190   AUTOMOTIVE EQUIPMENT

Date	Reference	Debit	Credit	Balance
10/1	Balance			$15,000

ACCT. 191   ACCUMULATED DEPRECIATION—AUTOMOTIVE

Date	Reference	Debit	Credit	Balance
10/1	Balance			($6,000)
10/31	GJ Adjusting Entry		$300	**($6,300)**

ACCT. 210   ACCOUNTS PAYABLE

Date	Reference	Debit	Credit	Balance
10/1	Balance			($4,960)
10/31	CD	$2,000		
10/31	GJ Adjusting Entry		$150	**($3,110)**

ACCT. 230   FICA WITHHELD

Date	Reference	Debit	Credit	Balance
10/1	Balance			($760)
10/31	CD		$760	
10/31	GJ Adjusting Entry	$760		($760)

ACCT. 231   FEDERAL INCOME TAX WITHHELD

Date	Reference	Debit	Credit	Balance
10/1	Balance			($2,600)
10/31	CD		$2,600	($5,200)
10/31	GJ Adjusting Entry	$2,600		($2,600)

ACCT. 232   STATE AND COUNTY INCOME TAX WITHHELD

Date	Reference	Debit	Credit	Balance
10/1	Balance			($640)
10/31	CD		$640	($1,280)
10/31	GJ Adjusting Entry	$640		($640)

ACCT. 240   OTHER ACCRUED LIABILITIES

Date	Reference	Debit	Credit	Balance
10/1	Balance			$0
10/31	GJ Adjusting Entry		$2,750	
10/31	GJ Adjusting Entry		$1,000	($3,750)

ACCT. 270   LONG-TERM NOTES PAYABLE

Date	Reference	Debit	Credit	Balance
10/1	Balance			($40,000)

10.6

ACCT. 290   PROPRIETOR'S CAPITAL

Date	Reference	Debit	Credit	Balance
10/1				($138,315)

ACCT. 291   PROPRIETOR'S DRAWING

Date	Reference	Debit	Credit	Balance
10/1	Balance			$5,000

ACCT. 299   PROFIT AND LOSS

Date	Reference	Debit	Credit	Balance
10/1	Balance			$0

ACCT. 301   SALES

Date	Reference	Debit	Credit	Balance
10/1	Balance			$0
10/31	CR		$27,690	($27,690)

ACCT. 310   CASH DISCOUNTS ALLOWED

Date	Reference	Debit	Credit	Balance
10/1	Balance			$0
10/31	CR	$320		$320

ACCT. 401   PURCHASES

Date	Reference	Debit	Credit	Balance
10/1	Balance			$0
10/31	CD	$2,940		
10/31	GJ Adjusting Entry	$1,500		$4,440

ACCT. 402   CASH DISCOUNTS EARNED

Date	Reference	Debit	Credit	Balance
10/1	Balance			$0
10/31	CD		$40	($40)

ACCT. 410   STAFF SALARIES

Date	Reference	Debit	Credit	Balance
10/1	Balance			$0
10/31	CD		$10,200	
10/31	GJ Adjusting Entry		$2,750	$12,950

ACCT. 415   PAYROLL TAX EXPENSE

Date	Reference	Debit	Credit	Balance
10/1	Balance			$0
10/31	GJ Adjusting Entry	$760		$760

ACCT. 420   AUTOMOTIVE EXPENSES

Date	Reference	Debit	Credit	Balance
10/1	Balance			$0
10/31	GJ	$250		$250

ACCT. 425   INSURANCE EXPENSES

Date	Reference	Debit	Credit	Balance
10/1	Balance			$0
10/31	GJ Adjusting Entry	$100		$100

ACCT. 427   RENT EXPENSE

Date	Reference	Debit	Credit	Balance
10/1	Balance			$0
10/31	CD	$1,500		$1,500

ACCT. 430   UTILITIES EXPENSE

Date	Reference	Debit	Credit	Balance
10/1	Balance			$0
10/31	CD	$720		$720

ACCT. 432   TELEPHONE EXPENSE

Date	Reference	Debit	Credit	Balance
10/1	Balance			$0
10/31	GJ	$150		$150

10.6

ACCT. 440   ADVERTISING EXPENSE

Date	Reference	Debit	Credit	Balance
10/1	Balance			$0
10/31	GJ Adjusting Entry	$1,000		$1,000

ACCT. 448 COMMISSIONS EXPENSE

Date	Reference	Debit	Credit	Balance
10/1	Balance			$0
10/31	CD	$200		$200

ACCT. 450 TRAVEL AND ENTERTAINMENT EXPENSE

Date	Reference	Debit	Credit	Balance
10/1	Balance			$0
10/31	GJ	$900		$900

ACCT. 501 OFFICE SUPPLIES AND EXPENSE

Date	Reference	Debit	Credit	Balance
10/1	Balance			$600
10/31	GJ	$100		$700

ACCT. 505 DEPRECIATION EXPENSE

Date	Reference	Debit	Credit	Balance
10/1	Balance			$0
10/31	GJ Adjusting Entry	$1,400		($1,400)

Preparing the Adjusted Trial Balance

After you've made your adjusting entries, you need to compute new balances for the affected accounts, unless you have an automated system. Sometimes it's easier to post the adjusting entries first to the trial balance, adding or subtracting to get new balances before posting to the general ledger. Either way, you need to confirm that the numbers in your adjusted trial balance add up before finalizing your general ledger.

SEE ALSO 11.3, "Preparing a Trial Balance"

To prepare the adjusted trial balance for The Hobby Company, its accountants took the adjusted account balances (bolded amounts) from the general ledger as follows:

THE HOBBY COMPANY
ADJUSTED TRIAL BALANCE
AS OF 10/31

Account Title	Account #	Debit	Credit
Cash in Bank	102	$18,165	
Petty Cash	105	$200	
Notes Receivable	130	$1,000	
Accounts Receivable	140	$3,410	
Inventory	150	$1,900	
Prepaid Expenses	160	$2,000	
Land	170	$90,000	
Building	175	$60,000	
Accumulated Depreciation—Building	176		$12,500
Machinery and Equipment	180	$25,000	
Accumulated Depreciation—Machinery and Equipment (sold 10/15)	181		$10,600
Office Equipment	185	$3,000	
Accumulated Depreciation—Office Equipment (sold 10/15)	186		$3,000
Automotive	190	$15,000	
Accumulated Depreciation—Automotive	191		$6,300
Accounts Payable	210		$3,110
FICA Withheld	230		$760
Federal Income Tax Withheld	231		$2,600
State and County Income Tax Withheld	232		$640
Other Accrued Liabilities	240		$3,750
Long-Term Notes Payable	270		$40,000
Proprietor's Capital	290		$139,075
Proprietor's Drawing	295	$5,000	
Profit and Loss	299		
Sales	301		$27,690
Cash Discounts Allowed	310	$320	
Purchases	401	$4,440	
Cash Discounts Earned	402		$40
Staff Salaries	410	$12,950	
Payroll Tax Expense	415	$760	
Automotive Expense	420	$250	

Continues

10.6

Continued

Account Title	Account #	Debit	Credit
Insurance Expenses	425	$100	
Rent Expense	427	$1,500	
Utilities Expense	430	$720	
Telephone Expense	432	$150	
Advertising Expense	440	$1,000	
Commission Expense	448	$200	
Travel and Entertainment	450	$900	
Office Supplies and Expense	501	$700	
Depreciation Expense	505	$1,400	
Totals		**$250,065**	**$250,065**

The totals for the adjusted trial balance differ from those in the original trial balance in subchapter 10.3 because of adjusting entries. The fact that the debit and credit balances still agree means the entries have been properly recorded and summarized. An entry still could have been omitted, but if the company is careful and thorough in its bookkeeping, most adjusting entries become regular monthly occurrences, reducing the chance of error.

10.7 Generating Financial Statements

The Income Statement
The Balance Sheet

The financial statements are generated from the adjusted trial balance. In this subchapter, you learn how to put it all together and generate an interim balance sheet and income statement. You'll also compute net income and transfer those earnings to the balance sheet as an increase in retained earnings.

The Income Statement

To prepare the income statement for the month, you can take the amounts directly from the adjusted trial balance, as The Hobby Company did:

THE HOBBY COMPANY INCOME STATEMENT FOR THE MONTH ENDED 10/31	
Sales	$27,690
Cash Discounts Allowed	$320
Net Sales	**$27,370**
Cost of Goods Sold	$4,400
Gross Margin	**$22,970**
Staff Salaries	$12,950
Payroll Tax Expense	$760
Automotive Expense	$250
Insurance Expense	$100
Utilities Expense	$720
Rent Expense	$1,500
Telephone Expense	$150
Advertising Expense	$1,000
Commissions	$200
Travel and Entertainment	$900
Office Supplies	$700
Depreciation	$1,400
Total Operating Expenses	**$20,630**
NET INCOME	**$2,340**

The Balance Sheet

The balance sheet is compiled with the asset and liability numbers. Note the amount in retained earnings (given a 0 balance in that account at the beginning) is equal to net income. Sometimes this calculation is done using a statement of retained earnings.

SEE ALSO 11.5, "Opening New Books"

THE HOBBY COMPANY
BALANCE SHEET
FOR THE MONTH ENDED 10/31/06

Current Assets

Cash*		$18,365
Notes Receivable		$1,000
Accounts Receivable		$3,410
Inventory		$1,900
Prepaid Expenses		$2,000
Total Current Assets		**$26,675**
Land		$90,000
Building	$60,000	
Accumulated Depreciation—Building	($12,500)	$47,500
Machinery and Equipment	$25,000	
Accumulated Depreciation—Machinery and Equipment	($10,600)	$14,400
Automotive Equipment	$15,000	
Accumulated Depreciation—Automotive	($6,300)	$8,700
Total Plant Property and Equipment		**$160,600**
TOTAL ASSETS		**$187,275**

Current Liabilities

Accounts Payable		$3,110
FICA Taxes Payable		$760
Federal Withholding Taxes Payable		$2,600
State Withholding Taxes Payable		$640
Other Accrued Liabilities		$3,750
Total Current Liabilities		**$10,860**
Long-Term Notes Payable		$40,000
Total Liabilities		**$50,860**

Owner's Equity	$139,075
Owner's Drawing	($5,000)
Retained Earnings	$2,340
TOTAL LIABILITIES AND OWNER'S EQUITY	**$187,275**

Note that cash on the balance sheet is composed of petty cash and cash in the bank. This is standard format for financial statements.

Having followed The Hobby Company through its monthly closing, you should have a pretty good idea of the steps involved. To review:

1. Close accounts and summarize transactions in various journals.

2. Post from journals to the general ledger.

3. Check to be sure general ledger totals agree with supporting documentation (subledgers for accounts receivable and accounts payable).

4. Put together a trial balance with the general ledger account totals. Don't worry if everything doesn't add up right away, because there are still adjustments to come.

5. Make adjusting entries for items like depreciation or liabilities you've incurred but not yet recorded.

6. Post those entries to the trial balance to arrive at the adjusted trial balance.

7. Check to see if adjusted trial balance adds up.

8. If it balances, post the entries to the general ledger and the adjusted trial balance numbers directly into your income statement and balance sheet.

10.7

The main difference if you have a computerized system is that your final statements or "reports" will be automatically generated from the entries you make. As a side note, you should keep a separate record of the general journal entries you make and all reconciliation reports. This will come in handy in the event you're audited or you need to review an adjustment or balance.

After that, you're done … for this month, at any rate. Now it's time to start over. In the next chapter, we look at the year-end procedures. That's when you'll officially close all your accounts and ready your books for next year.

Year-End Reporting

11.1 Year-End Closing Procedures

Steps and Timing
Reviewing and Reconciling Accounts
Summarizing to the General Ledger

This subchapter gives an overview of the process for closing your books at year-end. We discuss how to summarize financial activity for the **fiscal year,** as well as procedures you need to perform to help ensure that balances are recorded properly.

✓

A **fiscal year** is an accounting period 1 year in length. It doesn't necessarily coincide with the calendar year, although it is 12 months long.

Steps and Timing

All businesses must prepare year-end financial statements for tax preparation. Most of the work takes place in the month following your year-end month. For example, for a December year-end, you will likely complete the closing process in January.

Here are some of the main tasks involved in the year-end close:

- Closing payroll for the year and meeting governmental and reporting requirements by preparing required payroll tax returns.

- Closing out accounts and the general ledger and generating financial statements, including a statement of retained earnings and a statement of cash flows.

- Filing federal and state taxes and submitting tax payments to other agencies.

SEE ALSO 12.3, "Sales Taxes"

- Retiring old accounts.

- Preparing schedules and documentation for your outside accountant (or auditor if you work for a public company).

- Preparing **closing entries,** closing the general ledger, and opening new books for the next period.

✓

Closing entries are entries to close out revenue and expense accounts for the year and transfer any profit or losses to the balance sheet.

If your company files monthly financial statements, some of these procedures are no doubt familiar to you. Indeed, you perform many of the same tasks any time you close an accounting period, whether it's a month or a year. For the remainder of this chapter we'll explore the ways the year-end process is different.

SEE ALSO Chapter 10, "Monthly Closing Procedures"

Reviewing and Reconciling Accounts

At the end of the year you need to review and reconcile certain accounts. These include …

- *Cash.* You must reconcile the bank account and cash on your books. Remember to keep copies of these reports for your records whether you have a manual or automated system.

SEE ALSO 3.4, "Preparing a Bank Reconciliation"

- *Accounts Receivable.* Even if you don't prepare an aging schedule on a monthly basis, you need to do this at year-end to determine write-offs and/or what provision needs to be added to the allowance for doubtful accounts.

SEE ALSO 4.3, "Accounts Receivable"

- *Accounts Payable.* A review of outstanding bills at the end of the year is also recommended, for two reasons: making sure you're keeping up with payments, and confirming that all expenses are recorded in the proper period.

SEE ALSO 6.4, "Cash Disbursements"

11.1

- *Inventory.* You need to take an annual physical inventory to determine the actual quantity of inventory on hand at the end of the year. Any differences will be adjusted with an adjusting entry.

SEE ALSO 5.2, "Determining Inventory Quantity"

SEE ALSO 10.5, "Adjusting Entries"

- *Payroll.* In addition to updating employee accounts and benefits and preparing an accrual for wages and taxes incurred but not paid, employers also must file tax payments and certain reports with the government at year-end by preparing required payroll tax returns.

SEE ALSO 10.3, "Closing Employee Accounts"

SEE ALSO 12.2, "Payroll Taxes"

- *Fixed Assets*. Review any sales or additions to plant property and equipment to confirm they were properly accounted for. This includes preparing a schedule of fixed assets, which you can do automatically with most computerized accounting systems.

SEE ALSO 11.6, "Additional Reports"

If your company closes its books monthly, you'll find many year-end closing procedures are the same. Most of the major accounts—including cash, accounts receivable, inventory, and accounts payable—need to be reconciled. You'll also prepare a trial balance, record adjusting entries, and produce financial statements, ultimately closing revenue and expense accounts and transferring net income or losses to retained earnings on your balance sheet.

But different responsibilities come with the end of your fiscal year, too, such as making tax payments and preparing schedules and financial reports needed to meet federal laws for public companies or to give your accountant at tax time.

Summarizing to the General Ledger

As with a monthly or other interim period closing, you need to summarize the data from your journals—cash and sales, purchases and disbursements, and general—for posting to the general ledger. In addition, you should tally the balances in each account of your general ledger and reconcile these with your subledgers before putting together the trial balance as shown in the following diagram. This is a good way to double-check that all cash transactions have been properly recorded. With a computerized system, all these balances will have been automatically updated, but you'll still have to reconcile the accounts when you run your reports to be sure everything adds up and troubleshoot any errors.

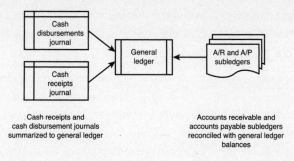

Cash receipts and
cash disbursement journals
summarized to general ledger

Accounts receivable and
accounts payable subledgers
reconciled with general ledger
balances

SEE ALSO 15.1, "Benefits of Computerized Accounting"

This diagram illustrates the information flow into the general ledger and some of its checks and balances. Totals are posted from the cash disbursements and cash sales journals to the general ledger account. At the same time, subsidiary ledgers track balances of individual A/R and A/P accounts. These balances can be compared to totals in the general ledger.

At year-end, you also need to prepare closing entries to ready the books for the next period. Some larger companies do this monthly, but yearly is more practical for most small businesses.

This diagram shows the year-end closing cycle from initial recording of transactions in the journal (1) to posting to the general ledger (2) to the trial balance (3) to adjusting entries (4) which are put on the adjusted trial balance and then (5) posted on the general ledger. Then you put the balance sheet, income statement, and statement of cash flows (6) together with the closing entries, which ready the books for the next period (7) and are posted to the general ledger.

11.1

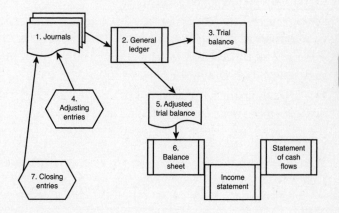

If you produce monthly financial statements: for asset and liability accounts, where the balance is updated monthly, the general ledger balances may be carried forward onto the trial balance and become the basis for the balance sheet.

For revenue and expense accounts, you can also carry the ledger balances forward onto the trial balance. If you want to produce an income statement for the year, adjusting these balances is sufficient. If you close your accounts monthly—which is more common for larger publicly owned companies—you'll have to add the profit and loss (P&L) for December to the previous 11 months to arrive at income for the year. (A computerized system will do this for you.)

If you only produce annual financial statements: Both asset and liability accounts and profit and loss account information can be summarized for the year directly from the general ledger balances. Small businesses with manual accounting systems are more likely to close accounts annually.

Whether you close accounts monthly or once a year, the information must still be summarized from transactions to journals to ledgers to financial statements. In the upcoming subchapters we take you through the year-end closing procedures step by step.

11.2 Adjusting Entries

Identifying Entries

Bad Debts

Inventory

As with other periods, when closing out the year, you need to be sure revenues and expenses are recorded in the proper period. In this subchapter, you learn how to determine the adjusting entries needed at year-end.

Identifying Entries

To identify necessary entries, you can start with the procedures we described in Chapter 10, including reviewing unpaid bills, prepayments, and depreciation schedules as well as looking back over adjusting entries you made in the past.

SEE ALSO 10.5, "Adjusting Entries"

In addition, you might find certain entries are more convenient to make only annually—adjustments to the bad debts allowance, for example, and to inventory after you've taken a physical count of what's on hand. Some companies also only record depreciation once a year.

You usually make these adjustments after running the initial trial balance. At year-end, it's sometimes helpful to make a spreadsheet showing the trial balance, adjustments, adjusted trial balance, and preliminary income statement and balance sheet all on the same page. This is known as a **trial balance worksheet.** This worksheet is useful because its format allows you to track changes in accounts. Columns for the trial balance, adjusted entries, the adjusted trial balance, balance sheet, income statement, and often the cash flow statement appear side by side, making the computations easy to follow. We've included a sample worksheet later in this chapter.

11.2

✓
_____

A **trial balance worksheet** is a schedule that allows you to take the trial balance through adjustments to the financial statements all on one page.

Bad Debts

Some companies write off bad debts monthly. Others do it only once at the end of the year. Whichever way you choose, you'll want to prepare an accounts receivable aging schedule.

SEE ALSO 4.3, "Accounts Receivable"

For example, Go Places Camping Gear, Inc., has the following accounts receivable at 12/31:

GO PLACES CAMPING GEAR, INC.
ACCOUNTS RECEIVABLE AGING SCHEDULE
DECEMBER 31

Customer	Balance 12/31	Current	31 to 60 Days	61 to 90 Days	Over 90 Days
T. Knight	$1,256	$1,256			
Peak Ventures	$5,230	$5,230			
C. Riley	$1,800		$1,800		
Scout Troop 51	$3,500	$3,500			
L. Hamm	$1,200		$700	$500	
J. Toombs	$3,920	$3,920			
P. James	$1,000				$1,000
A. Randolph	$1,550	$1,200	$350		
Totals	$19,456	$15,106	$2,850	$500	$1,000

Go Places management has recently had discussions with P. James regarding his account and received assurances it will be paid next month. Go Places won't directly write it off, but it will need to recognize bad debts expense for the year, as is its policy. It does this using the following calculation, with percentages based on past history of collectability:

Current	5%	$15,106	= $755
31 to 60 Days	6%	$2,850	= $171
61 to 90 Days	10%	$500	= $50
Over 90 Days	30%	$1,000	= $300
Total Write-Off			**= $1,276**

Many small businesses find it more efficient to simply write off individual accounts, or portions of them, when they go over 90 days. If Go Places used the direct write-off method and believes the P. James $1,000 account balance to be uncollectible, they would directly write off $1,000 to bad debts expense instead of using the allowance.

Larger companies tend to use an allowance for doubtful accounts, which is a reserve or contra account to accounts receivable. However, Go Places writes off bad debt amounts directly against accounts receivable and bad debts expense:

	Debit	Credit
12/31 Bad Debts Expense	$1,276	
Accounts Receivable		$1,276
To record bad debts expense for the year.		

If Go Places was to receive payment for a debt previously written off in another period, it would simply reverse the entry to bad debts expense or the allowance account and debit cash.

Inventory

Companies are required to take a physical count of their inventory at least once a year to verify the actual quantities in stock. Breakage, theft, and misclassification or other recording errors may result in on-hand inventory differing significantly from what's recorded on the books.

Go Camping closes its books in January and takes a physical inventory at the same time. Its physical count differed from the books by 100 units (cost each: $12), which were damaged in storage and unsellable. Go Camping made the following entry to adjust its books at year-end:

	Debit	Credit
1/5 Cost of Goods Sold	$1,200	
Inventory		$1,200
To adjust inventory as per physical count at 12/31.		

11.2

Companies with high-value inventory often keep a separate reserve for shrinkage and breakage. In that case, instead of recording any difference to cost of goods sold, it would be written off against the reserve account.

You should record adjusting entries in the general journal and post them to the general ledger from there. After you have posted all the adjusting entries, you're ready to prepare your trial balance.

11.3 Preparing a Trial Balance

Using a Trial Balance Worksheet

A Sample Trial Balance Worksheet

As with the monthly closing trial balance, the year-end trial balance is the rough draft of the financial statements for the year. In this subchapter, we show you how to prepare a worksheet that will take you from the trial balance through adjustments and onto the financial statements.

Using a Trial Balance Worksheet

When preparing financial statements, it can be very useful to have one schedule that shows the figures from the general ledger all the way through to the financial statements. This is the function of the trial balance worksheet. Although it can be used at the end of any period, it's particularly helpful at year-end as a way of summarizing the steps in the process and catching errors. Setting up a trial balance worksheet is fairly simple. Basically, it's just a way of putting every step of the summary and adjustment process onto one page.

The trial balance worksheet has several columns, with the trial balance taking up the first two-column section, followed by columns for adjustments, two columns for the adjusted trial balance, and final columns for the income statement and balance sheet. You can use either a 10- or 12-column worksheet, as shown in this partial trial balance worksheet:

GO PLACES CAMPING GEAR
TRIAL BALANCE WORKSHEET
12/31

Account	Trial Debit	Balance Credit	Adjustments Debit	Credit	Adjusted Trial Balance Debit	Credit	Income Statement Debit	Credit	Balance Sheet Debit
Cash	$500		$100		$600				$600
A/R	$400			$200	$200				$200

A Sample Trial Balance Worksheet

What follows is a trial balance worksheet prepared by Go Places Camping Gear, Inc.'s accountant at the end of the year.

GO PLACES CAMPING GEAR
TRIAL BALANCE WORKSHEET
AS OF 12/31

		Trial Balance		Adjustments		Adjusted Trial Balance		Income Statement		Balance Sheet	
		Debit	Credit	Debit	Credit	Debit	Credit	Debit	Credit	Debit	Credit
101	Cash	$5,695			(1) $55	$5,640				$5,640	
140	Accounts Receivable	$19,456			(2) $1,276	$18,180				$18,180	
150	Inventory	$12,080			(3) $1,200	$10,880				$10,880	
185	Office Equipment	$15,000				$15,000				$15,000	
186	Accumulated Depreciation: Office Equipment		$1,170		(4) $830		$2,000				$2,000
210	Accounts Payable		$1,685		(5-8) $1,635		$3,320				$3,320
240	Salaries Payable				(9) $1,870		$1,870				$1,870
290	Capital Account		$25,000				$25,000				$25,000
299	Retained Earnings		$4,649				$4,649				$4,649
301	Sales		$82,500				$82,500		$82,500		
401	Purchases (COGS)	$22,263		(3) $1,200		$23,463		$23,463			
410	Staff Salaries	$30,380		(9) $1,870		$32,250		$32,250			
421	Rent	$6,500				$6,500		$6,500			
425	Insurance	$640		(5) $200		$840		$840			
430	Utilities	$2,000		(6) $725		$2,725		$2,725			
432	Telephone	$260		(7) $540		$800		$800			
440	Advertising	$430		(8) $170		$600		$600			
460	Bad Debts Expense			(2) $1,276		$1,276		$1,276			
501	Office Supplies Expense	$300		(1) $55		$355		$355			
505	Depreciation Expense			(4) $830		$830		$830			
	Total	$115,004	$115,004	$6,866	$6,866	$119,339	$119,339	$69,639	$82,500	$49,700	$36,839
	Net Income							$12,861			$12,861
	Total							$82,500	$82,500	$49,700	$49,700

In this table, the adjusted entries are as follows (entries 5 through 8 can be done in one entry, debiting the expenses and crediting the total to accounts payable):

- Record purchase of supplies, directly written off to expense. (1)

- Bad debts expense write-off of $1,276. (2)

- Record change per physical inventory, which represents cost of goods sold. (3)

- Record depreciation expense on office equipment. (4)

- Record insurance bill—accrual; note total of entries 5 through 8 credited to accounts payable. (5)

- Record utilities bill. (6)

- Record telephone bill. (7)

- Record advertising bill. (8)

- Record accrued payroll. (9)

To prepare a trial balance worksheet, first compute the balances in the general ledger accounts and post balances to the worksheet in the Trial Balance Debit and Credit columns. Add the columns. If they don't balance—which is very common on the first try—look for errors. Be sure debits and credits are properly classified, look for transposed numbers, and so on.

Then prepare adjusting entries and put these into the appropriate Debit and Credit columns by accounts in the Adjustments section. Next, add the Adjustments Debit and Credit columns. If they balance, add to the account balances in the preliminary Trial Balance columns. Put the totals in the Adjusted Trial Balance Debit and Credit columns.

Finally, foot the Adjusted Trial Balance Debit and Credit totals. When they agree, you can take the assets and liabilities to the Balance Sheet section and the revenue and expense accounts to the Income Statement section to generate your financial statements.

By using a trial balance worksheet, you can follow transactions and adjust entries through the process because it puts all the information right in front of you. That makes it easier to trace back and forth from your financial statements if you need to, whether to make corrections or just to see how an account changed over the period.

11.4 Generating Financial Statements

The Income Statement

The Balance Sheet

The Statement of Cash Flows

In this subchapter, we look at producing statements for the year with a quick review of the balance sheet and income statement. In addition, we show you how to prepare the year-end statement of cash flows to find out how well you're managing your cash.

The Income Statement

When you've arrived at your adjusted trial balance, you're ready to compile your financial statements for the year. Here, too, the procedure is very similar to what you do if you generate monthly statements. If the totals of debits and credits in your adjusted trial balance are equal, you're ready to put together your income statement. You can do this by simply placing the numbers from your adjusted trial balance into the income statement format. Net income can be computed directly on the trial balance worksheet and carried forward to both the income statement and the balance sheet.

SEE ALSO 10.7, "Generating Financial Statements"

Using the trial balance worksheet, Go Places Camping Gear, Inc., prepared the following income statement for the year:

GO PLACES CAMPING GEAR, INC.
INCOME STATEMENT
FOR THE YEAR ENDED 12/31

Sales		$82,500
Less: Cost of Goods Sold		$23,463
Gross Profit		**$59,037**
Operating Expenses:		
Salaries	$32,250	
Rent	$6,500	
Telephone	$840	
Utilities	$2,725	
Insurance	$800	

Continues

11.4

Continued

Advertising	$600
Office Supplies	$355
Depreciation	$830
Bad Debts Expense	$1,276
Total Operating Expenses	**$46,176**
Operating Income	$12,861
Less: Income Taxes	$0
NET INCOME	**$12,861**

By taking the revenue and loss account totals directly from the adjusted trial balance and using the standard format, we are able to see Go Places Camping Gear posted net income of $12,861 for the year. Having computed net income, Go Places can now complete its balance sheet, which we show you in the next section.

The Balance Sheet

When you've completed the trial balance worksheet, you can put the numbers in the Balance Sheet column into your formal balance sheet. Remember, accumulated depreciation is classified as a contra account, not a liability, and should be deducted from plant assets in the Assets section. See, too, how net income from the trial balance worksheet is transferred to retained earnings to get the report to balance.

SEE ALSO 7.2, "Depreciation"

GO PLACES CAMPING GEAR, INC.
BALANCE SHEET
AS OF 12/31

Cash		$5,640
Accounts Receivable		$18,180
Inventory		$10,880
Total Current Assets		**$34,700**
Office Equipment	$15,000	
Less: Accumulated Depreciation	$2,000	$13,000
Total Assets		**$47,700**

Accounts Payable	$3,320
Accrued Salaries Payable	$1,870
Total Liabilities	**$5,190**
Proprietor's Equity	$25,000
Retained Earnings*	$17,510
Total Equity	**$42,510**
TOTAL LIABILITIES AND OWNER'S EQUITY	**$47,700**

Retained earnings of $4,649 + net income of $12,861

The Statement of Cash Flows

As you learned in Chapter 1, the statement of cash flows (or cash flow statement) shows how your company is using its cash and where this cash comes from. It gives you an idea of whether your business has enough cash to pay its bills and meet long-term obligations. In addition to its obvious value to you, a cash flow statement is useful to creditors, investors, customers, vendors, and others interested in the financial position of your organization.

SEE ALSO 1.1, "Accounting Basics"

Preparing a Cash Flow Statement

To put together a cash flow statement, you need to look at documentation and reports generated during the closing process for the period. You'll want to identify the sources and uses of cash, which fall into one of three categories: **operating activities, financing activities,** and **investing activities.** If you have a computerized system, this categorization will have already been done when you set up your chart of accounts, and you will be able to automatically generate a cash flow report.

✓

11.4

> **Operating activities** are those that primarily affect income, including sales and payments for products and expenses. These activities usually involve changes in current assets and liabilities.
>
> **Financing activities** involve changes in long-term liabilities and equity.
>
> **Investing activities** involve cash flows resulting from changes in investments or long-term debt.

The following table provides some examples of the different activities that fall into each category. You can use it as a reference when preparing your statement of cash flows.

Activity	Cash Inflows (Sources)	Cash Outflows (Uses)
Operating	Sales revenues Interest revenue	Pay to suppliers Tax payments Payroll Expense payments Interest payments
Investing	Sale of PP&E* Loan collections Sale of debt Sale of stock (held as investment)	Purchasing PP&E Making loans Purchase of debt
Financing	Selling own (company) stock Issuing debt	Paying dividends Redeeming one-term debt or stock shares

Remember from Chapter 7 that PP&E is property, plant, and equipment.

There are different ways to prepare a statement of cash flows for your business. We take you through a very simple illustration for Go Places Camping Gear. To do that, we need its income statement (presented earlier) and a comparative balance sheet, which shows ending balances for last year and this year.

GO PLACES CAMPING GEAR, INC.
COMPARATIVE BALANCE SHEET AS OF 12/31

	Year 2*	Year 1	Increase/(Decrease)
Cash	$5,640	$4,320	$1,320
Accounts Receivable	$18,180	$12,540	$5,640
Inventory	$10,880	$6,210	$4,670
Office Equipment	$15,000	$16,000	($1,000)
Accumulated Depreciation	($2,000)	($1,170)	($830)
Total Assets	**$47,700**	**$37,900**	**$9,800**
Accounts Payable	$3,320	$3,251	$69
Accrued Salaries Payable	$1,870	$0	$1,870
Long-Term Notes Payable	$0	$5,000	($5,000)
Total Liabilities	**$5,190**	**$8,251**	**($3,061)**
Retained Earnings	$17,510	$4,649	$12,861
Owner's Equity	$25,000	$25,000	$0
TOTAL LIABILITIES AND EQUITY	**$47,700**	**$37,900**	**$12,861**

In a real statement, the actual year would be the column heading.

The first amount you need to identify is the net increase or decrease in your cash. You can determine this by subtracting the cash balance at the beginning of the period (in this case a year) from the ending balance. We know we ended with cash of $5,640. The beginning balance was $4,320 per our comparative balance sheet. So we have a net increase of ...

$5,640 – $4,320 = $1,320

Now you must determine how much cash operations provided or used. One way of thinking of this step is that you're basically adjusting items recorded on the accrual basis to the cash basis or net income to net cash. So you'd be looking at cash actually collected on receivables, as opposed to both cash and credit sales.

For Go Places Camping Gear, the following adjustments need to be made to get net income to net cash. Again, we can pull these numbers directly from the comparative statement:

1. Increase in accounts receivable of $5,640 must be deducted.

2. Increase in inventory of $4,670 must be deducted.

3. Increase in accounts payable of $69 do not represent a cash outflow and must be added back.

4. Increase in salaries payable of $1,870 also must be added back.

Now you can determine cash generated or used by investing: a decrease in PP&E office equipment of $1,000 represents a source of cash. Next, you determine cash provided or used by financing: a decrease in long-term payables of $5,000 represents used cash.

To determine its cash flow, a company must identify the sources and uses of its cash. Because most companies record revenues and expenses on the accrual basis, certain amounts must often be adjusted to identify where cash is actually going and coming in from. In the next section, we show how these adjustments are made.

11.4

SEE ALSO 2.2, "Timing"

A Sample Cash Flow Statement

By putting these numbers into a standard format for the statement of cash flow, we come up with the following.

GO PLACES CAMPING GEAR, INC.
STATEMENT OF CASH FLOW
FOR THE YEAR ENDED DECEMBER 31

Net Cash from Operating Activities:	
Net Income	$12,861
Noncash Items Included in Income:	
Increase in Accounts Receivable	($5,640)
Increase in Inventory	($4,670)
Increase in Accounts Payable	$69
Increase in Salaries Payable	$1,870
Depreciation Expense	$830
Net Cash Flow from Operating Activities	$5,320
Cash Flow from Investing Activities:	
Sale of Office Equipment	$1,000
Net Cash Flow from Investing Activities	$1,000
Cash Flow from Financing Activities:	
Repayment of Long-Term Notes	($5,000)
Net Cash Flow Used by Financing Activities	($5,000)
Net Increase in Cash	$1,320
Cash at Beginning of Period	$4,320
Cash at End of Period	$5,640
NET INCREASE IN CASH	$1,320

Math check: if you have done your cash flow statement correctly, the net increase or decrease in cash at the end of the period should be the difference between the beginning and ending cash balances in your accounting records.

Go Places has a positive cash flow of $1,320. It earned income last year and currently has no long-term debt, which puts it in a healthy financial position. However, if it suddenly needed an infusion of cash, things could be tight, so the company should continue looking for ways to boost revenues and keep a line on expenses if it wants to grow.

11.5 Opening New Books

Closing Entries

The Profit and Loss Account

The Retained Earnings Statement

After you have completed the financial statements, only one step remains in the closing process—closing out temporary accounts and opening new books so revenues and expenses can begin accumulating again in the next period. In this subchapter, we discuss the purpose of closing entries, the accounts they affect, and how to prepare them, and how to open new books for the next period.

Closing Entries

All revenue and expense accounts are considered temporary holding accounts for activity during the period. As a result, these accounts must be closed at the end of the year so they have zero balances at the beginning of the next year. You will close them first into the **profit and loss account** and then transfer the resulting net income or loss into **retained earnings.**

✓

A **profit and loss account,** or income summary account, is the account all revenue and expense items are closed into before they become a part of retained earnings.

Retained earnings is the permanent balance sheet account used to reflect income and losses from each year since the business began. It's a part of owner's equity.

The Profit and Loss Account

11.5

To close out revenue and expense accounts, you must first transfer their balances into the profit and loss account. This is a matter of debiting revenue balances and crediting expense balances, as shown in the following journal entries for Go Places Camping Gear, Inc.

	Debit	Credit
12/31 Sales	$82,500	
Profit and Loss		$82,500
To close out sales account.		
Profit and Loss	$23,463	
Cost of Goods Sold		$23,463
To close cost of goods sold.		
Profit and Loss	$46,176	
Salaries		$32,250
Rent		$6,500
Telephone		$840
Utilities		$2,725
Insurance		$800
Advertising		$600
Office Supplies		$355
Depreciation		$830
Bad Debts Expense		$1,276
To close expense accounts for the year.		

These entries are usually combined into one entry, wherein the net difference is debited or credited to the profit and loss account. This would result in the same debits to sales and credits to cost of goods sold and individual expense accounts. The difference of $12,861 would be credited to profit and loss account 299.

Following the entry, the profit and loss account in the general ledger appears as follows:

ACCT. 299   PROFIT AND LOSS

Date	Reference	Debit	Credit	Balance
1/1	Balance			$0
12/31	Sales		$82,500	
12/31	Cost of Goods Sold	$23,463		
12/31	Operating Expenses	$46,176		$12,861

The next step is to transfer the balance in the profit and loss account to retained earnings. In some small businesses the profit and loss account is closed directly into the capital account. In the case of Go Places Camping Gear, the company closes accounts by transferring the profit and loss account balance to retained earnings.

	Debit	Credit
12/31 Profit and Loss Account	$12,861	
Retained Earnings		$12,861
To record net income for the year.		

It's worth noting here that most computerized accounting systems automatically adjust your income and expense accounts and post the net income to retained earnings. At the start of your new fiscal year, the retained earnings balance increases by the net income on your year-end balance sheet.

SEE ALSO 15.4, "Converting to an Automated System"

The Retained Earnings Statement

All public companies are required to prepare a retained earnings statement. The purpose of this statement is to show changes in this account during the year. These typically include the following:

- Net income or loss
- **Prior period adjustments** for errors that resulted in over- or understatements of income
- Dividend distributions to shareholders

✓

Prior period adjustments are adjustments for errors in past financial statements that must be corrected in current reports.

Retained earnings statements are also useful for closely tracking the entry of net income on the balance sheet. For example, assume Go Places had miscalculated cost of goods sold in the previous year. At the end of the current year, it would record the following correcting entry and retained earnings statement:

	Debit	Credit
12/31 Retained Earnings	$1,009	
Inventory		$1,009

To correct overstated income for previous year.

GO PLACES CAMPING GEAR
RETAINED EARNINGS STATEMENT
FOR THE YEAR ENDED 12/31/12

Balance 1/1/12, as Reported	$4,649
Correction: Overstatement of Net Income Due to COGS Error	($1,009)
Adjusted Balance, 1/1/12	$3,640
Add: Net Income (for Y/E 12/31/12)	$12,861
Less: Dividends	$0
Balance, 12/31/12	**$16,501**

After you've completed the retained earnings statement, you can adjust the balance in retained earnings on your company's balance sheet. If this were an actual error, Go Places would have to reduce inventory by $1,009 to $9,871 and retained earnings to $16,501 as noted.

After you've closed revenue and expense accounts for the year, you can transfer their balances into a profit and loss account. This account is then folded in retained earnings—an equity account on the balance sheet. Sometimes retained earnings may need to be adjusted with corrections or adjustments from the prior period. When this is done, its balance goes into the retained earnings general ledger account and the balance sheet.

11.6 Additional Reports

Summaries and Schedules

Other Documentation

In addition to the statements covered already in this subchapter, there are additional reports you might prepare at year-end. Some of these schedules assist you in analyzing accounts and performance; others help you get a jump on tax season. Here we list some of these documents and show you how to put them together.

Summaries and Schedules

Other useful reports focus on activity in particular areas and accounts. For public companies, some of these, such as the schedule of fixed assets or schedule of operating expenses, are included as part of the financial reports. If you have an outside accountant coming in or just want to better analyze your results, these additional schedules can be useful.

The Schedule of Fixed Asset Acquisitions

This schedule tracks additions to fixed assets to be sure costs are properly accumulated and monitored. A typical fixed asset schedule could look like the following:

GO PLACES CAMPING GEAR	
SCHEDULE OF FIXED ASSETS	
12/31	
Office Equipment	
Balance at 1/01	$16,000
Acquisitions:	
Disposition: 1/31/01	($1,000)
Balance at 12/31	$15,000
Accumulated Depreciation	
Balance at 1/01	($1,170)
Add: Depreciation Expense: 12/31	$830
Balance at 12/31	$2,000
Office Equipment Book Value: 12/31	$13,000

11.6

The schedule of fixed asset acquisitions can be used to check for proper asset valuation and calculation of depreciation. In addition, reviewing plant, property, and equipment can help you plan for upcoming repair and replacement costs.

SEE ALSO 7.1, "Property, Plant, and Equipment"

SEE ALSO 7.2, "Depreciation"

SEE ALSO 7.3, "Disposal of Fixed Assets"

The Schedule of Operating Expenses

This report provides a quick snapshot of a company's expenses. It's typically put together using annual expenses by type. Sometimes these are compared to prior periods. A schedule of operating expenses for Go Places appears as follows:

GO PLACES CAMPING GEAR SCHEDULE OF OPERATING EXPENSES 12/31	
Salaries	$32,250
Rent Expense	$6,500
Telephone Expense	$840
Utilities Expense	$2,725
Insurance Expense	$800
Advertising Expense	$600
Office Supplies Expense	$355
Depreciation	$830
Bad Debts Expense	$1,276
Total Operating Expenses	**$46,176**

You can also prepare this schedule as a comparative between years or between specific months of different years. The schedule of operating expenses is useful in computing taxes as well.

The Expense Report Summary

This document—again particularly useful for tax purposes—allows you to quickly analyze staff expenses. It can be done in a macro sense month by month for the company as a whole. You can also run expense report summaries that list expenses by account for each employee to get an idea if anyone's expenses are unusual or seem out of line compared to others.

GO PLACES CAMPING GEAR
EXPENSE REPORT SUMMARY—JUNE

Account	T. Rush	T. Lee	R. Aco	Total
Office Supplies	$150	$240		$390
Travel and Entertainment	$650		$1,500	$2,150
Automotive		$700		$700

Other Documentation

In this section, we cover some other useful reports you may have already prepared in the past. They're listed with references to the appropriate chapter, so you can find them easily.

Bank Reconciliation

Bank reconciliation does what it sounds like: brings your bank balance and your book balance in line. It's usually prepared monthly, so errors can be caught quickly. Auditors sometimes review previous reconciliations to check for unusual items or errors and verify that account activity is normal.

SEE ALSO 2.4, "Recording in Journals"

SEE ALSO 3.4, "Preparing a Bank Reconciliation"

The Accounts Payable Schedule

The accounts payable schedule lists payables by due date and can be used to evaluate how efficiently bills are being paid. It is also useful for confirmation requests.

SEE ALSO 6.2, "Accounting for Purchases"

11.6

Aging of Accounts Receivable

The accounts receivable aging schedule is prepared more frequently in big companies, where it's usually used to evaluate collections.

SEE ALSO 4.3, "Accounts Receivable"

Special Circumstances

This catchall category includes discontinued operations—such as losses or gains from dumping a product line or selling an unprofitable division. Also here are extraordinary items, which are material one-time items that are both unusual and unlikely to reoccur. In this case, *material* means big enough to matter—like the write-off of inventory after a major earthquake.

Tax Records

There's no time like after year-end to get the necessary records safely in a pile for tax time. In addition to receipts, invoices, and the like, you'll need tax forms and details of itemized deductions and a schedule or list of charitable contributions.

SEE ALSO 12.1, "Advanced Planning"

Closing your books at year-end needn't be that difficult if you follow the appropriate steps. You summarize transactions to journals and make any necessary adjustments to the general ledger. Accounts must be reconciled and balanced and financial statements generated, including the balance sheet, income statement, and cash flow statement. When this is complete, you can close revenue and expense accounts and prepare your books for business in the next period.

In addition, you'll want to ready yourself for tax season, gathering records and putting together schedules for items such as expenses and charitable contributions, so you won't have to scurry around at the last minute.

Taxes

12.1 Advanced Planning

What You Should Know

Where to Look

Where taxes are concerned, you'll find a little advanced planning goes a long way. In this subchapter, we tell you what you should know about taxes—even before you open up for business—and where to go to get the information.

What You Should Know

Anyone starting a business will quickly learn that they are required to pay taxes to a multitude of government agencies—and not just on income. Depending on the nature of your business you may also be responsible for payroll taxes, property taxes, sales taxes, and even excise taxes. What's more, the rules and regulations pertaining to these taxes are complex and unforgiving.

Few small businesses owners—particularly new ones—are prepared for the task of accumulating accurate information to pay and file these necessary returns. As a result, things slip through the cracks. You file a payment late or forget it completely. Your business is required to pay substantial penalties, not to mention the hours you'll have to spend going back and forth with governmental agencies trying to redress errors, omissions, and other problems.

That's why we can't emphasize it enough: Get educated first. Your simplest and most inexpensive solution to tax compliance is to acquaint yourself with the various tax requirements—*before* you begin operating the business. Because where taxes are concerned, ignorance is not an excuse.

As you can see in the following chart, you'll likely be filing more than a dozen tax returns to various agencies throughout the year:

TAX FILINGS

Agency	Type of Tax
IRS (irs.gov)	Federal income taxes
	Federal employee withholding
	FUTA taxes
	Excise taxes
	Self-employment tax
Social Security Administration (ssa.gov)	FICA
	Medicare

Agency	Type of Tax
State ([name of state].gov)	State income taxes State employee withholding SUTA taxes Sales taxes Business property taxes
Local Government County/City/Municipality (website can often be referenced from state or county site)	City or county income taxes Sales taxes

If this already seems like too much of a headache, talk with a good tax accountant. And be sure you have a thorough record-keeping system, so if nothing else, you'll be collecting the right data to sort out later.

Where to Look

The best sources for basic tax information and requirements are the websites of the government agencies responsible for collecting the taxes. For example, the IRS's website, irs.gov, has an excellent presentation of what's required of a new business, as well as a list of forms and publications you can download. Reviewing the forms you need to file can give you a heads-up on what kind of information you'll need to track for your return.

In addition, a copy of Circular E, Employer's Tax Guide, is available on the IRS website. This publication is required reading for a business owner and a handy tool for employment taxes. So if you weren't provided with a copy when you applied for a federal identification number, be sure to print one out and become familiar with the requirements.

You can find state taxing authorities through an internet search or at _____. gov—inserting your state's abbreviation in blank space. These sites provide specific information on state employment taxes, sales taxes, state income taxes, and the like, and often also have available the various forms you'll need to file. We cannot overemphasize the importance of researching these issues in advance. The following are good places to start for some specific tax types:

Payroll. Requirements for federal taxes, including FICA, Medicare, and FUTA, are spelled out in detail on irs.gov. Circular E and state websites have information on state payroll taxes.

Self-Employment. Requirements and details for making quarterly estimated tax payments are spelled out in form 1040-ES, which can also be found on the irs.gov website.

Sales. Look to your state, county, and local websites, since some locations are required to collect sales taxes for the state as well as the county and city. Invest in a handbook which summarizes sales tax requirements.

Business Personal Property. Details are usually summarized on the state website, which outlines how these taxes should be reported and paid.

Excise. Check out irs.gov, publication 510, for explanation of taxes or duties that must be paid on certain products such as fuel or in particular industries.

Income. These taxes are generally based on net income of the enterprise, adjusted by various governmental provisions. Federal and state governments publish a summary of these rules and regulations, which can be obtained directly or from irs.gov or your state government website.

Reporting and payment is required monthly, quarterly, or annually, depending on the particular tax, which we explain as the chapter develops.

You can usually find a good tax accountant by word of mouth or by asking vendors or other businesspeople you know. Most will be quite forthcoming with their recommendations, both good and bad. Generally speaking, you should look for a Certified Public Accountant (CPA), because of educational, experience, and business requirements—preferably one who has experience with a business your size. When you've found an accountant or firm you are comfortable with, have them provide a rough estimate of the services to be provided, costs and hourly rates, anticipated schedules, and delivery terms.

If you still decide to go it alone, keep in mind that the responsibility for sales, marketing, human resources, customer relations, and business development will also exert considerable demands on your time.

12.2 Payroll Taxes

Getting Organized

Required Withholdings

Required Tax Deposits

This subchapter is devoted to payroll taxes. Businesses must deduct a number of taxes from employee paychecks, including federal and state tax withholding as well as Social Security and Medicare. In addition, employers must make regular tax deposits and file returns. We provide guidance on what taxes you need to file and when.

Getting Organized

Employers find out in a hurry that the responsibilities of tax withholding, reporting, paying, and tax return preparation is a significant task with many potential dangers. First and foremost, you must have adequate records, and payroll checks drawn should be entered into a cash disbursements journal.

SEE ALSO 6.4, "Cash Disbursements"

As we noted in Chapter 8 during our discussion of payroll, you are also required to maintain individual earnings records for each employee. These records, which serve as the basis for computing taxable wages, include the information as shown in the following abbreviated employee earnings record. They also provide the data necessary to compute payroll deposits as well as required payroll tax returns and W-2s at calendar year-end.

EMPLOYEE EARNINGS RECORD

Name: <u>Larry Adams</u>　　　　　　　Social Security #: <u>305-44-5903</u>

Address: <u>1416 Cove Lane, Laguna Niguel, CA 92677</u>

Phone: <u>714-456-7891</u> Date of Birth: <u>11/13/71</u> No. Exemptions: 1

12.2

Pay Period Ending	Date Paid	Total Regular Hours	Over-time	Pay Rate	Total Pay	Social Security	Medi-care	Federal Income Tax	State Income Tax	Net Pay
2/1	2/4	40		$10	$400	$24.80	$5.80	$30	$9	$330.40
2/15	2/18	40		$10	$400	$24.80	$5.80	$30	$9	$330.40

At the end of the quarter, the totals from these columns for each employee can be used to complete the quarterly payroll tax filings. At the end of the year, completed employee earnings records are the basis for generating the W-2 report of employee earnings for the year.

Computerized systems not only keep employee earnings reports, but automatically generate the W-2.

Required Withholdings

As an employer, you must withhold several payroll taxes from employee paychecks and remit the monies to the respective government authority. These include FICA taxes (Social Security and Medicare) and federal and state withholding.

SEE ALSO 8.3, "Making Payroll Deductions"

SEE ALSO 8.4, "Employer Payroll Taxes"

Social Security Tax

For Social Security, you must withhold a percentage of the gross wages (Pay rate × Hours worked) up to a certain dollar amount. Wages in excess of that amount are not taxable for Social Security. At the time of this writing, employers are once again required to withhold 6.2 percent (up from 4.2 percent in 2011) of the gross wages on the first $110,100 earned for the calendar year. However, this wage base is periodically adjusted and an extension of the 4.2 percent rate is possible, so check the Social Security Administration website (ssa.gov) for current provisions. In addition, employers must pay a like amount out of their own pockets to match this tax.

Medicare Tax

For Medicare, you withhold 1.45 percent of the gross wages. Unlike Social Security taxes, there is no wage limit for taxability. This means all wages are taxable for Medicare. For simplicity, many businesses classify Medicare and Social Security together in a single account such as payroll taxes or FICA taxes. As with Social Security, employers must match this tax.

SEE ALSO 8.4, "Employer Payroll Taxes"

Federal Income Taxes

For federal income taxes, you withhold income taxes based upon the tables provided in Circular E, Employer's Tax Guide, on the IRS website. There you'll find tables that reflect various wages, pay periods, and exemptions.

Required Tax Deposits

Employers are required to make periodic tax deposits for Social Security, Medicare, and federal withholding taxes. In some cases, state deposits may be required as well.

Computing Tax Deposits

The requirements for timely tax deposits are rather complex, because they're based on various expected minimum amounts. Monthly deposits are required if the total tax deposits for the year (or deposits for the prior year) are $50,000 or less. The total deposit required for the month would be computed as follows:

Total Federal Income Tax Withheld (1)	$_____
Total Social Security Tax Withheld (2)	$_____
Total Medicare Tax Withheld (3)	$_____
Employer's Share of Social Security and Medicare Tax Withheld (2 + 3)	$_____
Total Tax Deposit Required	$_____

All federal tax deposits (including payroll, excise, and corporate income taxes) must be made electronically. Coupons and bank deposits, which were used prior to January 1, 2011, are no longer allowed. The easiest way to make these deposits is by using the U.S. Treasury's **Electronic Federal Tax Payment System (EFTPS).** Go to eftps.com to set up an account. Typically, the electronic funds transfer of your tax deposit must be before 8 P.M. by the fifteenth day of the month following the month for which the deposits were calculated. If the fifteenth falls on a nonbanking day, the deposit may be made on the next business day.

12.2

Semimonthly deposits are required if the total tax deposits for the year (or actual for the previous year) are $50,000 or more. The computation for the deposit is the same as for monthly deposits. However, the due date of the deposits is on the following Wednesday for paydays falling on a Wednesday, Thursday, or Friday, and on the following Friday for paydays falling on Sunday, Monday, or Tuesday.

Accumulation of $100,000 or more of taxes on any day during a deposit period must be deposited by the next banking day.

Failure to file electronically when required to do so incurs a penalty of 10 percent. Deposits not made on time will also incur an **automatic penalty,** so be sure to set up your funds transfer in a timely fashion.

✓
_____

The **Electronic Federal Tax Payment System (EFTPS)** is a free automated system for paying tax deposits which is provided by the U.S. Treasury.

An **automatic penalty** is an irrevocable fine levied by the IRS on an employer the instant a violation occurs.

SEE ALSO 1.4, "Establishing the Chart of Accounts"

SEE ALSO 8.1, "Setting Up Payroll"

Filing Tax Deposits

Following are the requirements for and timing of tax returns for payroll taxes:

Form 941. Filed quarterly, this form reflects total gross and taxable wages for the quarter, computation of total employment taxes, deposits made and liability, if any, at the end of the quarter. This return is due on the last day of the following month.

State withholding taxes. These are amounts withheld on gross wages at rates required by the state. Deposit requirements vary by state. Quarterly returns are also required.

Unemployment taxes—state. These vary by state, but generally are based upon a limited amount of taxable wages. Returns are required quarterly, due by the twentieth of the following month.

Unemployment taxes—federal (Form 940). The federal portion of unemployment taxes (6.2 percent) is computed on taxable wages (limited to $7,000) with a credit of 5.4 percent allowed for tax paid to the state. The net effect is a .8 percent tax on the first $7,000 wages paid to each employee. Form 940 is an annual return due on January 31 for the preceding calendar year. If your FUTA tax liability is $500 or less, you do not have to make a deposit. When the tax is cumulatively $500 or more, a deposit is required.

SEE ALSO 8.3, "Making Payroll Deductions"

Form W-2. Filing of this form is required annually on or before February 28. Copies are to be sent to employee, the IRS, the state, and the Social Security Administration.

Payroll taxes can be complex. Businesses must deduct a number of taxes from employee wages in addition to paying a few themselves. Employers are required to withhold federal and state income taxes, Social Security, Medicare, and sometimes disability. Businesses must match Social Security and Medicare with their own payments and pay federal unemployment insurance contributions, as well.

Because of the time and headaches involved, many companies opt to use an outside payroll service. Most computerized systems also make tax payments and file returns automatically. Whether you choose one of these options or manage your payroll taxes on your own, it's important to stay on top of them, as penalties for noncompliance or missing deadlines can be steep.

SEE ALSO 8.1, "Setting Up Payroll"

12.2

12.3 Sales Taxes

Sales Tax Rates

Sales Tax Collection

Paying and Recording Sales Tax

In this subchapter, we cover the ins and outs of sales tax, including finding rates, how to compute it, and where and when to pay.

Sales Tax Rates

Taxability and tax rates vary by state. For a quick look at current sales tax rates, go to the Federation of Tax Administrators (FTA) website at taxadmin.org for a listing by state. Income and other state tax rates are included here as well. You can also check your state's website for specifics.

Your state will specify what's taxable and what's exempt. You'll usually get a tax number when you register for a business license or permit with your state. Even if you don't sell products or merchandise, you still might be on the hook for sales tax, as some states levy a tax on services.

Generally, state forms and payments are required monthly or quarterly if amounts collected are below certain dollar limits. Be sure to find out what's taxable so you can charge and collect from customers on sales of covered products or services. Otherwise, you could end up paying the entire tax yourself.

Sales Tax Collection

Collection of sales taxes is typically the responsibility of the seller or purveyor of taxable services. In most states, you compute sales tax on the entire sales price. Additional add-on costs such as freight may not be included.

Computing Sales Tax

Because a sales tax must be computed on each individual sale, many retailers set up computer sales systems or cash registers to automatically record the tax. Most states require that sales tax be listed on the individual receipt as proof that it was not included in the sales price, so however you can streamline the system will make your work easier for you.

Generally, the computation of the tax will be the sales price multiplied by the tax rate, but in some states, a separate tax might be levied on certain items only.

You can also have city or county sales taxes, be required to pay taxes on transportation or fuel, or pay taxes for other special purposes. Be sure to check with your state.

About half of the states also give businesses a credit for collecting the tax, so this is definitely something you want to look into.

Sales Tax Exemptions

Certain necessities such as food, grocery items, and medicines are exempt from taxation. Other sales transactions that are usually not taxable include the following:

Selling merchandise for resale. If you manufacture and sell dresses to a retailer, you don't have to pay tax because the retailer collects taxes when he or she sells the dresses to the consumer.

One-off or occasional sales. This is if you're not in the business of selling and have a garage sale, for example. Requirements are usually that total goods sold for the year be below a certain dollar amount.

Goods sold to out-of-state buyers. Although there is movement afoot to change this with the explosion in internet commerce, currently many states have a use tax that is supposed to help compensate for lost tax revenue. This is self-reported and paid by the purchaser.

Goods sold to the government or for use in certain industries, such as farming. Or for purchases having a sales tax exemption certificate.

If this all seems like too much to keep up with, you might want to consider using an outside service to handle this for you—many do. It's also worth looking into some of the software packages available such as QuickBooks or Sage Peachtree Accounting to help you sort out state taxes. Typically, automated systems will compute sales tax payments *and* generate checks for the amount you owe. Some programs even automatically make payments.

SEE ALSO 15.2, "Evaluating Computerized Systems"

12.3

Paying and Recording Sales Tax

As we noted earlier in this subchapter, sales tax payment requirements vary by state. Monthly and quarterly payments are not uncommon, nor is paying taxes to more than one entity, as city and county governments often require you to remit them separately. You'll have to obtain your state's forms to see what you'll need, but most states want you to report gross sales, the tax rate, and taxes collected. When you enter your daily sales in the sales journal, you can also enter taxes collected.

SEE ALSO 4.2, "Adjusting and Summarizing Sales"

At the end of the month when you run the journal totals, you can post the taxes in the general ledger:

		Debit	Credit
12/31	Accounts Receivable	$3,108	
	Cash	$1,638	
	Sales		$4,520
	Sales Tax Collected		$226
To record monthly sales.			

When you remit the taxes to the state, you would make this entry:

		Debit	Credit
12/31	Sales Tax Collected	$226	
	Cash		$226
To record payment of sales tax.			

Sales taxes vary by state, as do reporting requirements. Even after you've determined the rates for state(s) in which you do business, you'll need to check what items are taxed, because there are often exemptions. In addition, depending on where you're located, you may be subject to county and city taxes.

When you've nailed down your obligations, it's important to keep good records. The IRS prefers to see receipts that separate sales price and tax and journals that classify sales tax and sales to separate accounts.

12.4 Income Taxes

Income Tax Basics

Sole Proprietor Taxes

Partnership Taxes

Corporation Taxes

Excise Taxes

This subchapter provides an outline of filing requirements for income taxes for different types of business. Because how you file varies by entity, we touch on sole proprietorships, partnerships, and corporations in the following sections.

Income Tax Basics

With the tax code as complex and constantly changing as it is, we can't possibly do more than scratch the surface in talking about taxes in one short chapter. We will, however, lay out some of the basics, so that even if you're turning everything over to an accountant, you'll have a general understanding of the subject.

The type of tax return you file depends on your company's business entity. If you're a sole proprietor or have a partnership, your income is still going to pass through and be reported on your personal income tax form. Corporations, with the exception of S corporation shareholders, pay income taxes as an entity. We explain the filing requirements for each of these entities in separate sections.

SEE ALSO 1.2, "Determining a Form of Entity"

Sole Proprietor Taxes

One of the benefits of being a sole proprietor is that you don't have to prepare a separate tax return for your business. Instead, your business income is reported on your personal income tax return.

Tax Forms

Usually, sole proprietors can file their taxes using Form 1040. You'll have to attach a Schedule C, the Profit and Loss from a Business form, on which you'll list the income and expenses of the business. During the year, you'll also need to file a Form 1040-ES to pay estimated taxes so you won't face penalties. It's more or less the sole proprietor version of federal withholding. The Form 1040-ES is filed quarterly.

12.4

Special Considerations

At tax time, you want to make a final check to ensure that you've included all business deductions and expenses. Make any of these adjustments before you file your tax return, as your filing requirements remain the same in terms of deadlines and extensions.

As a sole proprietor, you also need to pay self-employment taxes if your business profit totaled more than $400. This SECA (Self-Employment Contributions Act) tax is essentially the self-employed person's version of Social Security and Medicare tax, only double the FICA rate at 15.3 percent, because you're paying both the employer and employee portions. You can compute and file it using a Form SE from the IRS website.

Partnership Taxes

If you're a partner in a business, you report your income on your personal return. But first, you need to complete Form 1065, U.S. Partnership Return of Income, an informational return filed annually. Each of the partners should receive a copy of Schedule K-1, which essentially lists their individual shares of income.

The partnership entity doesn't pay taxes, so your income passes through to your own 1040. As a partner, you also need to add a Schedule E, Supplemental Income and Loss, to report the information from your K-1. Like sole proprietors, you are required to pay estimated taxes (Form 1040-ES) and self-employment taxes (Form SE).

Corporation Taxes

Corporations need to file a corporate tax return, Form 1120 or for Subchapter S Corporations Form 1120-S. (Download these forms and extensive instructions from the IRS website.) Corporations are also responsible for paying estimated taxes. The deadline for filing for the year is March 16—1 month before the individual deadline of April 16. An exception can be made if the corporation has a different fiscal year.

For tax purposes, a limited liability company (LLC) with more than one member is treated as a partnership, and member income also flows through to the personal return. Corporate shareholders who get a salary need to report this income (from a W-2) on their personal return.

Corporations also pay estimated taxes. As with individuals, corporations must remit these amounts four times a year. For corporations, this is typically on the fifteenth day of April, June, September, and December. For more detailed information and forms, visit irs.gov.

Excise Taxes

In addition to income taxes, some corporations are also subject to **excise taxes,** which are special taxes levied on certain businesses including communications and air transport; retailing; manufacturing; businesses owning and using heavy trucks, trailers, or tractors; and those producing chemicals that deplete ozone. There are a number of different excise taxes, targeting everything from using or mixing certain fuels, to environmental pollution, to the manufacturer of bows and arrowheads. Excise taxes are paid semimonthly using Form 720, however there are various schedules for certain types of taxes and/or credits. For more information, look up the most recent Publication 510 on the IRS website.

✓

Excise taxes are special taxes the government levies on certain businesses.

The type of income tax return you file depends on your business entity. Sole proprietor's report business income on their individual returns. Partnerships must file a special informational return and schedule K-1 but also report income on individual 1040s. Corporations report income separately on Form 1120, although LLC Corporation members' income flows through to their personal return.

Companies in certain industries such as air transport, communications, or those affecting the environment also face excise taxes, so it's important to check the rules to see if your business is responsible for any of these taxes as well.

12.4

12.5 Record Retention

Payroll Taxes

Sales Taxes

Income Taxes

Filing your taxes on time is only half the battle. This subchapter looks at the importance of retaining tax records in case of audits and lets you know how long you should hold on to what kinds of documents.

Payroll Taxes

Payroll records to keep include employee earnings reports, payroll registers, and check registers. Included in this information, you should have:

- Amounts of wages and pension payments
- Amount of employee tips
- Documentation of absence or sick pay
- W-2 forms returned as undeliverable
- W-4 forms
- Tax deposit forms and confirmation numbers from federal depository
- Details of fringe benefits

You are required to keep payroll records longer than most accounting records—a minimum of 6 years.

Sales Taxes

When paying sales taxes, keep copies of all tax filings, sales invoices, sales registers, and receipts listing tax collected. In addition, keep a copy of the check remitting the balance to the tax authorities as proof of payment. Keep these sales tax records for 3 years. For example, a company might keep a detailed monthly summary of daily receipts, separating the sales and sales tax. A partial summary for The Design Company is shown here:

THE DESIGN COMPANY
MONTHLY SUMMARY OF CASH RECEIPTS

YEAR: _____   MONTH: FEBRUARY

Day	Net Sales	Sales Tax	Daily Receipts	Deposit
1	$200	$10	$210	
2	$150	$6	$156	$366
4	$220	$11	$231	
6	$260	$13	$273	
7	$180	$9	$189	$693
10	$200	$10	$210	
11	$140	$7	$147	
13	$110	$5.50	$115.50	$472.50
15	$100	$5	$105	
16	$150	$6	$156	$261
22	$180	$9	$189	
26	$250	$12.50	$262.50	
27	$140	$7	$147	$598.50
Total	$2,280	$111	$2,391	$2,391

This schedule tracks both sales taxes and actual deposits, supported by deposit slips and individual sales receipts. Total sales and sales taxes would correspond to the credit to these accounts for the month of February. The monthly summary also clearly separates the portion of total deposits that are sales revenue and the portion that is to be remitted as sales tax (a 5 percent rate).

The important thing to remember in keeping track of sales taxes is to have adequate support for purchase price and revenues collected to avoid questions about underpayment of taxes.

Income Taxes

Keep files by year with documents supporting major expenses and purchases, sales invoices, fixed asset purchases, bank reconciliations, and financial statements—any documents supporting the computation of income.

12.5

The IRS has 3 years from the due date to audit returns, so you should keep records going back at least that far. The IRS can extend that limit under certain circumstances though, so we recommend you keep supporting documents at least 7 years and retain your tax returns permanently. Records for fixed assets should also be kept longer because these are long-term assets you expect to hang onto for awhile. Fixed asset records should include documentation supporting when the asset was acquired, the purchase price, how the asset is used in the business, and any supporting documentation (invoices, etc.) for additions or improvements made to the asset. If you're using accounting software, the same rules apply. You should keep back up copies of transactions and supporting documentation for the same length of time.

Although this may seem like a lot of paper to keep track of, remember the cost of unsupported income or transactions will be even higher if the IRS comes to call. When in doubt, don't throw it out.

The most important aspect of this chapter is that you must acquaint yourself with federal and state requirements for taxes. The penalties could be overwhelming, and you could be personally liable for nonpayment of federal payroll taxes, regardless of the form of your entity.

13

Analyzing Financial Results

13.1 Analysis Methods

Looking at Previous Periods

Other Comparisons

Ratio Analysis

Automating the Process

Limitations of Financial Analysis

You've completed the financial statements for your company; now it's time to take a deeper look at what the numbers mean. In this subchapter, we provide an overview of financial analysis and show you how to use it.

SEE ALSO 2.3, "Analyzing Transactions"

Looking at Previous Periods

Comparing data to a prior period—often called **trend analysis** or **comparative analysis**—is one way to put your company's financials into perspective. In comparative analysis, you're looking at the financial statements of the current period and at least one prior period and evaluating any significant or unusual increases or decreases. It's useful to look at changes in both amounts and percentages. Although larger companies may have the resources to do this quarterly or even monthly, if you can do it annually, you'll be in good shape.

√

Trend analysis looks at financial reports going back at least 5 years and sometimes as much as 10 or 20 years to identify what the trends are in operating data.

Comparative analysis involves comparing financial statements account by account to previous years to identify and explain any significant changes.

With trend analysis, you're usually comparing financial statements over a longer period of time—say 5 years at least. The goal here is to get a sense for the larger trends in performance. Are sales going up? Are expenses being held in line? Are receivable collections slowing?

Following is an example of comparative analysis for Star Shore and Company. Both the balance sheet and the income statement are compared with the previous year to gauge performance.

SEE ALSO 11.4, "Generating Financial Statements"

STAR SHORE AND COMPANY
COMPARATIVE BALANCE SHEETS DECEMBER 31

	Year 2	Year 1	Increase or (Decrease) During Current Year (Year 2)	Percent Increase or (Decrease)
Cash	$8,600	$7,500	$1,100	15%
Accounts Receivable	$12,800	$17,500	–$4,700	–27%
Inventory	$12,000	$10,000	$2,000	20%
Prepaid Assets	$4,500	$5,000	–$500	–10%
Total Current Assets	**$37,900**	**$40,000**	**–$2,100**	**–5%**
Property, Plant, and Equipment (Net of Accumulated Depreciation)	$13,500	$15,000	–$1,500	–10%
Total Assets	**$51,400**	**$55,000**	**–$3,600**	**–7%**
Accounts Payable	$6,900	$11,500	–$4,600	–40%
Long-Term Liabilities	$10,000	$12,000	–$2,000	–17%
Total Liabilities	**$16,900**	**$23,500**	**–$6,600**	**–28%**
Owner's Equity	$34,500	$31,500	$3,000	10%
TOTAL LIABILITIES AND OWNER'S EQUITY	**$51,400**	**$55,000**	**–$3,600**	**–7%**

STAR SHORE AND COMPANY COMPARATIVE
INCOME STATEMENTS FOR THE PERIOD ENDING 12/31

	Year 2	Year 1	Change Increase/ Decrease	Percent
Net Sales	$14,500	$15,000	–$500	3%
Cost of Goods Sold	$9,800	$9,100	$700	8%
Gross Profit	**$4,700**	**$5,900**	**–$1,200**	**–20%**
Operating Expenses	$2,600	$2,300	$300	13%
Income Before Interest and Taxes	$2,000	$3,600	–$1,600	–44%
Income Tax Expense	$120	$210	–$90	–43%
Net Income	**$1,880**	**$3,390**	**–$1,510**	**–46%**

13.1

If you look at the income statement, Star Shore and Company didn't appear to have a great year. Sales dipped slightly, and both cost of goods sold (COGS) and operating expenses grew significantly, resulting in a decrease in net income. At first glance, the slight decline in performance from the previous year doesn't appear to have affected the balance sheet as much. Receivables are down as expected, but debt is also down, suggesting that Star has had the wherewithal to pay down its loans.

Inventory has ticked up, which could reflect the impact of lower than anticipated sales. It might also mean that the company is carrying too much stock and levels might need to be reevaluated.

It looks like the owner's equity has gone up, although it is not attributable to net income, which decreased as well. This suggests that the owners might have increased their investment in the company to shore up cash reserves and pay down some debt and expenses.

To study this further and determine whether this is an off year or the start of something more serious, Star Shore and Company might want to consider doing a trend analysis going back 5 years or so.

STAR SHORE AND COMPANY
TREND ANALYSIS

	Year 1	Year 2	Year 3	Year 4	Year 5
Net Sales	$14,400	$14,200	$14,400	$15,000	$14,500
Gross Profit	$4,800	$4,900	$4,900	$5,900	$4,700
Net Income	$1,800	$1,900	$2,000	$3,390	$1,880

Even without converting these numbers to percentages, it's clear that last year—Year 4—stands out as a particularly good year for Star Shore and Company. Performance in the current year—Year 5—doesn't look quite so bad when you compare with Years 1 through 3. So is it the start of a downward trend, or was Year 4's stellar performance an aberration? This would bear more examination.

Other Comparisons

Certain types of analysis help narrow down the source of fluctuations in a company's performance. Have changes resulted from something specific your business has done or from factors that are affecting its entire industry? A retail store's sales might be trending up sharply with the rest of its industry during boom times, but its expenditures may still not be cost-effective when compared with its peers.

Looking at ratios between certain items on your own financial statements, as well as comparing your results to even larger companies in your industry, gives you a fuller picture of how you're doing.

What's Happening in the Industry?

Another method to examine how your business is doing is to look at the financial performance of the competition or averages for your industry published by sources such as Dun & Bradstreet, Value Line, Standard & Poor's, or RMA's Annual Statement Studies, which offer investment research, corporate/industry data, and other business information. Are your profit margins in line with what's expected? Are other companies in your industry experiencing a slump in sales or a spike in production costs? Looking at your company's performance side by side with industry competitors might give you a good idea.

Common-Size Financial Statements

Sometimes it helps to look at different accounts in relation to a key performance number such as sales. In **common-size financial statements,** all account totals are shown as a percentage of a certain item to get a fix on how your business is doing.

✓

> **Common-size financial statements** are balance sheet and income statements that show all items as a percentage of a key figure such as sales or operating income. This statement is often useful for comparing different-size businesses in an industry.

Let's look at an example. Kenner Bakery created common-size financial statements that show its income statement amounts as a percentage of sales.

13.1

KENNER BAKERY
COMMON-SIZE INCOME STATEMENT
FOR THE YEAR ENDED 12/31

Sales	$570,000	100%
Cost of Goods Sold	$427,500	75%
Gross Profit	**$142,500**	**25%**
Operating Expenses:		
Selling	$57,000	10%
General and Administrative	$45,600	8%
Total Operating Expenses	**$102,600**	**18%**
Income Before Income Tax	$39,900	7%
Income Tax Expense	$28,500	5%
Net Income	**$11,400**	**2%**

Common-size financial statements are particularly useful when comparing different-size businesses. If Kenner wanted to know how it was doing in comparison to Pain au France chain, for example, converting the statements and setting them side by side would show these results.

KENNER BAKERY
COMMON-SIZE INCOME STATEMENTS
FOR THE YEAR ENDED 12/31

	Kenner Bakery		Pain au France	
	Amount	% Sales	Amount	% Sales
Sales	$570,000	100%	$42,000,000	100%
Cost of Goods Sold	$427,500	75%	$27,300,000	65%
Gross Profit	$142,500	25%	$14,700,000	35%
Operating Expenses:				
Selling Expenses	$57,000	10%	$7,980,000	19%
General and Administrative Expenses	$45,600	8%	$4,200,000	10%
Total Operating Expenses	**$102,600**	**18%**	**$12,180,000**	**29%**
Income Before Income Tax	$39,900	7%	$2,520,000	6%
Income Tax Expense	$28,500	5%	$2,100,000	5%
Net Income	**$11,400**	**2%**	**$420,000**	**1%**

As you can see, Kenner's sales are dwarfed by the $42 million the Pain au France chain earned. The larger firm also has a heftier gross profit at 35 percent, perhaps due to lower costs from being able to buy in bulk and produce in large quantities. However, Kenner is doing a better job in terms of controlling selling and administrative expenses, and as a result, both its operating income and net income represent a slightly higher return on sales. So for a small company, it is not doing badly.

Ratio Analysis

Comparing different income and expense items can tell you much about the financial health of your organization. A number of simple formulas or **financial ratios** can help you uncover your company's hidden strengths and weaknesses. **Ratio analysis** helps you determine if you're earning an adequate return or if you have too much debt. In fact, this is the very tool banks, financial institutions, and potential investors turn to when deciding whether to invest or do business with you or any company.

√

> A **financial ratio** is a formula that shows the relationship of one amount to another in percentage terms. Financial ratios can measure liquidity, profitability, and economic health of a business.
>
> **Ratio analysis** is the process of using financial ratios to gauge the health, viability, and performance of an entity.

Ratios, as we discuss in upcoming sections, can be used to assess profitability, the ability of a company to pay its debt, and its liquidity. For example, say you want to look at the profitability of Kenner Bakery in the previous example. A good start is its gross profit margin. You can compute this ratio by dividing gross profit of $142,500 by sales of $570,000, which gives you 25 percent. Not bad for a bakery. But not quite as good as the impressive 35 percent gross profit ($14,700,000 ÷ $42,000,000) of the behemoth Pain au France chain. To do a complete analysis, of course, you need to look at more than one ratio, as we explain in the rest of this chapter.

Automating the Process

If you have a computerized accounting system, you'll likely be able to automatically prepare many of these analyses. Most accounting software programs can calculate year-to-year comparisons, measure liquidity, do ratio analysis, look at trends, and provide other useful data for making business decisions. The speed at which these computations are performed can also enhance your ability to move quickly to take advantage of opportunities and solve problems.

13.1

Some software programs and online offerings are even specifically designed for financial analysis, computing dozens of ratios and comparisons, as well as producing common-size financial statements and a variety of charts and graphs for reporting or presentations. In addition, some software makers, such as Sage Peachtree, offer business analytics that enable you to compare your results and challenges to those of other companies in the same industry.

Limitations of Financial Analysis

No matter which method you choose—and whether you're doing the work manually or by computer—it's important to remember financial analysis doesn't have all the answers. For starters, it's only as good as the numbers behind it. Choices in inventory method, credit policy, and a host of other variables all have an impact in how these numbers look when analyzed and can cause ratios and other measurements to vary. Financial analysis should be treated as one tool of many in evaluating the performance of a business and not as an oracle.

That said, informed analysis of financial results using comparisons and ratios can be invaluable in managing a company and assessing performance. In the next several subchapters, we look at some of the most commonly used ratios and what they tell you.

13.2 Assessing Profitability

Profit Margins

Return on Assets

Return on Equity

Earnings per Share

Price-Earnings Ratio

Your company made a profit last year, but is that the whole story? In this sub-chapter, you learn how to use ratios to look behind the numbers to assess how well things are really going.

Profit Margins

Profit margins are one of the first relationships you look at when you've completed your income statement. Margin measures return on sales and how well you're managing expenses. You can compute the profit margin a number of ways, depending on what you'd like to learn.

Gross profit margin gives you the margin return after deducting the cost of sales:

Sales – COGS ÷ Sales = Gross profit margin

Or again, using Kenner Bakery:

$570,000 – $427,500 ÷ $570,000 = 25%

Operating margin shows you your percentage return after COGS and operating expenses and is often thought to be a better gauge of overall performance, since it takes into account the cost of running the business.

Sales – COGS – Operating expenses ÷ Sales = Operating profit margin

$570,000 – $427,500 – $102,600 ÷ $570,000 = 7%

You can also compute the straight profit margin, which measures the relationship between your bottom line (net income) and sales:

Net income ÷ Sales = Profit margin

$11,400 ÷ $570,000 = 2%

13.2

In general, companies like discounters or supermarkets that do high-volume business have low profit margins. High-end, low-volume businesses such as luxury goods stores or aircraft manufacturers tend to have higher profit margins.

Return on Assets

Return on assets (ROA) tells you how much of a return you're making on your assets and is a pretty good measure of overall profitability. You can compute it as follows:

Net income ÷ Average total assets = Return on assets

As an example, Trident Engineering has income of $50,000 on sales of $867,000 for the year. Trident's average assets for the year ending 12/31 totaled $90,000. Its ROA would be 50,000 ÷ 90,000 = 55.5 percent.

Just because your company is showing a profit doesn't mean it's making the best use of the resources invested. Generally, the higher the ROA number, the better you're doing. However, firms that must invest substantially in machinery or other capital equipment tend to have lower average ROAs, and this is not necessarily a problem if prior to the investment it was determined the projected ROA was acceptable and/or necessary.

Return on Equity

Return on equity (ROE) measures profitability in terms of return on investment. As with the ROA, return on equity tells investors what they're getting back for what they put in. There are variations on this formula, but the simplest version is as follows:

Net income ÷ Average equity = Return on equity

Trident Engineering is a partnership with average equity of $65,000 during the year. This would put its ROE (Net income $50,000 ÷ Average equity $65,000) at roughly 77 percent.

As with the ROA, the higher the ROE number, the better you're doing. A ROE of 2, for instance, would mean you're earning a return of two times your investment. Because Trident is a new business, its partners are happy with its current ROE and expect it to improve in the future. Typically, all ratios involving net income and a balance sheet item use the average of the balance sheet item (for example, beginning assets at January 1 and ending assets at December 31 ÷ 2), but to keep the examples simple, we're just using the ending balance.

Earnings per Share

Earnings per share (EPS) is another version of return on equity. The difference is that EPS looks at return on individual shares of stock. This enables investors to see what kind of return they're getting on their specific investment—which is what makes it such a popular and widely used measure.

Here's the formula:

Net income ÷ Average shares outstanding = Earnings per share

While accounting for common stock is largely beyond the scope of this book, it's worth mentioning this ratio because it's so prevalent in the business world.

Price-Earnings Ratio

The price-earnings (P/E) ratio might be the one you hear about the most, although it has less to do with the performance of your company than how the stock market values it. To compute the P/E ratio, divide market value per share by the earnings per share:

Market value per share ÷ Earnings per share = P/E ratio

A high-price earnings ratio means your company is an expensive stock in terms of what it's earning. On the other hand, a low P/E could suggest the market undervalues your stock.

Profitability ratios, particularly when taken together, give you a good idea of what kind of return a company is earning, as well as a window into how it is managing both its assets and investments and controlling operating expenses. But this is far from the whole picture, as upcoming sections illustrate.

13.2

13.3 Determining Ability to Pay Debt

Debt to Assets Ratio

Debt to Equity Ratio

Equity to Assets Ratio

Times Interest Earned Ratio

Cash Debt Coverage Ratio

You want your company to make money, but not at the cost of too much debt. This subchapter helps you evaluate your business's reliance on creditors and investors and shows you how to measure your ability to pay them back.

Debt to Assets Ratio

To learn how much of your company's assets are financed by creditors, use the debt to assets ratio:

Total liabilities ÷ Total assets = Debt to assets ratio

By taking both current and long-term liabilities as a percentage of total assets, you are able to assess your ability to repay debt and how much leeway you have to withstand losses.

For example, if Trident Engineering has total assets of $80,000 and debt totaling $40,000, we could safely say that creditors provided half of its assets. Generally, the higher the debt to assets ratio, the more highly leveraged a company is said to be and the greater the risk it might be unable to meet loan payments as they come due should operations slow down. If Trident had total liabilities of $60,000 instead of $40,000, its debt to assets ratio would be 75 percent. The adequacy of this ratio depends on your particular company and its industry.

Debt to Equity Ratio

This ratio is another useful gauge of liquidity:

Total liabilities ÷ Total equity = Debt to equity ratio

As an example, say Trident had equity of only $15,000. Its debt to equity ratio would be $65,000 (debt) ÷ $15,000 for a 4:3 debt to equity ratio. This would indicate thin equity and a significantly overleveraged company.

Equity to Assets Ratio

The equity to assets ratio looks at how much of your company's assets are provided by equity, or how much investors are at risk if the company isn't profitable:

Total equity ÷ Total assets = Equity to assets ratio

To return to our Trident example, we would take:

$65,000 ÷ $80,000 = 8.1%

Like Trident's creditors, its investors are still on the hook for a relatively large chunk of money in relation to total assets. We know that Trident is a new business and investors have indicated they are satisfied with the company's return on equity, so this probably isn't a problem. New businesses aren't expected to immediately recoup their investments; if Trident has the same ratio in 10 years and the investors are less comfortable with performance, it could become more of a concern.

Times Interest Earned Ratio

Can your company make its current interest payments as they become due? The times interest earned ratio gives you an indication:

Income before interest expense and taxes ÷ Annual interest expense = Times interest earned ratio

When computing it, note that you take net income *before* interest and taxes, because interest is a tax deduction.

Cash Debt Coverage Ratio

This useful ratio measures your company's ability to repay its liabilities without liquidating the business. It tells you how long it would take to generate cash from operations to pay down debt:

Net cash from operating activities ÷ Average total liabilities = Cash debt coverage ratio

You can pull the net cash provided by operating activities from your company's annual cash flow statement. You can compute average total liabilities from interim financials or average the last 2 years' financial statements.

13.3

If Trident Engineering has average liabilities of $40,000 and generated cash flow from operations of $20,000, its ratio would be 0.50. This means it would take about 2 years to generate enough cash through operations. The higher the ratio, the less leveraged your company is.

13.4 Measuring Liquidity

Current Assets Ratio

Quick Ratio

Inventory Turnover

Accounts Receivable Turnover

Average Age of Accounts Receivable

Asset Turnover

Liquidity ratios measure your company's ability to pay its expenses and obligations in the short term as well as meeting any unexpected needs for cash. In this subchapter, we introduce some different liquidity ratios and show you how to use them.

Current Assets Ratio

The current assets ratio is one of the most common ratios. You can use it to measure your company's ability to pay short-term (or current) debt and expenses.

Current assets ÷ Current liabilities = Current assets ratio

If your company has current assets of $80,000 and current liabilities of $50,000, your current assets ratio would be 1.6 to 1. This means that for every $1 of current liabilities, you have $1.60 worth of assets.

How do you determine if your current ratio is adequate? Obviously, a higher current ratio gives you more breathing room, but that might not necessarily represent the best use of resources. The adequacy of your current ratio depends on your particular business and industry.

One drawback of the current assets ratio is that it doesn't specify what kind of current assets are included. Slow-moving inventory or prepaid expenses would not be as readily available to pay creditors as cash.

Quick Ratio

The quick (or acid test) ratio tries to remedy one of the drawbacks of the current assets ratio by including only those current assets that are extremely liquid—cash and equivalents (like short-term securities) and net accounts receivable. These are considered quick assets. This ratio is known as the acid test ratio because it's the most stringent liquidity test you can use.

Quick assets ÷ Current liabilities = Quick ratio

To compute the quick ratio using numbers from our previous example, assume current assets of $80,000 were composed as follows:

Cash	$18,000
Marketable Securities	$10,000
Accounts Receivable (Net)	$22,000
Inventory	$26,000
Prepaid Assets	$4,000

Using these numbers, quick assets would total:

$18,000 + $10,000 + $22,000 = $50,000

The quick ratio would be computed as:

$50,000 ÷ $50,000 = 1 to 1

This would result in a slightly more realistic but less comfortable ratio of 1 to 1.

SEE ALSO 3.1, "Classifying Cash"

SEE ALSO 4.3, "Accounts Receivable"

SEE ALSO 5.1, "Accounting for Inventory"

Inventory Turnover

Turnover ratios measure how efficiently and quickly assets can be converted into cash. Inventory turnover measures how many times, on average, inventory is sold during the period. Here's the formula:

Cost of goods sold ÷ Average inventory = Inventory turnover

To keep things simple, we'll assume our inventory averaged $30,000 over the year (computed by averaging beginning and ending inventory balances). COGS for the period was $105,000.

13.4

$105,000 ÷ $30,000 = 3.5

This means that inventory turned over 3.5 times during the year. You would then want to compare this amount to the average for your industry to see whether it was fast or slow.

As an added check, you can also compute average selling time by dividing 365 days by the inventory turnover rate:

$365 \div 3.5 = 104\ days$

You could also compare this figure to competitors and others in your industry.

SEE ALSO 5.2, "Determining Inventory Quantity"

Accounts Receivable Turnover

Accounts receivable turnover measures the liquidity of accounts receivable in terms of how often they are collected during the period. You can compute it using the following formula:

Net credit sales ÷ Average accounts receivable (net) = Accounts receivable turnover

With net receivables of $22,000, let's assume sales of $87,000, of which $72,000 are credit sales:

$\$72,000 \div \$22,000 = 3.27$

An accounts receivable turnover of 3.3 times seems rather low, but you would need to compare it to other companies in the industry to see if that is, in fact, the case. In general, the faster the turnover, the better. Some companies, however, particularly retailers, accept slow payments on credit that result in higher interest returns and, hence, have lower accounts receivable turnover rates.

Average Age of Accounts Receivable

You can also compute the average collection time for receivables by dividing the turnover rate by 365 days. This can be a useful ratio to use when evaluating the adequacy of bad debt allowance.

365 days ÷ Accounts receivable turnover rate = Average age of accounts receivable

Using the numbers from the previous example, we get:

$365 \div 3.3 = 111\ days$

You could conclude that receivables are collected on average every 111 days.

SEE ALSO 4.3, "Accounts Receivable"

Asset Turnover

This ratio looks at how well a company uses its assets to generate sales. It is computed as follows:

Net sales ÷ Average assets = Asset turnover

You can compute average assets using beginning and ending total assets for the period. For example, if your company had $170,000 in assets at the beginning of the period and $120,000 at the end, its average assets would be $145,000. Factor net sales of $560,000 into that, and you have:

$560,000 ÷ $145,000 = 3.86

This looks like a very healthy asset turnover, but because numbers can vary widely by industry, you would want to compare it to your competitors to truly gauge how you're doing.

13.5 Making Decisions

Measuring Costs and Benefits

Taking on New Business

Discontinuing a Product

How Many Must Sell?

Make or Buy?

All this financial data you've generated can also be useful for decision-making. Should you add a new product? Discontinue an old one? Can you afford to buy new equipment, or should you lease it? In this subchapter, we go over some simple ways to help you decide.

Measuring Costs and Benefits

Every choice you make about the course of your business is going to have a financial impact. Even something as simple as adding a new product, while offering potential revenue, also brings added expenses. To evaluate the potential costs and benefits of these different alternatives, you use what's called **incremental analysis.**

✓

Incremental analysis is the process used to evaluate the cost/benefit potential of different alternatives on future income.

If you operate a doll factory, Teeny Tots, the decision about whether to make or buy the clothing the dolls wear would be an example of an incremental decision. What you choose to do depends on a number of factors, including …

- The cost of making your own clothes versus the cost of buying, or the **relevant costs.**

- The loss of revenue from other products that could have been made when you were making clothing, or the **opportunity costs.**

- The costs already incurred, which would not increase if you started making doll clothing, or the **sunk costs.**

✓
_____

Relevant costs are the costs that are different in each alternative you're considering.

Opportunity costs are the potential benefits lost when choosing one alternative or course of action over another.

Sunk costs are the costs that would be incurred regardless of which option you choose.

By quantifying and comparing these factors, you should be able to arrive at an informed decision. The following sections show you how to use incremental analysis in making different decisions.

Taking on New Business

If you run your own business, from time to time you're likely to be faced with opportunities to expand or change your business. How should you evaluate them?

Let's use our doll factory example again. Assume you've already decided that setting up a separate production area to sew doll clothing or even hiring the additional workers needed would be prohibitive. But now, a customer is asking if you can increase his order by 1,000 more dolls a month. He usually has 5,000 but now he wants 6,000. The catch is that instead of paying the usual $5/unit cost, he wants to pay $3 for the additional 1,000. The dolls currently cost you $3.75 to make, broken down as follows:

Type	Cost per Unit
Direct Materials	$1.50
Direct Labor	$.70
Overhead	$.30
Selling Expense	$1.00
Administrative Expense	$.25
Total	$3.75

Assuming the same per-unit cost, it would appear that the additional 1,000 dolls will run you $3,750 to make. But remember, the customer only wants to pay $3 each for the additional 1,000, which would bring in only $3,000 in revenue:

1,000 × $3 = $3,000

13.5

At first it wouldn't seem worth it to make the additional dolls and sell them for $3, because unit costs appear to result in a $750 loss (selling price of $3,000 less $3,750 cost to make the additional 1,000). However, this is not the way you would analyze the problem, as we show in the following table:

	Cost per Unit	Cost per Additional 1,000
Direct Materials	$1.50	$1,500
Direct Labor	$.70	$700
Overhead	$.25	$250
Selling Expense	$1.00	
Administrative Expense	$.25	
Total	$3.70	$2,450

First, the overhead would be spread over a larger number of dolls lowering the per unit cost, lets say to 25¢ from 30¢ for both old and new dolls. Second, because there are no additional selling or administrative expenses associated with the order (the customer came to you), these costs are considered sunk costs and excluded from the computation. The relevant costs would include those that go into the product—direct material, labor, and overhead. These three combined add up to $2.45 per unit for a total cost of $2,450. When that price is subtracted from the sales price of $3,000, you can see you earn an additional $550 in profit.

Another cost you must evaluate is the opportunity cost of manufacturing the additional dolls. Your factory easily has the capacity and there are no other pending orders, so assuming no additional costs, you would still clear $550 by taking the order. You would most likely accept the additional order, priced as requested on a one-time basis.

When evaluating new business decisions, you should also take any changes in the gross margin into account as this would go directly to the bottom line. In our example, the added production does not significantly impact the gross margin, which remains at 25 percent. If it had significantly brought down the margins and profitability, this could impact the business even if you were not selling them at a loss, so it's worth keeping an eye on.

SEE ALSO 5.3, "Figuring Inventory Costs"

Discontinuing a Product

Sometimes what you need to decide doesn't involve new business as much as whether to continue with an old one. The same type of analysis you used in evaluating a new line can help you decide whether to discontinue a product as well. Once again, you'll need to weigh the relevant costs, opportunity costs, and sunk costs of each option.

Let's say Teeny Tots also produces custom-made dolls designed to look like their owners. The cost breakdown for these dolls is as follows:

Type	Cost per Unit
Direct Materials	$8.75
Direct Labor	$20.00
Overhead	$10.00
Relevant Costs	$38.75
Selling Expense	$1.00
Administrative Expense	$0.25
Total	$40.00

Last year, Teeny Tots made 200 of these dolls at a cost of $8,000 and sold them for $100 each for total revenues of $20,000. But these dolls required quite a bit of labor, which reduced the amount of time that could be spent on other Teeny Tots products. The company is now thinking of dropping the doll but doesn't know if it could make up the difference with its other products.

This would free the manufacturing capacity and labor to produce as many as 30,000 of the popular minidolls from the previous example, which retail at $5. Their costs break down as follows:

Type	Cost per Unit
Direct Materials	$1.50
Direct Labor	$.70
Overhead	$.30
Relevant Costs	$2.50
Selling Expense	$1.00
Administrative Expense	$.25
Total	$3.75

To decide whether to discontinue, you could look at the relevant costs of the custom-made dolls because the other costs are sunk costs and will be there anyway. That would give you total costs of $7,750 ($38.75 × 200) on revenues of $20,000 ($100 × 200) for a gross profit of $12,250.

13.5

The opportunity cost of continuing this line would be the amount that could be earned if the $5 retail dolls were made instead. Using the relevant costs of $2.50 for 3,000 dolls gives you costs of $7,500. The dolls could be sold at $15,000 ($5 × 3,000), which would bring in a profit of $7,500. All things being equal, Teeny Tots should probably continue the custom-made dolls even though they are expensive and time-consuming, because they bring in a higher profit than alternative products.

How Many Must Sell?

When you're looking at the costs for a new product, one of the first things you need to know is the **break-even point**—or the point when you will make money.

✓

The **break-even point** is the quantity at which the revenues you make from selling a product start to exceed the cost of making it.

Computing the break-even point is fairly simple. You need to know the unit cost of making your product, the sales price, and what your fixed costs are for the year. Then you can place those numbers in this formula:

Fixed costs ÷ [1 – (Average cost ÷ Average price)] = Break-even point

If your company sells coats priced at $100 that cost you $20 to make and your fixed costs are $40,000 a year, you could compute the break-even point as follows:

$40,000 ÷ [1 – ($20 ÷ $100)] = $50,000

To find out how many coats you would have to make, you would divide the break-even point by the price:

$50,000 ÷ $100 = 500 coats

If this is a new product you're considering, you should also consider the opportunity costs of choosing or not choosing to make it.

Make or Buy?

Sometimes you'll have to decide whether it makes more sense to make or buy a product or rent or own an asset. When faced with this choice, it's best to create a schedule to compare the costs of your options. For example, let's say a small businessman is trying to decide whether it would be more cost-effective to buy a computer system or purchase some components and build a custom-made one.

He or she would need to consider the costs of one versus the other as shown in the following table.

	Make	Buy	Incremental Increase (Decrease)
Purchase Price		$5,500	
Direct Materials	$1,000		
Direct Labor	$2,500		
Overhead	$1,000		
Total Relevant Costs	$4,500	$5,500	$1,000

At first glance, it would appear cheaper to build the computer system as opposed to buying it. But that's before we consider the opportunity costs of making and buying.

Let's assume that if the employees, materials, and overhead *not* going into making our own computer were diverted to other production with a potential to generate $2,000 in income. This amount then could be considered an opportunity cost of making the project and would change our analysis as follows:

	Make	Buy	Incremental Increase (Decrease)
Relevant Costs	$4,500	$5,500	$1,000
Opportunity Costs	$2,000		($2,000)
Total Cost	$6,500	$5,500	($1,000)

After considering opportunity costs, we can see that buying the machine would prove more economical.

This same analysis can be used to decide whether to buy or lease an asset as well. All you have to do is substitute a "Lease" costs column for the "Make" column.

Whether you choose to automate this process or do it yourself, financial analysis is a tool that can be used in a variety of ways, from evaluating a company's financial performance to helping a business owner make decisions about the future. But that doesn't mean it is foolproof. Ratios, comparisons, and cost-benefit analyses are only as good as the numbers being evaluated. And as with any formula or financial report, the numbers are only a part of the story. A healthy dose of judgment and business sense should always be factored in.

13.5

14

Budgeting and Forecasting

14.1 Budgeting Basics

Why Budget?

Types of Budgets

This subchapter explains how forecasts and budgets are used and introduces you to the different types of budgets you can make. You learn how budget data flows from forecasts, which budgets are most important, and how they all fit together.

Why Budget?

Not everyone is a big fan of **budgets.** It's understandable; budgets take a lot of work to put together and can leave you feeling constrained and like you've blown it if you don't follow them to the letter. That's why most accountants prefer to focus on **forecasting** rather than budgeting.

✓

A **budget** is a written plan laying out management's economic goals and setting up parameters and spending limits for the period.

Forecasting is the act of making predictions about financial outcome based on historical and current data. Budgets are based on forecasts.

We don't want you to think of your budget as something set in stone, where if you spend one more cent than what's allocated, you've failed. Instead, throughout this chapter we talk about a budget as a set of guidelines, not rules, based on the best forecasts at the time but always open to amendment as circumstances warrant.

Forecasting, done properly, can provide you with both a road map and a measure of security for the year. A road map because it lays out plans and projections for your company in economic terms. If you know what you expect to be spending and bringing in, it's harder to be surprised. And a budget can serve as a warning system, alerting you to any problems or variations as they occur. This enables you to react quickly and maintain more control over your business.

Types of Budgets

To be useful, a budget needs to be based on reality. As anyone who's tried to set up a personal budget can tell you, first you need to know how much money you have and expect to earn and what your expenses are. Only then can you set goals for saving and decide where it's possible to cut back. The budgeting process in business is much the same. You need data—projections of what you expect to come in and go out—before you can start setting down guidelines for spending.

You'll usually start the budget process a couple months before the new year—and before you get caught up in the closing process for the current year.

SEE ALSO 10.1, "The Closing Process"

SEE ALSO 11.1, "Year-End Closing Procedures"

There are several budgets you might find useful at your company or business. Your first budgeting task, however, is to set up the **sales forecast,** which is based on sales projections for the coming year. When you know what you hope to sell, you'll have a pretty good idea of what you need to produce. In a manufacturing company, this means forecasting your manufacturing needs for the year by setting up a **production budget.** When you've projected how much product you need, next you prepare the **manufacturing budget** to see how much it will cost you. In a merchandising company, you'll put together a merchandising purchases budget.

✓

A **sales forecast** is a company's best estimate of sales for the period.

A **production budget** shows quantities that must be produced to meet projected sales.

Manufacturing budgets project costs for budgeted production quantities.

The next area you need to look at is your expenses. You can prepare **selling** and **general and administrative expenses budgets** based on anticipated production levels and past history. Now that you have projected your costs, you can put together the **budgeted income statement.**

On the financial budget side, the **cash budget** is one of the most critical budgets you make, as it lays out both spending and earning plans. It draws on information contained in manufacturing and operating expense budgets, as well as from your sales forecast and budgeted capital expenditures. Looking at the balance sheet, you then might consider a **capital expenditures budget** if you plan on buying new equipment.

After you've completed all these specialized budgets, you put them all together into what's often called the **master budget.** Many companies even go so far as to

14.1

compile **budgeted** (or projected) **balance sheets and income statement** to further quantify forecasts.

✓

Selling and **general and administrative expenses budgets** estimate anticipated selling, general, and administrative expenses for the period.

A **cash budget** sets anticipated cash inflows and outflows during the year.

A **capital expenditures budget** estimates projected spending on plant assets or equipment.

A **master budget** is the main budget, piecing together sales, production, operating expenses, selling and administrative expenses, capital expenditures, and cash budgets.

A **budgeted balance sheet and income statement** project financial reports based on budgeted numbers.

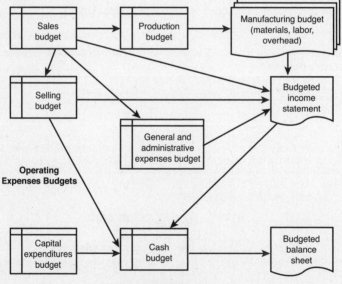

This diagram lays out some of the different budgets and shows how they connect.

In the following subchapters, we look at each of these budgets individually and show you how to put them together and use them.

14.2 The Sales Forecast

Forecasting

A Sample Forecast

The sales forecast is your starting point—the one that serves as the basis for the other budgets. In this subchapter, you learn about what goes into a good sales forecast and how to make one.

Forecasting

The sales forecast is a prediction of what you expect your sales to be in the upcoming year. Sales forecasts can be derived from any number of places—industry reports, economic reports, conversations with salespeople, customers, competitors, and so on. The idea is to use your best estimate of what you expect sales to be. This projection usually encompasses sales by product, territory, etc.

In both manufacturing and merchandising operations, it's best to start with the individual line or product, projecting per-unit sales and then multiplying by the sales price. Remember, even though these are only projections, budgeting sales too high can cause problems. You can end up with too much inventory, for example, that you end up discounting later. Many companies in cyclical businesses do quarterly budgeting to take slow seasons into account. Some larger companies put together monthly forecasts to keep on top of any unforeseen shifts in the market.

A Sample Forecast

To keep things simple, let's assume Soft Soundz Company markets and sells only one item—a musical sound system sold on the web and designed to go in infant cribs. Soft Soundz has come up with the following sales forecast for next year:

SOFT SOUNDZ COMPANY
SALES FORECAST
FOR THE YEAR ENDING DECEMBER 31

	Q1	Q2	Q3	Q4	Year
Units	1,500	2,500	1,400	4,000	9,400
Selling Price/Unit	$80	$80	$80	$80	$80
Total Sales (Projected in $)	$120,000	$200,000	$112,000	$320,000	$752,000

14.2

Soft Soundz's owner based these projections on past sales history, plus a slight increase after discussions with customers and individual salesman reports. The device has tended to sell better over the Christmas holidays and also in the second quarter, due to the high number of babies born in the spring. Sales are forecasted by quarter based upon anticipated units and the selling price. These figures now serve as the basis for Soft Soundz's remaining projections.

14.3 The Production and Inventory Budgets

The Production Budget
The Manufacturing Budgets
The Merchandise Purchases Budget

When you know the quantities you expect to sell, you're ready to calculate how much product you need to make or buy. In this subchapter, you learn how to set up budgets for production, manufacturing costs, and merchandise purchases.

The Production Budget

A production budget tells you how much you need to make to meet estimated sales demands. To compute production quantities needed, use the following formula:

Budgeted sales + Finished goods inventory desired at the end of period − Finished goods inventory at beginning of period = Goods to be produced

In the case of Soft Soundz, let's assume the company cut it pretty close with inventory last year and will only have about 30 units in stock at the beginning of the budgeted period. The company has adjusted sales up slightly but still would like to keep more of a cushion in ending inventory, say 300 units, which is about 20 percent of first quarter sales.

To arrive at goods to be produced, they would do the following calculation:

Budgeted sales + Ending inventory − Beginning inventory = Goods to be produced
9,400 + 300 − 30 = 9,670

The Soft Soundz production budget would appear as follows:

SOFT SOUNDZ COMPANY PRODUCTION BUDGET
FOR THE YEAR ENDED 12/31

	Q1	Q2	Q3	Q4	Year
Sales	1,500	2,500	1,400	4,000	9,400
Desired Ending Inventory	500	280	800	300	300
Units Needed	2,000	2,780	2,200	4,300	9,700
Beginning Inventory	30	500	280	800	30
Units to Be Produced	1,970	2,280	1,920	3,500	9,670

14.3

In this case, the finished goods inventory each quarter is determined by taking 20 percent of the next quarter's projected sales.

The Manufacturing Budgets

When you've computed units to be produced, you're ready to budget your manufacturing costs. Using the per unit cost as recorded in your inventory records and the units needed, you can prepare budgets for the materials, labor, and overhead costs that go into the product by using the following worksheets.

SEE ALSO 5.3, "Figuring Inventory Costs"

The Direct Materials Budget

This budget helps you decide how much raw material you need to purchase. You start by looking at what you need for expected production and what you already have in inventory. In this example, you're also budgeting a conservative cushion remaining in inventory after production of 10 percent of the next quarter production in case you go over or if there are delays in getting new product.

SOFT SOUNDZ COMPANY
DIRECT MATERIALS BUDGET
FOR THE YEAR ENDED 12/31

	Q1	Q2	Q3	Q4	Year
Units to Be Produced	1,970	2,280	1,920	3,500	9,670
Materials per Unit	2	2	2	2	2
Total Needed for Production (Pounds)	3,940	4,560	3,840	7,000	19,340
Add: Target Ending Pounds (10% Next Quarter Production)	456	384	700	400	400
Total Materials Required	4,396	4,944	4,540	7,400	
Less: Beginning Pounds	390	456	384	700	
Materials Purchases	4,006	4,488	4,156	6,700	19,350
Cost per Pound	$10	$10	$10	$10	$10
Total Cost Direct Materials Purchases	**$40,600**	**$44,880**	**$41,560**	**$67,000**	**$193,500**

SEE ALSO 5.3, "Figuring Inventory Costs"

The Direct Labor Budget

The direct labor budget also uses planned production quantities to determine how much labor should be forecast for each quarter. As the following table demonstrates, you need to know direct labor hours or direct labor costs per unit to complete this budget.

SEE ALSO 5.3, "Figuring Inventory Costs"

SOFT SOUNDZ
DIRECT LABOR BUDGET
FOR THE YEAR ENDED 12/31

	Q1	Q2	Q3	Q4	Year
Units to Be Produced	1,970	2,280	1,920	3,500	9,670
Direct Labor Hours per Unit	1.5	1.5	1.5	1.5	1.5
Total Hours Needed	2,955	3,420	2,880	5,250	14,505
Direct Labor Cost per Hour	$10	$10	$10	$10	$10
Total Direct Labor Cost	$29,550	$34,200	$28,800	$52,500	$145,050

The Manufacturing Overhead Budget

This budget projects the amount of indirect variable and fixed costs that will be incurred in the course of production during the year. To complete this budget, you need to carry over direct labor hours required from the direct labor budget.

SOFT SOUNDZ
MANUFACTURING OVERHEAD BUDGET
FOR THE YEAR ENDED 12/31

	Q1	Q2	Q3	Q4	Year
Variable Costs	1,865	3,260	1,640	8,750	15,515
Fixed Costs	7,000	7,000	7,000	7,000	28,000
Total Manufacturing Overhead	8,865	10,260	8,640	15,750	43,515
Direct Labor Hours	2,955	3,420	2,880	5,250	14,505
Manufacturing Overhead Rate per Direct Labor Hour	$3.00	$3.00	$3.00	$3.00	$3.00

Variable costs are those that fluctuate with production. Fixed costs are those that stay the same regardless of production levels. If we were costing actual inventory production instead of doing a forecast, we would apply these costs separately by period. But because this is a projection, we're using an aggregate rate based on total projected overhead for the year of $43,515 ÷ total projected direct labor hours of $14,505 or $3 per direct labor hour.

SEE ALSO 5.3, "Figuring Inventory Costs"

The Merchandise Purchases Budget

For companies that buy their goods as opposed to making them, the purchases budget takes the place of the manufacturing budgets. You would use the same sales and production forecasts as well as the computations involving beginning and required ending inventory to cost your merchandise.

As an example, say International Hats, Inc., plans to sell 140,000 baseball caps over the next four quarters. It starts out with an inventory of 7,000 hats and hopes to end up with about 5,000 at the end of the year. Each hat costs $1.

You could compute International Hats' cost of merchandise as follows:

Sales (Units)	140,000
Required Units in Ending Inventory	5,000
# Hats Required	145,000
Less: Hats in Beginning Inventory	(7,000)
Merchandise Purchases Required	138,000
Unit Cost	$1
Cost of Merchandise Purchases	$138,000

The other budgets and budgeted statements for a merchandising company (cash budget, operating expenses, capital expenditures, income statement, and balance sheet) would be the same as for a manufacturer.

14.4 The Operating Expenses Budget

The Selling Expenses Budget

The General and Administrative Expenses Budget

This subchapter shows you how to prepare budgets for selling expenses and general and administrative expenses. These schedules can be combined, but we show them separately to highlight differences in costs.

The Selling Expenses Budget

Selling expenses are those that are directly related to the sales, delivery, and marketing of a product. Common selling expenses include delivery costs, sales commissions, advertising expenses, and promotional expenses.

The first step in preparing a budget for selling expenses is preparing a schedule of what these expenses are for your company. Because Soft Soundz does most of its marketing over the internet, its selling expenses consist of advertising expenses and delivery costs. The company is a sole proprietorship with few employees, so it doesn't have sales salaries to include in these calculations.

After identifying selling costs, Soft Soundz must now determine whether they are fixed (meaning they remain the same whether they sell 1 item or 3,000) or variable (meaning they fluctuate depending on sales quantity).

Soft Soundz's delivery expenses depend on the number of systems sold and are considered a variable cost. Advertising is paid in a flat fee per month, regardless of whether it brings in sales, so it would be considered a fixed cost. Soft Soundz figures delivery costs at $2.50 a unit, while advertising for the year runs $6,000. (Advertising, being a fixed cost, would be divided evenly among the four quarters.)

We could compute delivery expenses using quarterly unit sales estimates as follows:

Quarter	Sales Units	Unit Cost	Delivery Expense
1	1,500	$2.50	$3,750
2	2,500	$2.50	$6,250
3	1,400	$2.50	$3,500
4	4,000	$2.50	$10,000
Yearly Total			$23,500

14.4

Soft Soundz could now compose the following forecast for selling expenses:

SOFT SOUNDZ COMPANY
SELLING EXPENSES BUDGET
FOR THE YEAR ENDED 12/31

	Q1	Q2	Q3	Q4	Total Year
Variable Expenses: Delivery	$3,750	$6,250	$3,500	$10,000	$23,500
Fixed Expenses: Advertising	$1,500	$1,500	$1,500	$1,500	$6,000
Total Selling Expenses	$5,250	$7,750	$5,000	$11,500	$29,500

The General and Administrative Expenses Budget

General and administrative expenses, also called G&A expenses, include office expenses and other costs of running the company that don't relate directly to producing or selling the product. Common G&A expenses include rent, administrative salaries, insurance, office supplies, utilities, and telephone charges.

To prepare a budget for G&A expenses, follow the same procedures outlined for selling expenses by first making a schedule of G&A costs and then determining which costs are variable and which are fixed. For Soft Soundz, none of the G&A expenses are variable. But the company does have fixed expenses of $80,000 for salaries, $30,000 for rent, and $5,000 for insurance.

The company's G&A Expenses Budget could be prepared as follows:

SOFT SOUNDZ COMPANY
G&A EXPENSES BUDGET
FOR THE YEAR ENDED 12/31

	Q1	Q2	Q3	Q4	Total Year
Variable Expenses	—	—	—	—	—
Fixed Expenses:					
Salaries	$20,000	$20,000	$20,000	$20,000	$80,000
Rent	$7,500	$7,500	$7,500	$7,500	$30,000
Insurance	$1,250	$1,250	$1,250	$1,250	$5,000
Total	$28,750	$28,750	$28,750	$28,750	$115,000

The operating expenses budget is usually done in two parts: the selling expenses budget, which covers costs like delivery and advertising, and the general and administrative (G&A) expenses budget. The totals from these forecasts are then carried forward to the budgeted income statement, discussed in the next subchapter.

14.5 The Budgeted Income Statement

Computing Cost of Goods Sold

Computing Budgeted Income

This subchapter discusses how to convert your forecasted sales and expense data into a budgeted income statement. Once again, the usefulness of this statement depends on how solid your forecasting is and how much things go as planned. Changing circumstances that effect costs or revenues should also alter your expectations.

Computing Cost of Goods Sold

When you've completed the sales and manufacturing and operating expense budgets, you're ready to project your net income for the year. But first you need to compute cost of goods sold. For a merchandising firm, this means multiplying units sold by the cost per unit. If your company is a manufacturer, you have to add your costs for raw materials, direct labor, and overhead and then multiply that figure by units sold.

Soft Soundz can compute cost of goods sold as follows:

SOFT SOUNDZ
TOTAL MANUFACTURING COSTS

Materials	$193,500
Labor	$145,050
Overhead	$43,515
Total Manufacturing Costs	$382,065

Total manufacturing costs ÷ Goods manufactured = Cost per unit
382,065 ÷ 9,670 = $39.51 (rounded to $39.50 for ease of computation)
($20 materials, $15 labor, $4.50 overhead per unit)

Total Units Sold	9,400
Cost per Unit	$39.50
Cost of Goods Sold	**$371,300**

14.5

Computing Budgeted Income

Soft Soundz now has all the pieces in place to put together its budgeted income statement for the year:

SOFT SOUNDZ COMPANY **BUDGETED INCOME STATEMENT** **FOR THE YEAR ENDED 12/31**	
Sales	$752,000
Cost of Goods Sold	$371,300
Gross Profit	**$380,700**
Operating Expenses:	
Selling	$29,500
G&A	$115,000
Total Operating Expenses	**$144,500**
Income from Operations	$236,200
Income Taxes (35%)	$82,670
Net Income	**$153,530**

Remember, the budgeted income statement is a projection. You're trying to get a sense for what performance might be given how much reality adheres to your forecasts. However, as with the other projected statements in this chapter, it can be a useful tool to help you stay on track.

14.6 The Cash Budget

Projecting Cash Flow

Preparing the Cash Budget

All your forecasts so far—sales, manufacturing, purchases, and expense budgets—contain cash flow data. This subchapter shows how to pull it all together to prepare your cash budget.

Projecting Cash Flow

The cash budget is one of the most important forecasts you'll put together, because it gives you an idea of what your cash position should be throughout the year. To complete the budget, you're going to need to draw data from all the budgets you've already prepared.

The essential format of the budget is this:

Starting cash balance

+ Cash inflows

– Cash outflows

= Cash balance before financing

+ Cash proceeds from financing (loans)

– Cash repayments

= Ending cash balance

Cash Inflows

Cash inflows include items such as receipts from sales, customer account payments, and proceeds from the sale of assets. To determine inflows for your company, look at your various budgets and statements from previous years. Put together a schedule of typical cash inflows. Then make an educated estimate of what these amounts are likely to be in the budget year.

Your biggest inflow is likely to come from sales. You can estimate collections based upon a percentage of the current month's sales and the previous months' sales. For example, Soft Soundz Company estimates that it collects 60 percent of sales in the current quarter and 40 percent in the following. This is how it would compute budgeted payments from customers.

14.6

SOFT SOUNDZ COMPANY
SCHEDULE OF PROJECTED COLLECTIONS

	Q1	Q2	Q3	Q4	Year
Sales	$120,000	$200,000	$112,000	$320,000	$752,000
Beginning A/R Balance	$50,000				$50,000
First Quarter	$72,000	$48,000			$120,000
Second Quarter		$120,000	$80,000		$200,000
Third Quarter			$67,200	$44,800	$112,000
Fourth Quarter				$192,000	$192,000
Total Expected Collections	$122,000	$168,000	$147,200	$236,800	$674,000

The amounts of expected collections for each quarter and the year can then be added to the cash budget. If you add sales ($752,000) to the beginning accounts receivable balance ($50,000) and subtract the total expected collections ($674,000), that gives you your accounts receivable balance ($128,000) on the **proforma balance sheet.**

✓

The **proforma balance sheet** projects the future rather than reflecting the past.

Cash Outflows

Cash outflows include any payments made to creditors or suppliers. Two places to look for cash outflows are the manufacturing costs budgets and the operating expense budgets. For budgeting purposes, let's assume Soft Soundz pays 50 percent of its raw materials expenses in the current quarter and the other half in the next:

	Q1	Q2	Q3	Q4	Year
Total Cost Direct Materials Purchases	$40,060	$44,880	$41,560	$66,360	$192,860

Using the raw material purchases excerpted from Soft Soundz's direct materials budget, we can compute payments made to suppliers using the following schedule:

	Q1	Q2	Q3	Q4	Year
Accounts Payable	$32,000				$32,000
First Quarter	$20,030	$20,030			$40,060
Second Quarter		$22,440	$22,440		$44,880
Third Quarter			$20,780	$20,780	$41,560
Fourth Quarter				$32,500	
Total Payments	**$52,030**	**$42,470**	**$43,220**	**$53,960**	**$191,000**

Soft Soundz pays direct labor; manufacturing overhead; and selling, general, and administrative expenses in the same quarter, so figures from those budgets can be brought directly forward to the cash budget.

Capital Expenditures

Capital expenditures, or the purchase of plant property and equipment, also affect the cash budget as an additional outlay. Further, if a fixed asset is to be sold, the proceeds must be included in the cash receipts section of the cash budget. Companies that expect to have a lot of activity in fixed assets often prepare a capital expenditures budget for the period.

Soft Soundz has projected two capital expenditures during the year: updated manufacturing equipment and land for a new office. These are detailed in the following budget:

SOFT SOUNDZ COMPANY
CAPITAL EXPENDITURES BUDGET
FOR THE YEAR ENDED 12/31

Asset	Q1	Q2	Q3	Q4	Year
Equipment		$30,000			$30,000
Land				$92,000	$92,000
Total Capital Expenditures		**$30,000**		**$92,000**	**$122,000**

Cash outlays for these projected expenditures will be carried forward to the projected cash budget.

SEE ALSO 7.1, "Property, Plant, and Equipment"

Financing Activities

The financing activities section is also sometimes referred to as the borrowing portion of the cash budget. Included here are any loan funds expected to be received or repaid. For example, if Soft Soundz plans to borrow $2,500 in the third quarter and expects to pay it back with interest in the fourth quarter, this is factored into the cash budget.

Preparing the Cash Budget

Based upon the data from the operating budgets and accompanying expense schedules, we can now prepare the cash budget for Soft Soundz. Assume Soft Soundz had a $43,000 cash balance at the start of the year:

SOFT SOUNDZ COMPANY
CASH BUDGET
FOR THE YEAR ENDING 12/31

	Q1	Q2	Q3	Q4	Year
Beginning Cash Balance	$43,000	$52,525	$64,685	$78,935	$43,000
Add: Receipts					
Customer Collections	$122,000	$168,000	$147,200	$236,800	$674,000
Total Cash Available	$165,000	$220,525	$211,885	$315,735	$717,000
Less: Disbursements					
Direct Materials	$40,060	$44,880	$41,560	$67,000	$193,500
Direct Labor	$29,550	$34,200	$28,800	$52,500	$145,050
Overhead	$8,865	$10,260	$8,640	$15,750	$43,515
Selling Expenses	$5,250	$7,750	$5,000	$11,500	$29,500
G&A Expenses	$28,750	$28,750	$28,750	$28,750	$115,000
Purchase of Equipment		$30,000			$30,000
Acquisition of Land				$92,000	$92,000
Excess (Shortage) of Available Cash Over Disbursements	$52,525	$64,685	$99,135	$48,235	$68,435
Financing					
Loans					
Repayments			$20,200		$20,200
Ending Cash Balance	**$52,525**	**$64,685**	**$78,935**	**$48,235**	**$48,235**

The cash budget is put together using forecasts for sales, customer collections, capital expenditures, manufacturing costs, and other expenses. One purpose of plotting out expected cash inflows and outflows is to help manage cash and avoid situations where you might have a cash shortage. If, for example, you'd planned both your capital expenditures for land and equipment in the first quarter, you would have come up with a negative cash balance and an excess of disbursements over available cash. Looking ahead can help you avoid this type of situation and make adjustments in your planning.

The cash budget is similar in some ways to the statement of cash flow. But always remember, the cash forecast is only a prediction, while the cash flow statement shows your actual cash position during the period.

SEE ALSO 11.4, "Generating Financial Statements"

14.6

14.7 The Budgeted Balance Sheet

The final part of the budgeting process is to produce a budgeted balance sheet for the period, which we show you how to do in this subchapter.

The budgeted or pro forma balance sheet shows your projected financial position at the end of a period, typically a year. You can prepare it using the balance sheet from the previous year as well as the operating and financial budgets you prepared for the current year.

By the time you're ready to put together the budgeted balance sheet, much of your work has already been done for you. Account balances for assets, liabilities, and owner's equity are derived either from financial statements for the previous year and forecasts for the upcoming year. Owner's equity comes from the previous year's balance sheet, for example, while cash is the forecasted ending balance on the cash budget.

SOFT SOUNDZ COMPANY
BUDGETED BALANCE SHEET
AS OF 12/31

Assets

Cash	$48,235
Accounts Receivable	$128,000
Inventory	$11,850
Total Current Assets	**$188,085**
Land	$92,000
Plant Assets	$30,000
TOTAL ASSETS	**$310,085**
Liabilities and Owner's Equity:	
Accounts Payable	$32,500
Owner's Equity	$124,055
Retained Earnings	$153,530
TOTAL LIABILITIES AND OWNER'S EQUITY	**$310,085**

The budgeted balance sheet, like the budgeted income statement, is a good start to plotting where you might go during the year. Having a plan—and in this case a projected end point—can help you stay on track and spot potential problems early on. But again, we emphasize that you are forecasting here, and nothing is set in stone. Business always has a few surprises in store; budgets are merely tools to help you better deal with them.

14.8 Automating the Budget Process

Manually preparing the detailed budgets we've described in this chapter can be a time-consuming process, which is why accounting software has been such a boon for many businesses. Even the most basic programs now give you the ability to project the future performance or financial position of your enterprise at the touch of a button. For small businesses in particular, this means the forecasting process no longer has to be a once-a-year exercise. By punching in a few numbers, business owners are now able to adjust their projections to actual circumstances and see how they're doing whenever it's warranted.

In addition to helping with midyear adjustments, an automated system makes it quick and easy to forecast profits and losses and project cash flows, two of the more useful pieces of information for business planning purposes. Note how the Sage Peachtree Accounting program allows you to compute cash flow for any period of time, even if it's just the week ahead.

Sage Peachtree allows you to get a snapshot of your
company's cash position for any period of time.

More advanced software applications can give you the ability to track budgets by different departments or cost centers, which can be beneficial for larger companies.

That said, it's important to remember that whether you're crunching the numbers yourself or having this done automatically, budgets are only as good as the assumptions behind them. Without a reasonable forecast for revenue and growth, it's impossible to establish a budget with any relevance. So focus first on your forecasting to come up with realistic goals and expectations. Having done that, you can create budgets to set some limits and parameters for spending. But even then, stay flexible.

Computerized
Accounting

15.1 Benefits of Computerized Accounting

The Benefits of Automating Your Books

What Accounting Software Can't Do

In a world of digitized data and instant information, a manual accounting system can seem like a throwback to another era. And yet, if what you have is still working for you, is it really necessary to go the automated route? In this subchapter we help you answer this question—laying out what accounting software can do for you and what it can't. We also discuss the factors you need to consider if you're thinking about computerizing your system.

The Benefits of Automating Your Books

Should you computerize your company's accounting system? With such a wide variety of simple and relatively inexpensive accounting software packages out there, it's difficult to ignore the benefits they offer. For small businesses in particular, computerizing your accounting system can be a boon to productivity, freeing up staff from some of the more tedious chores of bookkeeping, while helping your business as a whole run more efficiently.

In addition, automating the process can help you ...

Cut down on errors and make it easier to catch and correct mistakes. All the popular products have built-in error-spotting capabilities and check computations so any mistakes are hopefully caught early. With accounting software, you merely input the invoice data and the rest is done automatically. For example, at a sale, the invoice is printed and the amounts are entered into the sales journal and posted to the customer's ledger. At the end of the month, the Accounts Receivable module prints out an aging schedule, all at the touch of a button.

SEE ALSO 4.1, "Recording Sales"

SEE ALSO 4.2, "Adjusting and Summarizing Sales"

SEE ALSO 4.3, "Accounts Receivable"

Eliminate repetitive efforts. One example: In a manual system, you would record a bill received for a purchase in the purchases or cash disbursements journal, put the hard copy in the open invoice file, and record the amount to the vendor

A/P subsidiary ledger. When the bill comes due, you would approve it for payment and then write a check. With software, you might have to record the bill initially to accounts payable but the rest, including generating the check, may be done automatically.

Keep better tabs on how your business is doing. Because of how these software packages are designed, you can have instant income statements, debt summaries, accounts receivable aging schedules, and other documents that tell you what's going on in real time. Most of them now offer a customizable "home page" that displays account information, daily reminders, and financial data, and has tabs you can click on to quickly pull up any other reports or data you might need.

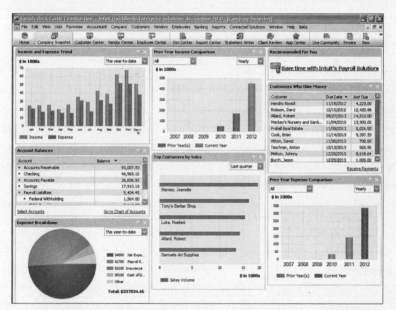

A home page like this one from Intuit QuickBooks Enterprise Solutions provides a snapshot of how your business is doing.

(Screenshot © Intuit, Inc. All rights reserved.)

Keep you up to date on bill paying and collection. Bill paying can be programmed so checks are written and processed. All you have to do is sign.

SEE ALSO 6.4, "Cash Disbursements"

Take care of much of the hard stuff while still giving you the financial information you need. All that complex summarizing from transactions to journals to posting in the ledger and ultimately generating financial statements is taken care of while you concentrate on running the business. At the same time, the calculations are

15.1

completely traceable and you can start at the income statement and dig all the way back to investigate a single transaction if you need to.

Give you better control over your business as a whole. Developing internal controls can be a breeze with access controls and other safeguards built into most software systems.

SEE ALSO 1.1, "Accounting Basics"

Note that in this chapter we'll primarily be discussing systems that automate your entire accounting process. Accounting software that handles specific tasks such as T-Value, which does present and future value calculations or certain taxes is covered elsewhere in this book.

SEE ALSO 9.1, "Time Value Basics"

SEE ALSO 12.3, "Sales Taxes"

What Accounting Software Can't Do

Not *every* company needs to automate its books. A simple business with few employees and an accounting system that's working fine might find the hassle of converting to and getting up to speed with a new system more trouble than it's worth. In addition, there are things that even the best accounting software program won't be able to do for you. So it's important to get your expectations in check before switching to an entirely automated system. Computerizing your books …

Won't guarantee accuracy. That's your job. Accounting software is just another tool, albeit one with built-in error-catching mechanisms. Still, your output is only as good as the input. If you enter data incorrectly or put it in the wrong account, you're still going to have problems producing accurate reports, no matter how good they look.

Can't solve all your problems. Yes, you can get reports at the touch of a button, customized so you can find out about the accounts or transactions you want to. But this alone won't make an unprofitable business profitable. Accounting data can summarize performance and highlight problem areas, but it's up to management to take in this information and make the business work.

Won't eliminate the need for any accounting advice. Again, no software package has all the answers, and some charge pretty steep prices for technical advice and support.

We recommend that you save yourself some headaches by having an accountant or someone knowledgeable about accounting set up your system for you. Be sure he or she walks you through the system and is on hand to help you with any start-up or beginner's glitches. One of the drawbacks of many of these accounting packages is that technical support doesn't come cheap. In some cases, it can cost as much as the software itself.

15.1

15.2 Evaluating Computerized Systems

Checking Out Potential Programs

Determining Your Needs

In this subchapter, we explain how to go about choosing software and deciding what you need it to do for your business.

Checking Out Potential Programs

This section is directed primarily toward small business owners who are computerizing their accounting records. Large companies likely are already automated and have much more complex, expensive, and often custom-made systems. At this point, you've probably talked to other businesses in your area and maybe your accountant, and perhaps you've done some research into some of the different accounting software packages out there. A variety of accounting websites and magazines (some included in Appendix B of this book) regularly review software and can help you evaluate what might fit your business. Free sites such as findaccountingsoftware.com or accountingsoftware411.com can also recommend appropriate software programs based on your needs.

Some of the most popular software packages for small businesses and start-ups are, in no particular order:

- QuickBooks, quickbooks.intuit.com
- Sage Peachtree or Sage Simply Accounting (Note: as of May 2012, both products will fall under the Sage 50 brand name), sagenorthamerica.com/Accounting
- AccountEdge, accountedge.com

Each of these companies is constantly updating their products, so you'll want to be sure you're reading information about the latest software. At present, you can still get a decent package starting at around $200 to $300.

In addition to selecting a product, you need to decide whether you want to purchase a product for downloading in-house or maintain your system online on the producer's website. This second option can be had at subscription fees as low as $9.95 a month. It also provides advantages in terms of accessibility and safety as we discuss later in this chapter.

As part of your research, you should check out the individual software manufacturers' websites. Many offer free trials that give you an idea of what the product looks like, how it works, and what it can do for your business.

SEE ALSO Appendix B, "Useful Resources"

Determining Your Needs

Don't forget, however, that these companies are in the business of selling products. Each of them will bombard you with an exhaustive list of all the tasks and reports you'll be capable of producing with their software—many of which you'll never use or have a need for. A better strategy is to sit down and figure out exactly why you want to automate your system and what you need it to do for you. If you're a small retail operation, your list might look like the following, and any fairly standard accounting software will meet your needs:

- Write checks and manage vendor payments
- Handle sales and account collection
- Process payroll
- Reconcile bank accounts
- Prepare monthly financial reports, summaries, and financial statements

If, on the other hand, you're a manufacturer, you'll require a system that does job costing, sophisticated forecasting, and can handle complex inventory valuation methods. This is a more advanced product.

Check out the list of features on the various programs to find the one that meets your needs. In addition, as we discuss later in the chapter, you can also customize these programs to suit your company.

15.2

15.3 Should You Do Your Accounting Online?

Accounting Web Applications

The Pros and Cons of Keeping Your Books Online

Here we explore why a growing number of companies are taking their accounting systems to the web and help you evaluate whether online accounting is for you.

Accounting Web Applications

When we wrote the first edition of this book 5 years ago, many business owners were leery of putting their accounting records online, let alone on another company's server. But since then, the ease of use and widespread acceptance of Google Apps and other software as service options have helped alleviate some of these fears while fueling an explosion in so-called "cloud computing." Makers of popular software programs like QuickBooks and Sage Peachtree now offer web-based applications, while newer developers including Kashoo (kashoo.com/homeb) and Less Accounting (lessaccounting.com) offer basic online accounting systems starting at $9.95 a month.

At the higher end, larger companies with more complex accounting systems turn to providers like Netsuite (netsuite.com/portal/home.shtml).

The Pros and Cons of Keeping Your Books Online

Using an online accounting system does offer several advantages. Among them:

Accessibility. Web-based software apps give you the ability to access your system from any computer, anywhere. In fact, some mobile apps allow you to work on the books from an iPad or other personal communications device. Authorized colleagues can access the system as well.

Added safety. As business owners have become more familiar with how online accounting works, concerns about security have given way to an added sense of safety. Access to your system is restricted by the latest technology, with only authorized users permitted to view your records. And even if your office or computer records are damaged, your accounting data is already backed up off-site if you have an online system. In addition, your own computer systems are at less of a risk of a virus because you won't be downloading software on them.

Web-based applications such as this QuickBooks App for iPad or iPhone make your accounting system accessible from anywhere at anytime.

(Screenshot © Intuit, Inc. All rights reserved.)

Less downtime. Most of the accounting systems offered in the cloud are guaranteed to be available 99.9 percent of the time. As a result, you're less likely to fall victim to system outage, which could make records inaccessible.

Speed. Fewer transactions need to be input as automatic feeds come from the bank, or you can take a picture of a receipt from a purchase or expense with a mobile technology which will put it right in the system. Some of the earliest adopters have been small companies without a dedicated IT person, in part because increased transparency and access have improved productivity and decision-making.

There are fewer disadvantages to choosing the online route for your bookkeeping. The most obvious is the need for internet access—if you don't have a dependable connection, your ability to get to your records could be affected. You're also at the mercy of the app/software maker for upgrades and the continued quality of the interface, so it's important to research carefully before you choose a service provider.

15.3

15.4 Converting to an Automated System

When to Switch?

From Trial Balance to Chart of Accounts

Creating Lists and Using Modules

Once you've decided to take the plunge and automate, you're going to need to decide when and how to do it. In this subchapter, we address timing and show you how to take your manual accounting system onto the computer.

When to Switch?

To the extent that you have a choice, converting just after the close of the year and before a new period begins is your best bet for a number of reasons. Most accounting software has you transfer account balances from the trial balance. Because you'll have just prepared one at year-end, you can simply take the numbers and plug them right in. You'll also have closed out your temporary (P&L) accounts for the year, so you won't have to carry forward year-to-date balances in revenue and expense accounts.

SEE ALSO 11.5, "Opening New Books"

If you've decided to switch over and can't wait that long, you can still do the conversion at other times. It will just be more complicated. To simplify your changeover, you should first focus on those transactions you'd most like to automate such as paying bills and recording sales and cash receipts, for instance. Then gather your files, documentation, and subledgers so you're ready to put this information into your new system.

From Trial Balance to Chart of Accounts

Procedures for setting up a computerized system vary depending on your choice of software, but the basics are pretty much the same. Much as you do in setting up a manual system, one of your first tasks is to put together a chart of accounts. This basically serves as a directory of your assets, liabilities, revenues, and expenses, listed in order of presentation and by account number.

SEE ALSO 1.4, "Establishing the Chart of Accounts"

One of the first differences you might notice between your manual and computerized systems is the account numbers. Most software programs have four- or even five-digit account numbers, whereas our chart of accounts has three-digit numbers:

CHART OF ACCOUNTS

Manual System	Computerized System
101 Cash on Hand	10000 Petty Cash
102 Cash in Bank	10100 Cash on Hand
105 Petty Cash Fund	10200 Checking Account
130 Notes Receivable	10300 Checking A/C Payroll
140 Accounts Receivable	10400 Savings Account
150 Inventory	11000 Accounts Receivable
160 Prepaid Expenses	11400 Other Receivables
	11500 Allowance for Doubtful Accounts
	12000 Inventory
	14000 Prepaid Expenses

Although you don't have to use all the accounts, we'd advise you to stick to the names, order, and account numbers in the software package you've chosen. There are ways to make changes in account names, but this often complicates recording transactions down the road. Your best bet is to make a note on your old accounting records referencing your new ones so you know which account balance went where in case you have to trace to a transaction that happened before you automated.

When you've keyed in your account balances and set up your chart of accounts, run a trial balance with the system to be sure all your entries have gone in correctly. You'll want to catch any errors before you move on. Then be sure the system has backed up the data. (Most now do it automatically.)

Creating Lists and Using Modules

Next, you can retrieve the supporting documents you'd gathered—invoices, unpaid bills, bank account reconciliation, and the like. You use these to create subledgers, often called **lists** in accounting software jargon. Most programs require you to enter data for all your customers and vendors (name, address, account number, beginning balances) and employees (name, address, Social Security number, deductions, exemptions, etc.).

15.4

✓

In an automated accounting system, **lists** are different groupings of like data, often the subledgers supporting balances in major accounts such as accounts receivable, accounts payable, and inventory.

Unpaid bills, for example, are keyed in to the system to develop a list of accounts payable. This essentially serves the same purpose as the file folder you kept of unpaid invoices, but with a bonus—the system automatically reminds you when the bills are due and can even be programmed to process them and write checks for payment.

SEE ALSO 6.1, "Accounts Payable"

It's worth noting here another difference between manual and automated systems—the terminology. These software programs break down accounts payable and disbursements, sales and accounts receivable, inventory, payroll, and the general ledger into what are known as separate **modules.** Instead of talking about tracing back to original postings or transactions, we talk about **drilling down** in modules to get to the initial transaction. For example, if you click on a customer balance in the Accounts Receivable module, a good program will give you details of the invoices that go into that balance. Clicking on the invoices will show you how the sale was recorded. You should also be able to trace back to the actual product or service billed. This helps promote accuracy and transparency.

Regular monthly journal entries for things like rent or depreciation and other recurring transactions are sometimes referred to as **memorized transactions,** in part because the system is set up to automatically enter them.

SEE ALSO 10.5, "Adjusting Entries"

✓

Modules are the different major functions of an accounting system and how accounting software is usually divided.

Drilling down traces an amount or balance on a financial report back to the initial posting or transaction.

Memorized transactions are recurring transactions such as monthly journal entries that a computerized accounting system makes automatically.

This is a lot to take in. To get a better idea of what this all looks like on screen, let's look at an example. The following screenshot from Sage Simply Accounting serves as the step-off point for any accounting functions affecting sales or accounts receivable. You can click on customers to get a detailed list of customer data and balances, check out information on sales taxes collected, record payments received on account or credits and returns, or look at an updated aging schedule of A/R. You could also decide to leave sales and receivables and go to one of the other sections noted down the left side: Vendors and Purchases (Accounts Payable), Employees (Payroll), and so on.

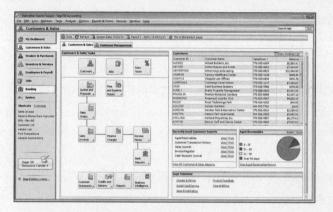

*This sample Accounts Receivable module offers instant access
and analysis of Accounts Receivable and Sales data.*

Again, we're not endorsing a particular software or maker here, but most are set up similarly. Expect to see something similar when looking at your computerized system.

15.4

15.5 Customizing and Using Your Software

Customizing Documents, Reports, and Forms

Software Add-Ons

Getting Used to Your New System

In this subchapter, we talk about how to customize your chosen software to suit your needs. Most accounting programs offer you the option of designing your documents, reports, and forms the way you want them. You can also add additional capabilities to most packages to make your accounting system work for you.

Customizing Documents, Reports, and Forms

Just as with any computer software, you can customize every document you want your system to generate. Each program offers a list of options in terms of templates, examples, and the like, for:

- Invoices

- Purchase orders

- Credit memos

- Sales receipts

Like the ones you probably purchased before, these documents are prenumbered so you can appropriately track them to record them in the individual accounts. For example, the AccountEdge software program shown on the next page allows you to go to the purchases register to find out which vendors you owe. You can then open the pay bills window and determine which invoices to pay and exactly how much to pay a given vendor when you're writing the check. Then you can print the checks and even email your vendors to let them know payment is on the way.

Accounting software also allows you to customize reports, so you can gather together any type of data for any period you'd like.

This sample screen from software program AccountEdge Pro 2012 enables you to write checks to pay bills with a click of a mouse.

(Screenshot reprinted with permission. AccountEdge is a registered trademark of Acclivity Group LLC.)

After you're done writing checks, for example, you might want to look at disbursements from the company checking account. Typically, there will be a notation that specifies the transactions shown are from the "current period." If you wanted to look at a prior period, you could simply click to change the date and then the two reports could be put side by side for comparison.

In addition, you also could sort the payments by amount instead of date, which would help you quickly zero in on what your biggest disbursements were for. Accounting software enables you to apply this sifting and sorting of data to financial statements as well. You can prepare statements when you want, for the periods you want.

One area where automation definitely enhances your system is in your ability to analyze data at any time very quickly, whereas with a manual system, there's often time for detailed financial analysis only once a year, if at all. You'll also have little excuse for not keeping tabs on how you're doing in terms of your budget because, again, these numbers will be a click away.

SEE ALSO 13.1, "Analysis Methods"

SEE ALSO 14.1, "Budgeting Basics"

15.5

Software Add-Ons

As time goes on and you become more comfortable with your software, you may discover you need a function that is not available in your system. Some of the more popular programs for small business, for example, only use one method for computing inventory, or don't have a fixed assets module. In this case, you will often be able to purchase additional modules or upgrades, or make some sort of a modification in the system. Check with your accountant or software provider for details. This is also where sites such as findaccountingsoftware.com, accountingsoftware411.com, and 2020software.com might be useful. All three offer free software recommendations based upon the type and size of your business as well as your particular needs.

Getting Used to Your New System

Your new system looks different, and you use slightly different terminology, but you might be surprised at how much of the process is the same. For example, you're still required to put in journal entries, although in the cases of recurring transactions, the computer takes over some of that burden.

In the meantime, even though you're not doing all the posting and summarizing yourself, the transactions somehow get totaled at the end of the period and you're able to balance the accounts and generate statements. Most packages take you step by step through the closing process. Here an income statement might be called a profit and loss summary, but it looks surprisingly like what you or your accountant used to labor over on the page.

SEE ALSO 10.1, "The Closing Process"

SEE ALSO 11.1, "Year-End Closing Procedures"

If you think a computerized accounting system will make your life easier, by all means look into it. But be sure to do your homework so you know what kind of software will work best for your business and whether you want to download the program or subscribe to a service that allows you to do your books online. Whichever option you choose, you'll also need to know how to adapt the software to your needs, and understand the costs involved. Automating your system can streamline operations in a multitude of ways, including increasing efficiency, reducing errors, and taking over many of the more tedious and repetitious accounting chores to leave you to focus on your business. But even the best system, whether manual or automated, is only as good as the information you put into it.

```
8:37 AM                        Mark's Atomic Graphic Designs
12/15/12                          Profit & Loss Standard
Accrual Basis                  January 1 through December 15, 2012
```

	Jan 1 - Dec 15, 12
Ordinary Income/Expense	
Income	
Sales	55,197.50
Total Income	55,197.50
Expense	
Advertising	275.00
Car and Truck Expenses	50.00
Commissions and fees	300.00
Contract labor	985.00
Customer discounts and refunds	35.00
Fuel	985.53
Insurance (other than health)	608.39
Interest (other than mortgage)	1,568.00
Office expenses	2,620.32
Postage and Delivery	15.00
Rent of other business property	9,003.41
Repairs and maintenance	2,836.20
Supplies	1,432.25
Taxes and licenses	10,139.20
Travel	255.00
Utilities	448.24
Total Expense	31,556.54
Net Ordinary Income	23,640.96
Other Income/Expense	
Other Income	
Other Income	12.00
Total Other Income	12.00
Other Expense	
Other Expenses	1,380.00
Total Other Expense	1,380.00
Net Other Income	-1,368.00
Net Income	**22,272.96**

This sample QuickBooks–generated profit and loss report looks a lot like the reports you used to generate on paper. Using accounting software, either online or downloaded on your computer, can make your work easier and more efficient.

15.5

Glossary

absorption (or full) costing   Including all costs associated with production in determining inventory value.

accounting cycle   The time period from the execution of a transaction to its ultimate reflection in the financial statements.

accounts payable (A/P)   Amounts owed to suppliers and other creditors that must be paid within a certain period.

accounts receivable (A/R)   A verbal promise by a customer to pay the seller an amount by a certain time.

accounts receivable aging schedule   A way of categorizing receivables to see how much is outstanding and for what period of time. With this, you can see who is paying, who isn't, and what amounts are in danger of becoming uncollectible.

accrual   A revenue or expense that has occurred but not yet been recorded in the accounting records. Accrued revenues have been earned but not yet paid.

accumulated depreciation   The contra account that shows how much of an asset has been written off to expense.

adjusted trial balance   Rough compilation of the balance sheet and income statement after adjusting entries have been posted to general ledger.

adjusting entries   Journal entries typically made at end of the month to be sure costs and revenue are matched and recorded in the proper period.

allowance for doubtful accounts   A reserve for accounts receivable that are expected not to be collectible.

amortization   The gradual reduction of the value of an asset or expense account over the time you benefit from its use. Accounts such as intangible assets and deferred charges are amortized.

annuity   A stream of equal payments made at equal intervals.

assets   Items owned by a business.

automatic deposits   Amounts automatically debited directly to your bank account on a regular basis. This is often how payroll is handled.

automatic loans   Amounts advanced by a bank to cover potential overdrafts. Also called automatic overdraft protection.

automatic penalty   An irrevocable fine levied by the IRS on an employer the instant a violation occurs.

bad debts expense   Monthly charge for accounts receivable expected to be uncollectible.

balance sheet   The financial report that lists a company's assets, liabilities, and owner's equity, providing a snapshot of its financial position.

bank errors   Amounts that might have been recorded incorrectly. Such errors require a call to the bank to notify them of the error.

bank reconciliation   The evaluation of the differences between the cash on the books and cash in the bank.

bonding   Purchasing insurance in the event of employee theft or dishonesty.

bonds   Debt instruments issued by the government or a company that can be sold to raise money.

book value   The difference between the cost of an asset and its accumulated depreciation.

break-even point   The quantity at which the revenues you make from selling a product start to exceed the costs of making it and all other operating expenses.

budget   A written plan laying out management's economic goals and setting up parameters and spending limits for the period.

capital expenditure   Purchases of fixed or plant assets.

capital lease   A lease that has the substance of a purchase and is recorded as an asset on the balance sheet.

cash   Any funds on hand or in the bank, as well as cash equivalents and petty cash.

cash discounts allowed   An account used to record a percentage reduction in price earned by a customer who pays his or her bill within a certain time. Sometimes referred to as sales discounts. Discounts for payment terms are not the same as discounts for sales volume, specials, etc.

cash equivalents   Short-term investments, such as CDs and Treasury bills, that can be easily converted into cash and have an original maturity of no more than 3 months.

cash flow   Measures the changes in cash as opposed to revenues and expenses.

chart of accounts   The list of all the different accounts a business has.

closing entry   An entry to transfer balances in temporary capital accounts for revenue, expenses, and the capital drawing account to the income summary account, which is folded into retained earnings on the balance sheet.

collusion   When two or more employees conspire to embezzle money or otherwise defraud the company.

comparative analysis   The process of comparing financial statements account by account to previous years to identify and explain any significant changes.

consumer credit   When the customer pays with a credit card and a third party handles collections and remits the money to the company, less a fee.

contra account   An offset account deducting a reserve or other amount from another account so both amounts can be shown on the financial statements. Examples include sales discounts and allowance for doubtful accounts.

cost   The purchase price of an asset plus the charges to put it into service. This is also referred to as the cost basis.

cost of goods sold (COGS)   Often called cost of sales, this is the cost of merchandise or product sold to the customer.

credit   The right side of an account. For an asset it represents decreases; for a liability, increases.

credit memorandum (or credit memo)   The document given by the seller to a buyer of merchandise to let him know that his account is being credited for a certain amount (typically, the price of the item returned).

cross-foot   To add a row of numbers to be sure the columns balance.

current asset   An asset expected to be held less than 1 year.

current ratio   A measure of liquidity that divides assets by liabilities.

debit   The left side of an account. For an asset, it represents an increase; for a liability, a decrease.

deferral   The postponing of recognition of revenue or expenses. Deferred revenue is a liability representing income received but not earned. Deferred expenses are expenses recorded as an asset until recognized in subsequent periods.

deferred income taxes   The difference between income tax paid and income tax recorded on the income statement for financial purposes.

depletion   The write-off of a natural resource like timber, oil, or gas as it's extracted or used.

deposits in transit   Deposits made before the end of the month but not reflected in the bank statement. These amounts must be added back into the bank balance.

depreciation   Used to account for the decline in value of an asset through wear and tear, deterioration, and obsolescence, by allocating its cost over its useful life.

direct labor   Labor costs directly attributable to a product.

direct materials   Raw materials directly related to a product.

direct write-off   An outstanding account taken off the books because the customer is not expected to pay.

discount   When the rate of interest paid on a bond is less than the market rate, that bond was acquired at a discount.

dividend   A distribution of corporate profits to stockholders.

double entry bookkeeping   A method of accounting in which every transaction is recorded to at least two accounts.

drilling down   Tracing an amount or balance on a financial report back to the initial posting or transaction.

earnings per share   The amount of net income per share of outstanding stock.

Electronic Federal Tax Payment System (EFTPS)   The mandatory automated system for paying tax deposits if prior year tax payments were more than $200,000.

electronic funds transfer (EFT)   Payments automatically deducted from you account.

embezzlement   The process of stealing cash from a company while trying to cover it up by omitting transactions or otherwise falsifying accounting records.

employee earnings record   An ongoing record of employee earnings and deductions for the year.

equity   The excess of total assets over total liabilities.

exempt   Employees who do not get paid overtime. No matter how many hours they work, their pay is at a quoted rate. Exempt employees are usually, but not always, salaried workers.

expenses   The costs of doing business.

extraordinary item   An income statement item that's both unusual in nature and rare in occurrence.

face value   The amount of principal a bond issuer must pay. For example, in a $100,000 12 percent bond, $100,000 is the face value.

factoring   Selling a receivables to a factor for financing purposes.

federal depository bank   An institution authorized to accept federal tax deposits.

Federal Insurance Contributions Act (FICA)   The law that established both Social Security and Medicare taxes.

federal unemployment tax   A payroll tax paid by the employer to fund unemployment insurance.

federal withholding tax   The amount of estimated income taxes withheld from employees' compensation.

financial ratio   A formula that shows the relationship of one amount or account to another in percentage terms.

finished goods   Manufactured goods that are complete and ready for sale. Finished goods include raw material, labor, and overhead costs.

first in, first out (FIFO)   A method of inventory costing where the oldest inventory is assumed to be sold first.

fiscal year   The business year for accounting purposes.

fixed assets   Another term for plant, property, and equipment or plant assets.

fixed costs   Those expenses that do not fluctuate with activity levels.

foot   To add the sum of a column of numbers; the totals in the purchases journal, for example.

forecasting   Making predictions about financial outcome based on historical data and projections from current data.

freight-in   The shipping charges paid by the purchaser. These become part of the cost of the product.

future value (FV)   The amount you'll have at some future date if you invest a sum or sums of money at compound interest. This can also be called the future amount.

general journal The book to record corrections to accounts.

general ledger A company's complete set of accounts, which shows increases and decreases in each individual account and their balances.

Generally Accepted Accounting Principles (GAAP) The rules accountants must follow when preparing financial statements. They're handed down by the Financial Accounting Standards Board, the rule-making body for the profession.

goodwill An intangible asset representing the excess of the purchase price for a company over its fair market value.

gross pay The total pay earned before taxes and other deductions.

gross profit The difference between sales and the cost of goods sold.

imprest system (or imprest account) A method of controlling expenditures by setting up a fund at a fixed amount and requiring supporting documentation for reimbursement to replenish the fund to the fixed amount.

income Profit; the difference between revenues and expenses.

income statement The financial report that shows revenues less expenses to arrive at net income.

incremental analysis The process used to evaluate the cost/benefit potential of different alternatives on future income.

indirect costs Those costs that cannot be directly tied to a specific product but are allocated to the entire manufacturing process.

intangibles Assets that lack physical substance, such as a brand name or goodwill.

interest The amount paid for the use of money.

internal controls The system of procedures and policies that help safeguard a company's assets and reduce the risk of irregularities or errors in it financial records.

International Financial Reporting Standards International rules stating how certain transactions and events should be reported in financial statements to make them more comparable across borders.

inventory Items held for resale or products that will go into the manufacturing of goods to be sold.

journal   Also known as the book of first or original entry, it is the first place a transaction is recorded or "journalized." It's also the only place where the entire transaction is recorded together with an explanation. This is called a *journal entry*.

kiting   An attempt to hide a cash shortage in one account by depositing a check from another and exploiting the float time between then and when it clears the bank.

lapping   Illegal activity where an employee deposits a customer check in his personal account and then uses the next payment to reduce the previous customer's bill.

last in, first out (LIFO)   The inventory system that assumes the newer items are sold first.

leasehold improvements   Depreciable changes or alterations to a leased property.

leases   Agreements in which one person or entity (lessee) is guaranteed rights to use a piece of property or land belonging to another (the lessor) for a specific period of time in return for payment of a rental charge.

lessee   A person or entity who pays to lease a property.

lessor   A person or entity who owns a property being leased.

liabilities   Money owed by a business.

liquidity   A company's ability to meet debt payments and operating expenses.

lists   In an automated accounting system, these are different groupings of like data, often the subledgers supporting balances in major accounts such as accounts receivable, accounts payable, and inventory.

lockbox system   A process of having customers remit receipts directly to the bank as a cash safeguard measure.

long-term assets   Assets not expected to be used within the year.

long-term liabilities   Liabilities not expected to be paid within the year.

marketable securities   Stocks or other investments that can be readily sold on an open market.

master budget   The main budget, pieced together using forecasts for sales, production, operating expenses, selling and administrative expenses, capital expenditures, and cash budgets.

material Refers to whether an amount is significant in relation to the business.

memorized transactions Recurring transactions, such as monthly journal entries, that a computerized accounting system makes automatically.

merchandise inventory The inventory for a retailer or wholesaler.

modules The different major functions of an accounting system and how accounting software is usually divided.

monthly service charges The amount a bank charges to process an account.

net income The bottom line revenues less all expenses, including interest and taxes.

net pay Your pay after (net of) deductions for taxes and benefits; your take-home pay.

net sales Sales less discounts and returns.

nonexempt employees Those employees not exempted from overtime pay. They're required to be paid extra if they work more than 40 hours in a week. Nonexempt employees are typically hourly workers, but not always. Some salaried workers, particularly in jobs covered by union contracts, are also nonexempt.

notes payable A written promise to repay a company a certain amount by a specified time in the future.

notes receivable A written promise by a customer to pay seller an amount by a certain time. Also called a promissory note.

NSF checks A check received that's drawn on an account with insufficient funds to cover it.

operating cycle The average length of time between when a company buys inventory and receives cash proceeds from its sale.

operating expenses The costs of running the business, generally selling, general, and administrative.

operating income Revenues less cost of goods sold and operating expenses.

operating lease A lease in which rent payments are expensed monthly and the asset is returned to the lessor at the end of the lease period.

opportunity cost The potential benefits lost when choosing one option or course of action over another.

outstanding checks   Checks that have been written but not yet cleared the bank by the date of the statement.

overdraft   A check written for an amount exceeding the balance in the bank account; the proverbial "bounced" check.

overhead   Expenses related to the production process such as rent, utilities, or insurance. These costs are usually allocated based on direct labor hours or materials used in a product.

owner's equity   The owner's investment in the business.

periodic inventory system   A method of accounting for inventory where it is not updated during the period.

perpetual inventory system   An inventory method in which purchases are debited to inventory so the balance is continually updated.

petty cash   A small fund, typically $100 or less, kept on hand to meet miscellaneous expenses without going through the payment approval process.

physical inventory   The process of taking an actual physical count of the items you have in inventory.

plant, property, and equipment (PP&E)   The tangible assets you need to operate your business. You might also hear them called *plant* or *fixed assets*. They're typically big-ticket items you plan on holding for at least a year.

premium   When the rate of interest paid on a bond exceeds the market rate, we say a bond is bought at a premium.

prepaid expense, prepayment   An asset representing the amount paid in advance for future expenses.

present value (PV)   The amount you'd have to put in now to get a future sum or sums assuming compound interest.

prior-period adjustments   Adjustments for errors in past financial statements that must be corrected in current reports.

profit and loss statement (or income statement)   The financial report that shows a company's revenues and expenses and net income or loss for a period.

purchase order   A formal document authorizing order quantity, time, and specifics.

purchase returns and allowances   Credits for goods returned to the vendor or additional amounts discounted by the vendor because of problems with the goods.

quick ratio   A liquidity measurement that looks at the relationship between assets that are most easily convertible to cash (cash, marketable securities, and accounts receivable) to current liabilities.

raw materials   The components, ingredients, and parts that go into making the company's product. The steel needed to make cars, for example, would be considered a raw material.

receivable   An amount owed to a company for goods purchased or services rendered.

reconcile   To check that account totals agree with supporting data or calculations.

relevant costs   Costs that vary depending on the course of action you choose.

residual value (or salvage value)   The estimated value at the end of an asset's useful life. Salvage value is not used in depreciation for income tax purposes.

retained earnings   An equity account where earnings or losses are recorded.

revenue recognition principle   A principle that holds that sales revenue should be recorded when earned, when services are performed or goods are exchanged.

revenues   The proceeds from sales or services. Often referred to as sales or sales revenue.

sales returns and allowances   Returns of merchandise and allowances for defective or damaged goods.

shrinkage   A decline in inventory quantities due to breakage, damage, or loss.

skimming   An illegal process wherein an employee or business pockets part of cash receipts before recording a smaller amount in the books.

sole proprietor   A single owner of a business.

statement of cash flows   A financial report that shows actual cash activity for the year.

sunk costs   Costs that would be incurred regardless of a business's course of action, i.e., producing one product versus another or discontinuing a product line.

T-account   A general journal account with debits on the left and credits on the right.

temporary holding account   An account where amounts are recorded because the proper account or allocation of the funds is unknown.

time value of money   The concept that there's a difference between $1 today and $1 sometime in the future.

trade credit   When a customer buys something on account for which he or she agrees to pay a certain amount within a certain time.

trademark (or trade name)   Intangible assets representing the value attached to a name or logo.

trading securities   Shares of stock or bonds purchased for resale in the near future.

transaction   A business event that alters a company's financial position.

trend analysis   The process of comparing financial reports for at least 5 years to identify performance trends.

trial balance   The first rough figuring of balance sheet and income statement accounts to see if debits and credits are the same.

uncollectible accounts   Amounts customers are unlikely to pay.

unearned revenues   Liabilities representing amounts received in advance of selling goods or performing services.

useful life   An estimate of the asset's expected productive life.

variable cost   A cost that fluctuates based on production levels.

vendors   Suppliers.

voucher   An authorization form, usually prenumbered, that's required before a check can be approved for payment.

voucher register   The journal for recording all vouchers as bills are received and approved.

wages   Earnings paid to hourly workers.

work in process (W-I-P)   The second stage of manufacturing inventory, which consists of product partially made or assembled. For example, a truck wheel assembly or unpainted pottery would be work in process. Work in process includes the cost of raw materials used plus any labor or overhead costs expended to date.

Useful Resources

The following list of organizations, government agencies, and websites can provide you with additional information on accounting-related issues.

Accounting Software 411
3943 Irvine Boulevard #110
Irvine, CA 92602
accountingsoftware411.com
This website provides a searchable database for accounting software resources.

AccountingWEB
accountingweb.com
Sift Media
9449 Priority Way W Drive, Suite 150
Indianapolis, IN 46240
1-866-688-1678
This general site for accountants offers free registration, a section on accounting questions, advice, and links to a variety of accounting-related resources.

The American Institute of Certified Public Accountants (AICPA)
1211 Avenue of the Americas
New York, NY 10036
212-596-6200
aicpa.org
The AICPA's website has a consumer section with useful information for entrepreneurs and small businesses on setting up a business, break-even analysis, taxes, and more.

Dun and Bradstreet
103 JFK Parkway
Short Hills, NJ 07078
800-234-3867
dnb.com
Dun and Bradstreet offers business information, credit evaluation, and management services.

Financial Accounting Standards Board (FASB)
401 Merritt 7
PO Box 5116
Norwalk, CT 06856-5116
203-847-0700
fasb.org
The FASB is accounting's governing body. Check its website for information about new accounting rules or changes in existing rules.

Find Accounting Software
800-827-1151
FindAccountingSoftware.com
This website is a free and independent service of CPA Online that will help you find the accounting software that works for you.

Internal Revenue Service (IRS)
111 Constitution Avenue NW
Washington, DC 20224
irs.gov
The IRS answers tax questions and provides downloadable tax forms, tax guides, and other useful information on its website.

Intuit
Customer Contact Center
2800 East Commerce Center Place
Tucson, AZ 85706
520-901-3000
intuit.com
Software developer of accounting programs including, QuickBooks, TurboTax, and Quicken.

National Association of Small Business Accountants
6405 Metcalf Avenue, Suite 503
Shawnee Mission, KS 66202
866-296-0001
smallbizaccountants.com
The association offers accounting information for small businesses as well as accountant referrals.

The Risk Management Association
1801 Market Street, Suite 300
Philadelphia, PA 19103-1628
800-677-7621
rmahq.org
This organization provides annual statement studies that offer source of comparative data that comes directly from financial statements of the small and medium-size business.

Rutgers Accounting Research Center
Rutgers Business School
1 Washington Park
Newark, NJ 07102
raw.rutgers.edu
Rutgers Accounting Web (RAW) offers one of the most comprehensive accounting websites, with an exhaustive list of links to accounting associations, government agencies, journals, and other resources.

Sage Accounting Solutions
Sage North America
866-996-7243
sagenorthamerica.com/Solutions/Accounting
Long-time developer of accounting software including Sage Peachtree, Sage Simply Accounting, and Sage 50 products.

Securities and Exchange Commission (SEC)
100 F Street NE
Washington, DC 20549
sec.gov
The SEC is the regulatory body for public companies. Go to its website for info on filing requirements, rules and regulations, forms, information involving registration or sale of securities, and interpretations of accounting rules and regulations. Here you can also access filings for public companies.

Small Business Administration (SBA)
409 Third Street SW
Washington, DC 20416
1-800-U-ASK-SBA
sba.gov
This government agency administers small business loans and provides information on business financing, managing, taxes, and other small business concerns.

Social Security Administration
6401 Security Boulevard
Baltimore, MD 21235
ssa.gov
Here you'll find information for employers and the option of online W-2 tax form filing.

Standard & Poor's
55 Water Street
New York, NY 10041
212-438-1000
standardandpoors.com
This financial ratings agency offers comparative data, industry resources, etc.

Tax and Accounting Sites Directory
taxsites.com
This is a useful aggregator of tax information, with plenty of links to state and federal information.

Time Value Software
PO Box 50250
Irvine, CA 92619
1-800-426-4741
timevalue.com
Provides software (*Tvalue5*) for present and future value computations, mortgages, loans, leases, and investment yields.

Value Line
220 East 42nd Street
New York, NY 10017
valueline.com
This website provides corporate research, industry, and investment analysis.

Index

C

D

F

G–H

Q–R

S

U

V

W–X–Y–Z